WILFRED BION

HIS LIFE AND WORKS 1897–1979

WILFRED BION

HIS LIFE AND WORKS 1897–1979

GÉRARD BLÉANDONU

Translated by Claire Pajaczkowska

Foreword by R.D. Hinshelwood

OTHER
Other Press
New York

Library of Congress Cataloging-in-Publication Data

Bléandonu, Gérard.
    [Wilfred R. Bion. English]
    Wilfred Bion : his life and works, 1897-1979 / Gérard Bléandonu ; translated by Claire Pajaczkowska ; foreword by R. D. Hinshelwood.
      p. cm.
    Originally published: London : Free Association Books ; New York : Guilford Press, 1994.
    Includes bibliographical references and index.
    ISBN 1-892746-57-3
    1. Bion, Wilfred R. (Wilfred Ruprecht), 1897-1979. 2.
Psychoanalysts—Great Britain—Biography. 3. Psychoanalysts. I. Title.

    RC438.6.B54 B5713 2000
    150.19'5'092—dc21
    [B]

                                  00-028346

WILFRED BION

This is the first full biography and the first comprehensive exposition of the most interesting and arguably the most influential figure in recent psychoanalysis. It is particularly welcome, since Bion's ideas are often found to be difficult of access. There is no substitute for immersing oneself in his writings, but an introduction is surely a useful beginning, something which no one has hitherto undertaken with respect to the complete works.

Bléandonu takes us through Bion's personal and intellectual explorations and gives clear expositions of his key concepts, including work groups and basic assumption groups; psychotic processes; the grid; epistemology; catastrophic change; abandonment of memory and desire; the mystic; ultimate truth. Finally, he guides the reader through the fantasy writings in the *Memoir of the Future*, the masterpiece that is Bion's autobiography and his final writings, including the posthumous *Cogitations*. The book is a *tour de force*.

GÉRARD BLÉANDONU is a community psychiatrist in a suburb of Lyon. He is the author of work on group therapy, and is writing a book about dreams.

CLAIRE PAJACZKOWSKA is Senior Lecturer, School of the History and Theory of Visual Culture, Middlesex University, and translator of *Freud or Reich? Psychoanalysis and Illusion*, by Janine Chasseguet-Smirgel and Béla Grunberger (Free Association Books).

R.D. HINSHELWOOD is Clinical Director, The Cassel Hospital, London, and author of *A Dictionary of Kleinian Thought* and *Clinical Klein*, both from Free Association Books.

CONTENTS

FOREWORD

R.D. Hinshelwood

Bion's writing often intimidates; therefore we have a surprising hesitancy over interpreting his views. Only Leon Grinberg (with colleagues) and Donald Meltzer have gone into print in any prominent way. And that is in spite of Bion's enigmatic and ambiguous way of writing; it calls for interpretative secondary sources to develop it. The many ideas which he deliberately leaves half-formulated, the evocative and limping style of his fiction-writing (if it is fiction), and the often humorous kind of gestural asides to clinical material would seem to invite being filled up with flesh and blood and passion. And indeed they do. It is what Bion intended; he wanted to work his readers so that they produced their own responses, their own hard learning, instead of his. But the task that he seems to require of his readers is so personal and idiosyncratic that there is a sense of being in the closet with him in a private contemplation. It feels unseemly to fill out the ideas in one's own way for public consumption.

What Gérard Bléandonu has created is a sense of the corpus of Bion's work as a whole, and he has set it in an episodic sketch derived from Bion's autobiographical experience of his own life. We can see here just how much Bion's *oeuvre* transcends Freud and Klein before him, and the work of subsequent Kleinians after him. And this is because Bion was interested in the tangential task of the meaning of psychoanalysis itself in our culture, and especially within a philosophical tradition. Bléandonu has done us an important service in steering a way through the philosophical interests that influenced Bion, and the sources that he drew on. Bion the philosopher comes through strongly; he was a theory-builder, and only on the way a therapeutic psychoanalyst. That estimation contrasts with the overview we have cultivated, as practising psychoanalysts and psychotherapists, in order to exploit Bion's ideas in therapy. His work as a whole is balanced between the two, but leaves us bemused; too philosophical to draw together a clinical school of psychoanalysis, too clinical to make an impact on philosophers as he truly wished. Bléandonu manages to sit astride the two.

The book is structured simply: an initial review of Bion's childhood; a review of his work on groups, and during World War Two; the period of his work on psychotic patients; an epistemological phase; and a final and brief section on the late 'fictional' trilogy. The first section is tantalizingly sketchy, though evocative, as in fact are Bion's autobiographical texts. One day a fully researched biography will mould into a perceptible form those hesitant links we barely glimpse here: the one that peeps out occasionally from his Indian upbringing with his *ayah*; his psychoanalytic mysticism that involved abolishing memory and desire (surely inspired by his roots in the East); and his later entry into the 1970s culture of Los Angeles where he would once gain have encountered oriental religion and mysticism.

I suppose all biography linking formative influences and the later professional achievements is risky, especially when written for psychoanalysts; and especially, perhaps, about a psychoanalyst. Perhaps Bléandonu is right to leave that mostly aside – and to leave us to fill in our own surmises, just as Bion would have done. For this book stays with the achievement. The section on groups informs us of the relation between basic assumptions and the ideas of J.A. Hadfield, Bion's first therapist. Bion as a 'Hadfieldian' before he was a Kleinian is intriguing and important; but we are again left with all the questions open for us to fill in – what *was* all this social psychology that was around at the time for the Army and its psychiatrists to use? What really *is* the status now of these early ideas on groups after the redrawing of group life in Bion's return to groups in 1970, a much more psychoanalytic (and Bionian!) approach?

Bléandonu's discourse on Bion's ideas about psychosis rivets us to the texts; that *grid* is laid out carefully and explained meticulously, perhaps more explicitly than Bion does himself. How the idea of links, and attacks on them, emerges as the great nuclear idea for the rest of Bion's working life is given proper importance. Our nose, however, rarely lifts from the grindstone and we seldom have a moment to survey the surrounding context of work going on elsewhere; we have to call a check on our sense that Bion's developing ideas were a hermetically sealed process, without influence from outside. This intellectual biography follows Bion himself towards suppressing debate on the influences that pressed on him. For Bion appeared to present himself as being in isolation, generating his ideas *de novo* in a process of spontaneous generation; a guru linked in with 'truth' in a way that ordinary mortals are not. We know this to be untrue; psychoanalysts especially know it. Yet reputations are still made, and biographies written and sold on the basis of it.

The next section of the book does, in contrast, give more context. This, perhaps the most important section, describes Bion's attempt to create an extensive psychoanalytic epistemology. Here the background of logical positivism and British analytical philosophy is sketched in, and one gets the feeling that this is Bléandonu's greatest interest in Bion. It gave me, for the first time, a picture of Bion's vast ambition as a philosopher – as opposed to his identity as a psychoanalyst who had stumbled into philosophical territory, which is the way I might previously have described it to myself. This topic of Bion the epistemologist is surely a subject that longs for as extended an exploration as Bion the psychoanalyst.

The final section, unfortunately but not necessarily cursory, deals synoptically with the fictionalized version of psychoanalysis in Bion's trilogy of 'novels'. I suspect that Bléandonu has reacted as I do to them – with an irritation at their numbing density and wanton confusion. There must be a resistance to tackling them at the end of such an exhausting exposition of the previous phases of Bion's life. I can sympathize with this. After the challenging journey of Bion's professional and philosophical work, to take on something as remote as Joyce's *Ulysses* – and not written with half the wit, style or conviction – makes the reader wilt, let alone the biographer.

Most people take parts of Bion and develop their own views; then work, clinically or philosophically, with what they have produced from the bit they have taken away. In contrast, Gérard Bléandonu has made an extraordinarily inclusive attempt to cover the ground from the early work on groups (and even before), to the very last work on the fictionalization of psychoanalytic theory. It is, in a relatively short book, and with a glittering clarity of style, an impressive achievement.

Bléandonu's coverage is comprehensive and as valid as any, though the manuscript is written as if it were a definitive reading, which it cannot be. With such a standardizing text, Bléandonu has been faced with the paradox of making an exegesis of a work that trembles only for interpretation. His choice was between defining and explaining in the style of a standard secondary source, or free associating as Bion would have demanded. He has managed, as far as I believe it is possible, to take the side of straight exposition, of the 'telling it as it is' point of view. And a didactic text will be of great relief to many people (many students) who have struggled with Bion. But a Foreword is possibly the right place for a warning: do not be beguiled by Bléandonu's straightforward writing. After you have finished here go back to some of the real thing. Until then you can really know nothing of Bion. We could have asked Bléandonu to contest the ideas more, we could have asked him to cloak the ideas in their surrounding psychoanalytic debate, raging through the 1940s to the sixties. Had Bléandonu discussed the possible alternative readings that could be made, that might have been made, then the impression of a definitive text would have been mellowed. But then we would have had solid academic porridge; we would have lost all the tantalizing, foggy potentiality of Bion – just the quality which attracts us and infuriates us, which limits Bion's work, but which extends our own imaginations.

Perhaps this reading is better for coming from the Continent, where philosophical occupations are more present in the culture and in professional life. In Bléandonu's presentation Bion sought for a grand and unifying theory of everything. Or is that just a continental reading of Bion in continental terms? Nevertheless, this is the first really good and comprehensive guide through the oscillating components of Bion's soaring intellectual and professional achievement, and his agonized and restless soul.

Even so, there is a curious quality to reading about a British psychoanalyst through a French-speaking author. It feels as though one of our own has been repatriated, rather like Bion's own return to this country to die, after his exile in Los Angeles. One can only regret the timidity of us British not being the first to make the effort to lay off the taboo of the sacred texts. This book is surely a formidable achievement; equally surely it forms the grounding for the next effort that will inevitably be made to ensnare such a free spirit.

WILFRED BION
HIS LIFE AND WORKS 1897–1979

INTRODUCTION

Wilfred Ruprecht Bion ranks with Sigmund Freud and Melanie Klein in the psychoanalytic tradition. His theory of groups remains as relevant today as when it was first conceived, at the end of the Second World War. Later, his outstanding clinical skills extended the analytic understanding of psychoses. Having developed his theories of thinking, Bion went on to reconceptualize psychoanalytic epistemology. Finally, towards the end of his life, he wrote an unusual autobiography and a trilogy of imaginative fiction. This innovative narrative form put the finishing touch to a lifetime's work entirely dedicated to psychoanalytic truth. His writing has been received with enthusiastic admiration and irritated rejection in equal measure; often judged on hearsay, as reading it demands effort and introspection. However, the investment of intellectual effort demanded of the reader is amply repaid with extraordinary insights and real intellectual pleasure.

Bion's style is a mixture of dazzling illuminations, provocative aphorisms and tiresome digressions. Underscored by contradiction, it obliges readers to choose either timid or risky interpretations, and does so in order to avoid oversimplification, and defy paraphrasing. It could be compared to an uncut diamond, and the reader, in search of the illumination of its refracted light, is drawn into a labyrinth of obscurity. Bion's writings create links between psychoanalysis and such diverse fields as philosophy, mathematics, physics, art and mysticism. To our contemporary age of narrow specialization, Bion brought back the ideal of the Renaissance man.

To those who met him, Bion seemed an extraordinary person,

unlike others in his manner of speech, in his style of writing and in his behaviour. While he emerged as a leader of the Kleinian Group, he nevertheless remained fundamentally a solitary man. His own work has never been institutionalized as a school or group, unlike that of Freud and Klein. Bion's work was never written with the aim of establishing master–disciple relations; rather, it lives on in the minds of creative readers.

It is not my aim to review the entirety of Bion's work – this would be a massive undertaking – but simply to set out some of its forms and contents. My objective is to reveal the meaning of given texts in relation to the development, the historical context and the internal economy of Bion's *oeuvre*. Such a triple perspective reveals the work's structural unity. Yet it is this very unity which constitutes the greatest impediment to the average reader, as it tends to produce the sense of a hermetic text. Bion's thought runs the risk of being reduced to a meaningless jargon of catchphrases: basic assumptions, alpha function, container–contained. This is precisely what Bion hoped to avoid; he always maintained that his writing should be forgotten in order that each reader might discover its meaning within themselves. This remains the task of the reader, however much books such as this one aim to facilitate the process of reading Bion.

In order to give an overview of Bion's lifework we have divided it into four 'seasons' of production: first the period of group psychology, then the clinical work which centres on psychosis, then the writing on questions of epistemology, and finally his immersion into literary art. Bion's work forms a whole, and to some extent we have had to generalize its predominant themes in order to avoid too much repetition, or perhaps because we found no inspired method of homogenizing its complexity. There is some continuity between the four seasons of work and the equivalent periods of the lifespan they traverse. Bion came to psychoanalysis fairly late and, burning with an almost adolescent impatience, he made his way through at quite a pace. During these four periods of work he lived – or relived – the four seasons of a lifespan. Springtime began after a mid-life crisis, whereas winter was cut short by death.

The autobiography of a well-known psychoanalyst is a rare thing indeed. Bion, who had been rather constrained by a dry intellectualism throughout his career, chose, at the end, to pour out (almost) everything about his life. He sought clinical truth, grasped the final truth, and then began a search for aesthetic truth. Bion's life proved as rich, as varied, as spontaneously or wisely lived as his work. In both the life and the work we can perceive similar flaws, similar silences, similar mistakes, but also similar achievements, similar qualities and ultimately the same greatness. We have therefore sought to follow the thoughts of the contradictory, changing, immutable individual, as well as those of the more 'official' author of the books. 'This play of shadow or reflection which a person himself tends to project around himself out of defence or bravado' (Marguerite Yourcenar, *Mishima ou la vision du vide*. Paris: Gallimard, 1980). Nevertheless, our aim has been to find the core reality within the work that Bion chose to write and to publish.

PART 1:
THE YEARS OF APPRENTICESHIP

On setting out to write an account of Bion's life, we come up against a threefold problem. First of all, since no books and few articles, memoirs or testimonies have been published about him, we have had recourse to a single main source of information: his autobiography. And we are reminded of the limitations of this by the well-known principle of Roman law 'One witness is no witness', and the popular French adage 'Whoever hears only one bell hears only one sound'. Secondly, as Bion tended – perhaps because of his Kleinian training – to privilege psychic reality over other realities, we might be led to overlook the importance of social and cultural reality, especially since we are now some fifty years and hundreds of miles away from most of the original events and settings. Lastly, we render the account of thoughts written in the first person into a third-person narrative. In the preface to his autobiography Bion maintains that he wants to tell the truth, the whole truth, believing that he is writing a historical account of what 'really happened'. However, autobiography, as a genre, is based on identity; its interest and value lie in what it alone is capable of expressing. It need not necessarily bear any resemblance to historical reality.

1 ORIGINS AND CHILDHOOD

Readers who first encounter Bion's work through the autobiography will find, on the first page, the Bion family crest and motto. The motto, *Nisi dominus frustra*, indicates their faith: 'Without God there is no purpose' (the same motto was chosen by the city of Edinburgh). A verse from Psalm 127 underscores the theme: 'Except the Lord build the house, they labour in vain that build it; except the Lord keep the city, the watchman waketh but in vain.' Since Bion chose to represent himself historically in terms of his paternal ancestry (his autobiography was published after his death), it is all the more surprising that there is no discussion of the Bion family in the book. Only in some of the letters to his fiancée, written during the months of their engagement, do we find any information about them. In one letter Bion tells her that the family name can be traced back over several generations. The Bions served in India, in the police and in government. They were descendants of Huguenots who emigrated from the Cévennes to England via Switzerland (Saint Gall).[1] At least one thing seems clear: Bion happened to be born an Anglo-Indian and wished, to the very depths of his being, to remain one.

In the autobiography the adult narrates, organizes and controls the text. The adult describes the child's point of view, but does not give him the voice of a first-person narrator. Childhood re-emerges only through the framework of an adult's memory. The childhood spent in India is remembered by a highly educated man who had always maintained a great interest in social and economic affairs, a student of history who sought to apply his theory of group psychology in social terms. In the letters written to his children towards the end of his life, we find a man who is quite aware of contemporary events in Britain and the USA. When his love of India was rekindled, he augmented his memories and knowledge by reading Birkenhead's biography of Kipling, for example (Bion, 1985, p. 227). Finding out about life in India at the beginning of the twentieth century, Bion traced the life of his father. His father was still alive, but Bion's identification with him had always been conflicted. The autobiography is our only source of information about Wilfred's childhood, but its narrative unfolds through the consciousness and cultural, social and political concerns of a wise old man.

Bion warned his fiancée that she was about to join an awful family; first, because 'they are all, as far as I am aware without exception, completely cracked! This is more difficult because they possess a sort of cunning that has kept them out of the loony bin' (1985, p. 79). Bion had not kept track of them all, so he concentrated on telling her about those who were particularly important to him. He began with his paternal grandfather, Robert Bion, who was 'some sort of missionary in India'. This grandfather had three, or maybe four, sons. Bion hardly knew one of his uncles, who worked for the Indian railways, as he disappeared abruptly and permanently from his life. The three remaining brothers married three sisters from the Kemp family, and each had several children. Bion knew little about his mother's family, except for the fact that they were 'probably missionary, or "off" missionary in the sense that builders and decorators talk about "off" white when they mean cream coloured'. This intermarriage was, according to Bion, proof of the family's complete madness. There were also another uncle and aunt, although young Wilfred had not met their children, his cousins, who also had the Bion surname but, strangely, were 'quite sane'.

The letters describe the oldest uncle as 'a horrid little man who was happily as incompetent in his meanness as he was in his work', who allowed a senseless piety to dominate his private life entirely. At the end of his life he had a temporary moment of sanity in which he understood that he had wasted his life, and following this realization he became 'so cross with everyone and everything' that he was 'shut up in a loony bin'. His wife is described simply as formidable and handsome. The two younger brothers, on the other hand, were, in their respective spheres, as brilliant as they were 'impossible'. The youngest was the only one of the three to 'become enormously wealthy by Bion standards' as an indigo planter. Despite his 'Anglo-Indian merchant's ignorance of culture and indifference towards everything except hard work and personal comfort', he seems to have been sympathetic to his nephew (1985, p. 87). Two of his sons were killed in action during the First World War, and this undoubtedly meant something to Bion, who had fought throughout the same war. Whatever their limitations, these families were able to mitigate to some extent the emotional deprivation which the young Bion suffered in Britain.

Wilfred Ruprecht Bion was born on 8 September 1897 in Muttra in the Punjab. This province became a British colony in 1847 as part of the final colonial expansion. The Punjab, a very fertile region, had been the cradle of great Indian civilizations; it had also been the pathway of the majority of invasions of the Ganges plain. This province, in the north-west point of the Indian subcontinent, is crisscrossed by five rivers (from which it derives its name) which flow into the Indus. The monsoon affects the whole of India; in the Punjab, however, the rainfall is irregular, requiring extensive irrigation before the province could develop its important wheat production.

Colonialism can be roughly divided into two periods: a phase of imperialism from 1858 to 1905 and a phase of reform from 1905 to 1937. Wilfred Bion lived in India towards the end of the imperialist phase (corresponding, roughly, to the end of the Victorian era). Lord Curzon is considered to have been one of the greatest viceroys of India (1899–1905). His greatest fault, however, was his complete inability to acknowledge and recognize the development of new social movements. He poured scorn on the idea that the educated classes of the indigenous peoples might be entitled to have a say in the running of their own public affairs. Other high officials had welcomed the creation of the Indian National Congress, and had benefited from its advice. Curzon's strengths outweighed his faults. Every branch of his administration was affected by his policies, and at that time India enjoyed peace, prosperity, and a status which has never since been equalled. It was the acme of the British administration.

Bion's father, the fourth and youngest of the brothers, played a significant part in this period, working as a civil engineer in irrigation. His country's welfare was a matter close to his heart, and he worked part-time as secretary to the Indian Congress (Lyth, 1980, p. 269). His wife seems to have been a more ordinary person who devoted herself to the home. On arriving in Britain, Bion had the feeling of belonging to a family that was not very well off. Once, at school, he was chided by the matron for spoiling his shoes: 'Your parents are poor; they cannot afford to buy you new shoes every term!' Bion's response was to think: 'Who had said they were poor? They never told me.' Of course his parents did not live in opulence like the uncle on the plantation, but his father was one of the high-salaried engineers. Moreover, their position as part of the colonial class gave them significant advantages, and their standing as Big Game hunters conferred a certain status within Anglo-Indian society.

Bion's childhood was clearly marked by one event, the relatively close arrival of a baby sister, Edna. Wilfred and Edna proved to be the couple's only children. Bion's autobiography opens with a description of the brother and sister united in a shared fondness for their Indian *ayah*. He wonders even if they might not have been fonder of her than of their parents. He found their mother 'a little frightening', because of her unpredictable moods. Comfortably sitting on her lap, feeling warm and safe, he could suddenly feel cold and frightened: 'as it was many years later at the end of the school service when the doors were opened and a cold draught of night air seemed to sigh gently through the sermonically heated air'. In the evening they would gather round the harmonium while their mother picked out hymns. The young Bion seems to have lived in a world of marked contrasts: 'Intense light; intense black; nothing between; no twilight' (1982, p. 18).

His relationship to his father seems to have been characterized by a greater contrast still. The first memory of his father recounted in the autobiography describes Wilfred seeking admiration and approval, but eliciting the opposite reaction. From his earliest years the child Wilfred tended to ask question upon question. He remembers having completely spoiled his father's attempt to read him *Alice in Wonderland* because of his endless questions about it. Wilfred soon realized that his father was a 'sensitive' man, and discovered what could floor him or make him beside himself with rage. He wished he could rival or equal his father's powerful character. Bion devotes an entire chapter to the description of Big Game hunting in the bush. His father was renowned as a hunter.

The boy's oedipal fantasies were activated by the intensity of the dramatic atmosphere; a tigress prowled the area for several nights in search of the tiger that had been killed in the hunt.

The boy yearned for more substantial and united parents: 'indeed made in a formidably robust and uncompromising mould' (1982, p. 15), to provide limits for his imagination. Young Bion's vivid imagination added vertiginous perspectives to the most mundane realities. He baffled his mother by inquiring about the 'simply city', which turned out to be his version of the 'simplicity' he heard about in his bedtime prayers. One birthday, his father had ordered an electric train from London, one of the first such toys to be marketed. At first he was delighted by his son's interest in electricity, thinking that it was a nascent interest in engineering. Unfortunately, the barrage of questions put to him by his son soon stupefied him. The boy was still pursuing his own original associative train of thought, and was trying to find out more about 'electric city'. Bion remembers: 'I made up my mind to keep my questions to myself' (1982, p. 24). To a small boy, living in a house entirely lit by oil lamps, the concept must have seemed mysterious indeed.

The Bion parents had such absolute religious principles that they could not tolerate deception, or anything but the truth. Wilfred was often reproached for telling lies. The first chapter of the autobiography contains a recollection of a trivial quarrel with his sister. Who was lying? It was Wilfred who was spanked, across his father's knees. The quarrels with Edna often became real conflicts requiring parental intervention. Bion considered his sister to be a 'bitch', identified her with all sorts of wild animals in his imagination, and took a wicked pleasure in attacking them. He was immediately overwhelmed with remorse and guilt, so that he often managed to get himself punished by his father. His father believed in corporal punishment – or, as Bion puts it, in the principle of *'faire la sagesse entrer par le cul'*.[2]

Eventually Wilfred changed his tactics and developed a new strategy of imitating his enemy. He learned 'how to curl himself into a tight ball of snowy innocence and launch himself, with a small piece of ice in the middle, at his foe'. Wilfred and Edna quarrelled for years. Finally he decided to keep his distance. This won him a double victory. Edna began to demand imperiously that he play with her, thereby giving him the power to frustrate her. At the same time he could thwart his father's ambition for tenderness and loyalty between brother and sister. With hindsight Bion thought that their mother's love was probably more authentic than that of their father; the latter loved only his image of his children, an image of his own making, whereas her love was not an 'attitude'. Their mother could tolerate having to raise two nasty brats, while their father became 'bitterly resentful of anything that imperilled his fiction'. The siblings managed to fool strangers whenever social contact was relatively superficial and brief. In retrospect Bion thought that they had become 'an accomplished and unpleasant pair of liars, smooth and quick to see what our betters expected of us and to provide accordingly' (1982, p. 28).

Meanwhile, Wilfred's imagination was gaining the upper hand. He began to talk to 'Arf Arfer'. Through this onomatopoeic transformation of 'Our Father' he created an imaginary respondent for himself. 'Arf' began to turn up, unbidden, in his thoughts, daydreams and nightmares. He was present on all important occasions. He was loosely related to the Jesus of hymns, but also derived from the incomprehensible laughter of grown-ups: 'Arf Arf Arf!'. 'Arf Arfer's' power began to wane around the time when young Bion started school, about four years of age, at which point he met boys of his own age and came across rules other than those of his own family. With school Wilfred's life began, for the first time, to include something of a twilight as well as the intense contrasts of chiaroscuro that fired his imagination: it was the dawning of intelligence. However, another mysterious threat began to loom on the horizon: he discovered that in four years' time he was to go to school in England.

The following two years seemed to drag: nothing happened. His mother seemed sad, and although Wilfred questioned her anxiously, she replied, 'Why should I be sad?'. Nevertheless, he knew: 'But she was'. Wilfred also knew that he was not brave. Nor, perhaps, could he be as brave as the courageous Big Game hunter who had married his mother. The previous year his parents had made him a gift of an air rifle of his own. The loading mechanism entailed opening the rifle and folding it in two. Once, while it was being loaded, the two halves snapped shut on his thumb, and there was blood everywhere. His mother rescued him, and he was given a 'real bandage like a real soldier'. Seventy years later Bion gazed at the scar and could not recall having been anything but a sissy.

It was not only Jesus, 'Arf Arfer' and wild tigers that populated

Wilfred's imagination. Coming home from school with his *ayah* one day, he glimpsed two girls playing an erotic game with their tongues and, had he been allowed to, he would have been pleased to watch. One day he discovered the 'pleasure of masturbation by lying on my stomach on the floor and wiggling'. Once again his sister disappointed him – she could not share the game, nor the pleasure. He next tried to communicate the importance of his discovery to his mother. But she 'sneaked' to her husband, and the couple came to catch him out. 'I felt horribly guilty.' Wilfred was surprised, however, by their quiet tenderness. He soon returned to his 'wiggling', and was again caught out. This time he was given a therapeutic bath. This was repeated on the following two days, whereupon he became a thoroughly cleansed Christian.[3]

India made an indelible impression on the young Bion. He was never to return, but he maintained a passionate interest in the country throughout his life. A man who was usually so intellectual and so reserved records an open sensuality at that time: the blazing sun, the intense blue of the sky, the fullness of the monsoon, the midday silence of the siesta, the piercing cries of the birds, the great trees with their hanging leaves. Within this exotic nature the boy discovered the delight of playing trains. The intense heat produced a fine white dust; one nonchalant kick was rewarded with a cloud rising in the air. A few kicks and clouds of 'steam' rose from the locomotive (a 'real' one rather than the 'electric city' of father's toy train).

When he woke at night, frightened by 'Arf Arfer', his mother told him to go back to sleep and forget him. These days were coming to an end. One day he saw the son of family friends, desolate and afraid because he was leaving for England, and understood that his days in India were numbered. His life so far had taught him that it was better to keep his mouth shut. His father took him on a visit to the fortress home of an Indian ruler in Gwalior, south of New Delhi, a long way from the Punjab. Train journeys were slow, and the boy had time to develop an intimacy with his father. During the visit Wilfred felt he had a premonition of the future. They came across a trap for catching tigers, which used a live kid as bait. Wilfred was horrified, and thought how awful it would be to be the kid, and once again discovered that he was a crybaby. He was mortified at being such

a disappointment to the Big Game hunter who had hunted with
famous people such as King George V. How could his parents
have produced such a coward? Was it something to do with
'wiggling'?

2 THE SCHOOLBOY EXILE

'The mores of the class system of middle and upper class families and in the civil service of the empire were such that children, particularly boys, were sent off quite early to "public school". Wilfred Bion was one of the many victims of this now questionable custom, and was accordingly sent off on his own to England at the age of eight' (Grotstein, 1981, p. 2). There can be no doubt that this was a terribly painful experience which affected him for the rest of his life.

His mother made the long journey with him. They set off by train, interrupting the journey to visit Delhi and New Delhi. Crossing the steep slopes of the Ghats, they eventually arrived at the railway terminus, Bombay. A long sea crossing brought them to Britain. Another train journey and Wilfred was left, alone, in the playground of Bishop's Stortford College prep school. He immediately felt that he was powerless before the boys, whose natural cruelty was activated by the arrival of a new boy from India. As an old man Bion evokes the horror of this experience by his frequent use of adjectives such as 'ghastly' and 'gloomy'. The awful first day of exile seemed to go on for ever. As soon as he was in bed, he broke into sobs. One of the boys in the dormitory asked him why he was crying. Bion did not know what to say. He finally accepted the solution that it was 'homesickness'.

Every weekend seemed endless, aggravating his feelings of isolation and abandonment. As a schoolboy Bion felt that he was dying. Every Sunday the boys would go to church wearing Eton suits, and mortarboards with bright blue tassels. The sermon gave him brief respite from his tormentors, although the same could not be said of the Holy Scriptures when, compared to daily life, the Word of God seemed 'worse than useless'. Sunday lunch was not bad, but it was ruined by anticipation of the rituals of bullying that followed. In the gymnasium, where the tuck boxes were kept, the smaller boys (of whom Bion was one 'for an age') were made to crawl from one end of a high horizontal pole to the other. He could not bear to see the eager faces of the boys below watching and waiting for a faltering move.

Another feature of Sundays was the walk. Led by the taciturn headmaster, they walked the same three miles each week. To deter stragglers, a punishment of doing sums had been instituted. The thought of having to start the week by doing sums could bring a second wind to the weariest of boys. Bion learned to imagine that he owned a little railway that ran alongside the walk, which could just hold his friends. He, of course, was the engine driver. The fantasies of 'Arf Arfer' gave way to a more socialized fantasy life. His imagination was also fired in chapel, where they sang military hymns with the music master on Sunday evenings.

Before bedtime, prayers had to be said, kneeling at the bedside. One day, as he and his friend Freddie arrived late for nightly prayers, Freddie made him see the funny side of the whole ritual, and they dissolved in laughter. Seventy years later Bion still wondered whether it was immanent justice that struck down the unrepentant sinner. He recalls the punishment that followed this hilarity: Freddie was carried off by an undiagnosed appendicitis. From then on it was impossible to forget Freddie, 'punished for ever in the cemetery nearby'.

Alone in his bed Bion felt disappointment, frustration, bitterness and feelings of abandonment resurfacing in him. If the bed was not too squeaky, he would abandon himself to a session of 'wiggling'. This was so delightful that he could have laughed. One day a master caught him 'wiggling' in class – he dealt with the matter kindly, simply telling the boy that it might cause him to be 'sent away'.

Religion tormented the young Bion, because it made him fear worse punishments for 'wiggling'. On one occasion something unusual happened in chapel. After the service, the headmaster began to preach about a conspiracy of silence: 'If you knew that one of you, however esteemed he was for his games and work, was putting poison in the food of another boy, you would go to one of the masters and tell him. Yet when a boy is poisoning the mind of another, you say nothing.' As soon as the sermon was over, Bion tried to find out about this poisoning: he learned nothing except that he was a 'chump' in his ignorance. Later he found out that a boy from the senior school next door had been expelled. As the same punishment had been served on Adam and Eve, it must be something to do with 'wiggling'. Expulsion from the Garden of Eden meant death to this boy. He was convinced that it was his sin that had cast him from the Eden of India.

The young Bion used several activities to fight against feelings of loneliness and the despair of homesickness. The 'awful' weather made him yearn to hear the hymn 'Summer suns are glowing'. His schoolmates could not understand why he kept requesting this hymn while it was pouring with rain. But for Bion, who was yearning for the intensity of the monsoon, the murky dampness of the English drizzle was not rain. If only it *would* rain 'like when you heard it coming, roaring and hissing, and moaning and sighing over the trees and the grass in the distance till suddenly there it was'. The rain would burst and be followed by real sun. From time to time the boy received a brief visit from his mother. Was he unhappy? He shook his head. Did he like it there? He nodded. But when she gave him gifts, the special treats he had enjoyed in India, he absolutely refused to take them back to school.[4]

Until the age of twelve Bion was a boarder at the prep school annexed to the senior school. As he turned twelve he anticipated the new departure of starting at the main school. Soon he would be one of the big boys. Looking back, it seemed that one aspect of the playground game of trains that summer was symptomatic of this anticipated change. The boys, who had a craze for this game, organized themselves into two railway lines. 'Impelled by some memory of glorious dust', Bion tentatively joined in. He discovered at once that he had 'outstanding gifts as a locomotive'. Suddenly, wanted by both teams, he emerged from the hitherto well-preserved anonymity of the Sunday-walk game. The glory went to his head, and he was accused of 'showing off and swanking'. The glory had no sooner arrived than it was gone, and the boy returned to his private world of insignificance and obedience. 'But I had tasted what it was to be wanted – almost famous and loved' (1982, p. 49). He was to rediscover this pleasure when he become a captain of team sports, and eventually a leader within his chosen profession.

Another incident, from around the same time, convinced the young Bion that a real change was in the air. He joined a group of a dozen or so boys who, much to everyone's surprise, suddenly attacked the two team heads of the train game. Not only were the leaders deposed, but there was no retaliation, as feared and anticipated. One of the boys was promoted to the main school 'because he was judged too big – that is, too big a bully – to remain in the prep'.

Another source of help in making the transition from junior to senior school was Bion's friendships with two particular boys. He was often welcomed by their families over the holidays. It is interesting that in his autobiography Bion devotes as many chapters to memories of time spent with these boys and their families as he does to school life. Moreover, the atmosphere and mood of the text changes – it is more relaxed, the horizons expand, the prose becomes more complex and almost lyrical. Although it is often controlled by humour, the tone occasionally attains a relaxed confidence. Bion openly expresses gratitude to the kind people who offered him material comfort, sympathy, even a certain affection, and enabled him to have experiences that helped his maturation. 'Mrs Hamilton and Mrs Rhodes, both in their different ways, helped to make my last year at prep school one in which I began to break through what I see in retrospect to have been an intolerable exo-skeleton of misery' (1982, p. 54).

Bion acknowledges that school-age boys can achieve 'only a rudimentary form of love', and so it was for Heaton Rhodes, Dudley Hamilton and himself. The two boys were very different, as were their respective families. This contrast and complementarity proved an enriching experience for Bion, in his final prep school year. The Rhodes family belonged to a very prosperous rural bourgeoisie; both parents could trace their ancestors back through three or four centuries of Yorkshire history. The family lived at Archer Hall, a large farmhouse on a hilltop surrounded by fields. The little village nearby was populated entirely by Rhodes employees. It must have been painful for the boy when his hosts asked after his parents. He had managed to forget them in order to avoid the pangs of homesickness that overwhelmed him whenever he thought of them. He bitterly resented the ritual of writing the weekly letter home. His defensive forgetting was facilitated by the 'ruthless and austere' character of his hosts' lifestyle, which was reminiscent of his life with his parents. At Heaton's, however, there was an abundant variety of food never encountered at school. He also had a share of the affection that Mrs Rhodes generously bestowed upon her numerous children. Like Mrs Bion, she played harmonium while the children sang hymns. The family attended the parish church every Sunday.

Bion did not try to conceal the fact that he identified more with the Hamiltons than with the Rhodes family. They also ran a farm, but on a larger and more lucrative scale. Their wealth – embodied, for Bion, in their magnificent Bollet automobile, which rivalled the magnificence of the locomotives of his imagination – introduced him to a different world, one that 'literally and metaphorically stank' with money. Young Bion admired Mr Hamilton's perspicacity, business sense and keen, alert manner. The boy would burst out laughing, in genuine mirth, at his jokes and stories. He was also falling in love with Mrs Hamilton. Idealization always glows through happy memories: 'I must have felt Mrs Hamilton's personality as spring to my prep school winter' (1982, p. 54). The boy very much enjoyed being in this huge house, full of beautiful things. The children usually played outdoors in the garden, with its large lawns and huge cedar.

Wilfred and his friend Dudley were reaching the awkward age where parents' patience and affection is sorely tested. The two accomplices found that their games were not without malice. They tried to catch birds using bird lime. They almost set fire to the house playing war games with toy soldiers, miniature cannons and real gunpowder. Another pastime was to chase the cat, lure her under a large earthenware flowerpot, then smash the pot with a croquet mallet, releasing a terrified animal. On one occasion the boys decided to replace the cat with Dudley's youngest brother Colin, but fortunately for them, Colin would not play. These games were eventually brought to an end because the gardener complained about his flowerpots. Mrs Hamilton thought them cruel.

The last straw was when the boys built an 'aeroplane' from the gardener's bamboo canes. Again the parents intervened in the nick of time, as the boys were about to hurl themselves from the roof into a thirty-foot drop to the garden below. As he listened to Mrs Hamilton talking tenderly to Dudley, Wilfred realized that they might have seriously injured or even killed themselves. Only after he had become a parent himself did Bion realize what a responsibility he must have been for his hosts.

'Living with the Hamiltons typified luxury, warmth, almost sybaritic pleasure' (1982, p. 75). One night in bed, waiting for Dudley to come to bed, Bion saw Dudley suddenly discard the towel he had round his waist. He straddled Wilfred as if challenging him to wrestle. Bion remembers that he had no physical response, only a sense of boredom and anticlimax. These feelings communicated themselves to Dudley, who soon gave up trying to provoke a struggle. With the hindsight of an old man Bion explained that in this incident as a boy he was experiencing a deep and silent fear of the changes that were taking place within him. It was only much later that he, like the other schoolboys, realized that he was going through the changes of puberty. The autobiography assures us that the pre-adolescent boy had not understood what was happening with Dudley, even if his analyst, years later, insisted that he had known. Bion simply experienced fear, guilt, frustration and furtiveness – what he termed the contributors to 'an absolute hatred and loathing of sexuality in any form'. Wilfred and Dudley gradually avoided their friendly tussles. Never again was he intimate with Heaton.

That September Bion was once again a new boy, but this time he was with his friends at the main school nearby. This was at the beginning of the twentieth century, and Bishop's Stortford College was one of the public schools that went back to the Victorian era, a time when the middle classes had sufficiently large incomes to maintain such schools, to form a homogeneous, coherent elite known as 'the Establishment'. (Bion later accords the Establishment a significant place in his intuitive understanding of groups.) At the beginning of the twentieth century the Establishment already constituted a dominant minority, recognizable through its traditions, education and social behaviour. It controlled the future of the nation. Education maintained this tradition through inculcating a social apprenticeship in the public schools. Children of the middle classes could hope to join the Establishment if they made their way through one of these exclusive institutions. It was with this hope in mind that the Bions had sent their son to such a school. Being a boarder at Bishop's Stortford, as at any other public school, meant conforming to strict discipline. It was this authoritarian education that Great Britain imposed on its colonial empire.

In the nineteenth century public schools aimed to produce practising Christians, but by the twentieth these links with the Church had begun to loosen. It may be that many children had a happy emotional experience there, but certain practices and certain moments could be particularly unpleasant: fagging, bullying, gossip, 'jokes' and pranks, the pressure to conform, the obsession with sports and games. Above all, the homesickness of young children separated from home, and the massive repression of sexuality, have been amply documented as negative experiences (Gathorne-Hardy, 1977).

At the threshold of adolescence Bion started at the main school, anxious about once again becoming a new boy. He tells his readers how he was chosen to fag for two sixth-formers, on the basis of his friendship with Rhodes, because the latter had the push and drive necessary in a competent fag. Bion had grown into a large, dreamy boy with a deep voice. He remembers that at the time he was incapable of making toast without burning it, or of making sure there was enough milk for the sixth-formers' breakfasts. Therefore he frequently had to borrow cans of evaporated 'Swiss' milk from other boys, and was duly nicknamed 'Swizz'. After two terms the sixth-formers could stand it no longer: 'To my great relief I was sacked and returned to the obscurity of the school common room. I was *no good* – a failure for which I was profoundly thankful' (1982, p. 76). In this passage Bion gives us an insight into the depth and complexity of his personality. He was grateful to be able to merge back into the obscurity of the mass of schoolboys. He had experienced something similar a few months earlier, when he was stopped from being the locomotive in the train game. However, the use of the verb 'sacked' perhaps connotes the feeling of loss of self-esteem at the return from distinction to anonymity. It is a verb that Bion uses to describe the frustrations and setbacks in his military career in the medical service in the Second World War.

Bishop's Stortford College had a reputation for being less traditional than other public schools. Once Bion had become an eminent psychoanalyst, he maintained that the school was 'enlightened and ahead of its time'. First, sex *was* sometimes mentioned. The headmaster considered the school 'intact as a kind of gigantic sexual pressure cooker', and kept it under the vigilance of two or three masters of unimpeachable integrity. These professionals, aided by a system of boys of similar outlook – albeit less established – formed a network of 'honourable spying'. They detected any steam that escaped from the pressure cooker, and reported it at once to the appropriate authority. 'At this point the big guns came into action, although loosing off only small-arm ammunition in the form of a cosy sexual talk.' Bion was to have direct experience of this when he too, much to his surprise, was invited to 'have a cup of tea' with one of the masters.

At the beginning of the century, religion still played a significant part in the daily routine of school life. The sensitive adolescent blew hot and cold about religion, oscillating between the celestial beatitudes of the elect believers and the darkness of Hell, the threatening yet exciting world of the outcast. Gradually Bion developed a hatred of religion which was not only ineffectual but also seemed to create obstacles to sexual pleasure. His ambivalence verged on duplicity, as every Sunday afternoon he went to the voluntarily organized prayer meeting. Bion was impressed by the sincerity of the boys who prayed so hard to God. He wanted to be like them – not least because the most important among them were also the best athletes in the sixth form. Maybe a good religious vow, Celestial Selection Committee willing, would guarantee membership of the water-polo team! In any case, a few Sundays later he was selected for the polo team, as he had wished.

The public schools had enthusiastically encouraged sports and team games for decades. Bion felt that he instinctively turned to physical activity as an outlet for sexual energy: 'Games were substituted for sex' (1982, p. 92). By the time he arrived at the main school he was already proficient at all games except cricket. He trained hard, and soon became first-class at everything. This was a significant gratification of his self-esteem, and brought him the respect of his peers. Furthermore, his abilities reassured him that 'wiggling' had not damaged him. Bion liked swimming and water polo. It was soon evident that he was as adept at rugby. He came nearer to playing for the sake of the game than he did to working for the sake of school work.

In 1914 Bion was seventeen, and had been at the same school for eight years. He did not seem to be in any hurry to leave. Secretly, he wished he could become an international sportsman at Oxford or Cambridge. The usual continuation of public-school education was a move to one of the prestigious universities. Academic work was one of Bion's weak spots. Sadly, he thought of his finances: he would have to win a scholarship. He decided on history. Finally he wrote to his parents, but received the negative reply he had anticipated. He did go to Oxford to sit the scholarship exams, but his knowledge did not match his desire. Neither was his family poor enough for him to be entitled to an exhibition.

Soon talk of war began to seep through the protective doors of the public school. The masters seemed to think that the events in Agadir and Germany were more important than the syllabus. The question 'Do you think there will be a war, sir?' became more and more frequent. At the beginning of the second term of the 1914–15 academic year, the war was not only a question of talk. The exciting sounds of an army band drew the boys to the gates. For the first time they saw a division of the Territorial Army march by in columns. From that point on Bion found it even more difficult to concentrate on his school work, even though he was a prefect. His dreams of glory soon turned to ashes. Of what use was being captain of the First XV at rugby and captain of the swimming team, when the heart had gone out of inter-school contests? His final year at school ended in an anticlimax – it was an angry, unhappy young man who left Bishop's Stortford College.

Nevertheless, Bion retained a very good opinion of his school. The main school was 'well disciplined and extremely enlightened. It can stand comparison with any other known to me since. It was lively intellectually and emotionally' (1982, p. 85). The school had furnished the child, then the adolescent, with a competence in general knowledge. Bion made good use of this in his later work. It also provided him with an excellent education of the type that enabled him to recognize other members of the 'Establishment' at a glance. The school had refined his language and his accent. As he embarked for England, his mother had advised him to remember to pronounce his H's, to distinguish himself from 'badly educated' people. At public school Bion had noticed the absence of swearing. He often asked his family's or his friends' parents' advice on correct pronunciation. Correct pronunciation was thought to be an indispensable component of good manners, those of a 'gentleman'. Bion had rubbed shoulders with wealthy intellectuals of the upper middle classes and had adopted their tastes, aspirations and mores.

3   THE GREAT WAR

No sooner was school over than Bion took the train to London, where he was met by his parents. Although he was slightly afraid of the doors closing behind him, he yearned for freedom. His parents were happy to see their son again, yet the prospect of mobilization for war loomed ominously over their reunion. Bion admitted that military music had the power to move him – its sonorous violence simultaneously stimulated and soothed him. The following morning he went to the Territorial Army recruiting office, and was devastated at being rejected.

At the hotel with his parents the atmosphere left much to be desired. Wilfred suspected his parents of reproaching him for being hostile, resentful and selfish. His father made it clear that he could not understand how his son could be rejected by a nation at war, and contacted a family friend 'with connections'. An opulent dinner was followed by successful intervention on his son's behalf. On 4 January 1916 Bion joined the armed forces. He had joined up with an awareness of the probability of dying, as he returned to school that very afternoon to share out his books and belongings among friends. He was convinced that he would never need them again (Pines [ed.] 1985, p. 387). Bion's uniform was 'baggy, itchy and hot', although his mother was proud to see him in it. The comparative comfort of the Officers' Training Unit was much appreciated. Thanks to his sporting abilities, he did very well and had no difficulty in passing his exams at the end of the course.

Bion described himself as 'hard-headed, timid, gloomy and revolting', adding that he felt alienated from his fellow training officers by his 'immaturity, queerness, nonconformity; drawn to

them by the same difference' (1982, p. 112). He then went to the
Tank Battalion, via Bisley transit camp. The schoolboy who played
at locomotives had become the driver of armoured vehicles. The
mood became serious; most of the men in the camp had already
been in active service at the front. Bion had the right to one
weekend pass. He spent the weekend visiting his mother in
London. It was horribly evocative of the prep school weekends.
She was preoccupied with him as a child, while he wished only to
be seen as a soldier.

Bion was commissioned and posted to the 5th Tank Battalion at
Bovingdon, Wool. He had opted for adventure in choosing to work
with a new weapon that was still shrouded in secrecy. The term
tank, meaning reservoir, had been used by the British to confuse
German spies. The first British tank, the Mark 1, was brought into
service on 1 February 1916. It was an impressive 40-ton mass,
although its bullet-proof armouring was vulnerable to shrapnel and
shells. Its mobility left much to be desired; the 105 horsepower
vehicle could reach two or three miles an hour on roads, but no
more than one mile an hour across land. The range of action was
limited to seven miles. At first sight the tanks reminded him of
nothing more than the primitive machinery of the tiger traps near
Gwalior that had frightened him as a child. He felt that this camp
presaged something ominously real, unlike the 'ramshackle,
temporary and amateur' quality of his previous camps. At
Bovingdon, even a fresh sublieutenant like himself was expected
to become an officer. One day the great news was announced: the
battalion was being sent overseas. 'How I wished my mother could
see us as we marched down to Wool station' (1982, p. 116). His
mother had followed him down to Wool, and was staying in a
rented cottage in the village.

The embarkation for Le Havre took place on a lovely sunny day,
and the mood was euphoric. Gradually the euphoria was replaced
by a dull, anxious routine. How could he envisage a destination as
mysterious as 'the front'? The not knowing was unbearable; stories
and rumours were circulated. Already an extraordinary transformation had taken place. Bion, the inveterate inquirer, had caught the
passive resignation of his peers: 'we did not ask questions requiring
answers. It was wiser to sleep'. Bion grew acutely aware of the gulf
that separated the officers from the men. The latter travelled in
different-class train compartments. He was also aware of the

difference between the believers and the non-believers. Bion and four others were believers: 'In the view of other members of our company we were "pi" or just plain humbug'. Yet they were all heading for the front. No sooner had they disembarked than everyone waited for something to happen. 'We had not even begun to realize that nothing happens in war, or – which comes to much the same – nobody knows what happens' (1982, p. 120).

The troops would have to tolerate the cold and the wet for a long time to come. They would often have to throw themselves into wet mud to protect themselves from shell fire. The prospect of imminent action had created deep and relentless fear. Most of them began to wonder how it was possible to survive exposure to such hell. One day it was the turn of Bion's section to go into action. The tanks were being sent in to help an infantry division by 'clearing up' a couple of German pillboxes. The ruins of a town were sighted; it could only be Ypres. They were stationed in Belgian Flanders on the famous 'Salient' where, between 1914 and 1918, so many battles were fought and so many lives lost. Their orders were to carry gas masks in case of an alert. Writing his autobiography, the veteran mourned the fact that names such as the Salient and the canal (from the Yser to the Lys) were only islands in the mists of the memories of a few people, when they had meant so much during the Great War.

Nightfall brought the first reconnaissance mission to an end. There were many yet to come, and the next morning Bion set off again with an officer, Quainton, another 'pi' and a good friend. The terrain was unrecognizable, bearing no resemblance to the map: there was nothing to be seen; no trenches, redoubts, fortifications or machines. Bion noticed that his hands were trembling, and was annoyed to find that he could not control them. The sound of a sudden explosion made them dive into the muddy earth, until they realized that the explosion was a hundred yards or so away, and therefore of no immediate danger to them. Bion blushed with humiliation – he was so obsessed with the fear of being thought a coward. He tried to walk away with as much casualness as he could muster. A new anxiety grew as they tried to find their objective, the Steenbeck, those notorious fortifications that had been such an obstacle to the British troops.

Despite returning empty-handed, the officers brought the two tanks to the rendezvous detailed for the attack. They arrived at the appointed hour, and the column of eight tanks set off immediately. Sixty years later, the details of the events of that night were still etched clearly in Bion's memory. He found himself in his familiar nightmare. As tank leader he was positioned in front, outside, signalling to the driver through his front flap: 'The tank commander's private fear now possessed me – that I would fall wounded, unobserved by the crew and so be driven over by the tank' (1982, p. 130).

How was he to locate on the map the mudbath in which his tank and its crew were wallowing? Bion was convinced that he and all or part of his crew were going to die. The tank hit an obstacle and tried to override it. The transmission went, and the engine was freewheeling. The whole crew tumbled into the mud. The sergeant pulled Bion out of the way just in time to avoid a bullet in the head. Under the shock of intolerable emotion, Bion had the sensation of floating about four feet above his body. This depersonalization automatically gave him a sense of security. The potential danger of this kind of security was that one could remain unaware of imminent death. Bion followed his training instructions and ordered the formation of a 'strongpoint' between the tank and the enemy. There, with their equipment, ammunition and Lewis guns, they stayed from morning to dusk. They were relieved when they recognized some British soldiers retreating. An officer gave them orders to withdraw to company headquarters.

Bion was worried about his indifference to death. Writing about his experiences, he found that fragments of exact actions, intonations, events, all seemed indelibly etched on his memory. The verb 'etch' should be taken literally, as Bion had always had an unusually visual memory. Scenes of the war were retained in his memory with the same clarity as the dispatches of a war correspondent writing for a readership. Then everything seemed to vanish, in a matter of days after the events themselves. It was as if nothing outside the 'here and now' of his continuing life could exist. The emotions returned with great intensity as he wrote his autobiography and recollected the memories. Writing provided a way of absorbing the surplus emotions that had been preserved intact.

One day the tank division was posted to a landscape of chalky hills. In the train they discovered that their destination was

Cambrai. The great railway junction there was a nerve centre of the German Army's communications network.

At Cambrai British command sent into action practically all of the Royal Tank Corps, supported by 300 planes and eight infantry divisions. The battleground seemed to Bion to resemble a diagram. The tanks were so perfectly complemented by the infantry's artillery that the whole might have been a commanding officer's dream. The Germans, struggling painfully to hold the front, were in a state of confusion. The only resistance point was the village of Flesquières, and it was to this village that Bion aimed his tank at top speed – four miles an hour. The exhilaration came to an abrupt end when an explosion sounded from the rear of the tank. It stopped.

The tank had been hit by a shell. It had narrowly missed igniting ninety gallons of petrol. An NCO reported to Bion that there were no officers left, asking him to take command of the infantry. Bion accepted but, aware that he knew nothing about infantry fighting, he asked the NCO to stay with him as adviser. They managed to hold their positions, although some of the infantry had to yield some ground. They lit their marker flares when British reconnaissance planes flew over. That was the end of Bion's part in the battle of Cambrai.

The following day Bion discovered that the battle was over. He gave an account of the troops' actions, was congratulated, and the Major said he was going to recommend him for the Military Cross. His colleagues congratulated him and were surprised at his dismay. Bion found it difficult to be publicly distinguished from the group, even when he had done everything to deserve it. In his heart of hearts he was afraid of being thought an impostor, especially as a rumour was circulating that one British officer had been firing at the Highlander troops from the roof of his tank. The Major informed him that a report from the 51st Infantry Division confirmed his own account, and that he was being put in for the Victoria Cross. Bion felt guilt and embarrassment as he glimpsed the envious and disgruntled glances of his peers, as if every officer was wondering: 'Why him? Why not me?'. His embarrassment was even greater when he faced his own tank crew, who had shared the danger with him. The junior officer was to undergo a further interview with the General before being recognized for 'valour'.

As the battalion had no more tanks, it was withdrawn to winter quarters to be re-equipped. Bion was made section leader. For him the winter of 1917 was 'horrible' – as, indeed, it was for so many others. The camp had a sordid atmosphere, and it was dilapidated. Bion was the only officer to have retained some of his men, who had been with him from the start. Where were the others now? The 5th Battalion, to which he had been so attached in England, was now almost entirely restaffed. Since Cambrai, something had changed irreversibly. The officers calculated that they had lost over a third of their men and officers in each action.

Overwhelmed by an unbearable tension that seemed to be pulling him towards death more than life, Bion had, instinctively, strengthened his attachments to his old comrades, his crew and the 'pi' group. But every attachment brought with it the experience of being torn apart and having to make new attachments: 'we were swallowed up amongst so many new boys that we hardly existed' (1982, p. 182). Bion clung on to the few friendships that fate, impenetrable and obscure, permitted him. Quainton, a lively and brilliant man, who was a Quaker, enabled him to maintain a difficult relationship with God. It was with Quainton that he went to the services at the chapel hut at the bottom of the camp. One day Quainton went on leave, and never returned. In a letter to the battalion he wrote that he had ended up in a 'loony bin' following a car accident. He had been diagnosed as suffering from 'shell shock'. Some of the men assumed that this was shrewd malingering, although Bion knew that Quainton was not a fraudulent man. This news greatly increased Bion's anxiety, as since his school days he had been afraid that he might lose his mind. Throughout the war there had been no question of masturbation or sexual desire, as all reserves of energy were expended in physical activity.

The early months of 1918 dragged by. Nothing was happening. Locked into a war of positions, the 5th Battalion prepared to dig trenches in the frozen ground. It was amid this gloom and despair that Bion received the news: he was given leave to return to London to receive the Distinguished Service Order. Bion had to admit he was happy: 'I could hardly believe it . . . Second Lieutenants with DSO's were rare birds anyway' (1982, p. 188). About sixty men and officers received decorations during that investiture at Buckingham Palace. Bion was by far the youngest officer there. As soon as the ceremony was over, the young officer avoided the reporters and press photographers to greet his mother, who was waiting outside.

'It seemed a shame that she had not been allowed in to see and share the glorious moment which was in fact so much hers and so little mine' (p. 190).

As before, the leave for which he had so ardently wished left him with nothing but fierce unhappiness. Faced with her son's morose taciturnity, his mother felt defeated and helpless. Bion, too, was embarrassed by his own hostile silence. The only relief came when she was able to express her misery, and cry openly. Luckily or unluckily, the newspaper headlines announced a Great New German Attack: all soldiers to be recalled.

At the age of nineteen, nobody could bear the prospect of a return to Hell. Bion felt that he and his mother were behaving like automata. By eight in the evening neither could stand any more, and they each withdrew to their hotel room. The following morning they did not talk; each had withdrawn. He went alone to join a crowd of soldiers in uniform.

Bion was dismayed to find that his battalion was to be made into a reserve force for the French infantry. In the next few months he had plenty of time for self-reflection, and was more inclined to introspection than to conversation. He had idealist goals of being a perfect officer. He could not always achieve such ideals, as his training had been in the armoured division and he was now working with infantrymen. Every inadequacy, imaginary or perceived, gave rise to self-accusations of being only a decorated schoolboy in uniform. At least he no longer yearned to prove himself brave; he wanted only not to disgrace himself. As a section commander he discovered the problems of loneliness and isolation. Peering into the no-man's-land before him, he had the disorientating experience of isolation, living in waking reality what had been familiar to him in childhood nightmares. Bion and his men stayed in their trench positions for three weeks. When they were relieved, the lieutenant was amazed to find fifteen out of the twenty still alive. It was the first time the losses had been so low.

We have selected these war memories for several reasons. First, Bion was unlucky enough to belong to one of the generations decimated by the Great War; the war so named after the scale of destruction and number of lives it claimed. The participation of the United States of America made it the first world war in history. In the course of its four years, some sixty-five million men faced battle, and the British Empire mobilized some nine million soldiers, of whom 90,000 were killed in action. Bion remained profoundly affected by this terrifying and cruel ordeal for the rest of his life. Its effect on his life is evident in the autobiography, which is largely centred on his experiences of this war. Secondly, the memories provide much more than the 'retro' mood of compelling or tragic narratives. In later years Bion used his psychoanalytic talents to explore the extreme, the unbearable, and also the rich emotions of this time. In the light of these experiences, his theses on the relationship between thinking and action, on the container and the contained, his thoughts on claustrophobia and on lying, his enigmatic concepts of 'the terror without name' and 'reversal of the alpha function', acquire extraordinary reality and depth. Finally, Bion never wrote better than when he was recollecting lived experience, either his own or that of his patients. Totally without pretension, he writes in a lively, funny, precise, evocative, dense, elliptical prose style: in other words, this is *real* writing.

After their infantry experience the armoured division were sent to billets in one of the villages close to the central workshops. It was a comfortable billet. Bion was now a lieutenant, the top of his rank at the age of twenty-one. This entitled him to a room of his own, with clean sheets. He had a new uniform, which fitted him well. He was also entitled to new underclothes, which meant that for the first time he was free from making the agonizing choice between being warm and itching with lice or being 'free of bites and blue with cold'. The comfort of the clothing and the civilian housing greatly improved morale. A pleasant routine was re-created.

Eventually General Foch took over command of the Allied forces, and he launched the 'second battle of the Marne' on 18 July. British troops joined the offensive in August, under direction from General Haig. Once again in the armoured division, Bion had to put up with the fact that the infantry were not making much use of this new weapon. As the operation was top secret, the manoeuvres began at night. Officers were instructed that the operation was on a large scale, located at Amiens. Bion volunteered to accompany the officer on reconnaissance mission. The two of them set out on a beautiful clear, hot afternoon. Bion began to take bearings with his compass 'as my way of keeping fear at bay and giving myself something to do'. The very numerous compass bearings also proved useful later for the manoeuvres of the tank division.

Bion's imagination constructed scenarios of what might happen. His fantasies were abruptly interrupted as he heard the first engine starting up, and he was gripped by an acute fear. 'Sooner or later my parents would be bound to have the telegram announcing my death; the war had only to go on long enough. Already I had exhausted my quota of chances of survival' (1982, p. 247). The tanks had left their departure point and Bion found himself with two men, brothers, in a shell hole. How were they going to reach the agreed rallying point now that the enemy had unleashed a barrage of fire? One of the brothers disappeared in the fog; the other had half his chest blasted away. Bion could not make out his bearings. Suddenly the bombardment ceased, and the night and fog were replaced by daylight and sunshine. It was a marvellous day, 'just the day for a battle' – the ground was suitable for tanks. Bion made his way to the rendezvous point in the nick of time. All the objectives were reached. For the first time the British had achieved a victory without losing more than a third of their men. It was the first time since disembarking at Le Havre that Bion saw troops marching in columns. They were walking towards the valley of the Luce.

Throughout the war Bion had encountered lies. The propaganda of governments trying to shield the population from the actual situation; half-truths, euphemisms or distortions from commanders seeking to avoid losing face or status; pious lies, too, addressed to the families of those killed. So much unbearable truth to be avoided. Bion was questioning the attitude of some of his superiors, as it was said that they were more concerned with personal kudos than with the safety of their troops.

A little later Bion was overjoyed to be in London, on leave, in a Turkish bath. He was listening to two old fellows discussing the war news in the evening paper. Bion hoped that the Turkish bath would cleanse him of all the filth and grime accumulated during the war. As he fell asleep there, he was plagued by all the repressed feelings and memories swirling in his mind. Try as he might to keep a comfortable distance from his disturbing inner world, he seemed to have become a mortuary for all the dead of his battalion. They haunted him with reminders of his obligations: 'The old ghosts never die. They don't even fade away; they preserve their youth wonderfully' (1982, p. 264). These ghosts were becoming vampires, draining his entire life's blood. With only the outward appearance of life left, Bion was convinced: 'I? Oh yes, I died – on August 8th 1918' (1982, p. 265).

Bion went to Cheltenham, where his mother was staying in order to be near his sister at school. He thought that both the school concert and the town were very nice. But he felt withdrawn, able to maintain only a superficial contact with the people there: 'Relations with anyone I respected were intolerable, notably with my mother; I wanted nothing except to get back to the Front just to get away from England and from her' (1982, p. 266). Leaning out of the train window to say goodbye to his mother, he warned her that the door was filthy. His mother, close to tears, again replied: 'Everything is dreadful . . . I mean nothing is really cleared up nowadays.' And on that note they parted. This goodbye at the station later became evocative, for Bion, of the final separation from his mother. She died a few months before the outbreak of the Second World War. It was as if, that day, Bion had taken his final leave of her.

Bion rejoined his battalion at Blangy. The war situation had altered profoundly in favour of the Allied forces, and victory rather than defeat seemed likely. But having been so repeatedly disappointed, they did not dare trust in the hope that the end of the war might be in sight. Bion seemed to relax for the first time since his recruitment. He liked and respected both his colonel and his company commanders: 'regular soldiers, efficient, quiet, unspectacular' (1982, p. 279). He could identify with them. He was now a captain, and a bright red ribbon was added to the DSO as he was awarded the Legion of Honour by the French government for his part in the action of 8 August.

The end of the war was imminent, but Bion was in the action literally until the last minute. All the officers had been notified that the ceasefire would take place at eleven o'clock, on the eleventh day of the eleventh month. He watched incredulously as the Germans spent the last five minutes firing all the ammunition they had left. The British replied with a 'proper barrage', and it was like the Somme again. How many lives were lost in that last 'little joke'? Fate then let fly the Parthian shot to the young man who wished to be liked by his troops and to have the respect of his superiors. The troops were close to mutiny because the rations were bad. Bion explained that the shortages would not last long, as they were due to the army giving up part of its rations to feed the civilian population. A little later Captain Bion was informed by his Sergeant Major that the troops were refusing to go on parade. Bion managed to get them on parade only by ordering the Lewis gun crews to turn their sights on the barracks. When they paraded he could see their glances of 'anger, resentment, humiliation'.

Christmas 1918 reaffirmed Bion's conviction that people will use 'anything to hold at bay the dark and sombre world of thought'. Demobilization followed shortly after the festivities. The train that took them back to London had no lights. Someone protested: 'Ruddy heroes when you're wanted; so much muck when it's finished'. When he left the army, Bion began to realize that the war had imposed responsibilities that were beyond his capacities, his training and his education. 'Though we did not realize it, we were men who had grown from insignificance to irrelevance in the passage of a few short years' (1982, p. 286).

4 THE YEARS OF TRAINING

Bion wasted no time – the day after demobilization he went to Oxford University. He did not find it difficult to gain admission. He mentioned his sporting achievements and his two military decorations, and was offered a place. He chose to read history. From the outset he was overwhelmed by the aura of intellectual brilliance with which Oxford was surrounded, and undermined by a feeling of inferiority. Other students had come from schools with more famous names, from homes with a university tradition. It was the opposite for him. His sense of inferiority exaggerated the esteem in which he held the university: 'Oxford was kind and tolerant . . . Oxford was marvellous'. It was close to this *alma mater* that he came to die at the end of a long life.

One tragedy of the aftermath of war is that the men who return to civilian life often feel alienated. Although Bion liked university, he suffered from isolation and demoralization. 'Peace time was no time for me. I did know, however many pretty ribbons I put on a wartime uniform, wartime also was no time for me. I was twenty-four; no good for war, no good for peace and too old to change' (1985, p. 16). The terror of realization would often burst out in sleep as a nightmare. Night after night he dreamed he was flattened on his stomach, clinging by his nails to a slippery slope. A raging torrent flowed at the foot of the slope: the muddy stream of the Steenbeck (the impassable German fortress). It was towards this that he was slipping. He would wake covered in sweat. Daylight barely dissipated the terrifying darkness of his subterranean world. 'Was I going crazy? Perhaps I *was* crazy.'

From 1919 onwards Bion read history at Queen's College. There he met H.J. Paton, a professor of philosophy through whom he became interested in the work of Kant. This encounter with philosophy was to have a lasting impact, particularly evident in the psychoanalytic epistemology he formulated in his fifties. Alongside his studies Bion continued to devote himself to sport; he reached a high level of competence. As captain of the Oxford University swimming team he led them to second place in the annual list of prizewinners. He also played for the rugby team, which topped the inter-university league in 1919, winning a blue. For the rest of his life he regretted not having been able to play in the varsity match because of a torn cartilage in his knee.

Bion was awarded his degree in 1921. He seems to have been quite proud of it, as he added he letters BA to the initials of his military decorations whenever he used his full name and title. Beause of the war he had entered university halfway through the year, and had thus completed his studies short of the usual three years. He was therefore not entitled to the honours degree he had hoped for, in order to be able to follow an academic career. Later, however, he told his friends that he had no regrets over not having pursued an academic career. Bion decided to improve his knowledge of French language and literature, and spent 1921–2 at Poitiers University. Although he read French fluently, he did not consider himself capable of speaking it. He maintained his admiration of French literature, and his later writings are studded with quotations in the original French. He later cited his year at university in France as a preparation for writing his book *The Dream* (see Lyth, 1980, p. 231). Since he had to earn a living, Bion decided to become a schoolteacher after all. He returned, as a teacher, to his old school at Bishop's Stortford.

His arrival there in 1922 had quite an impact – as the boys met a young man (barely twenty-five years old), built like an ox, decorated with military and sporting honours. His impassivity and brusque speech initially caused some intimidation, which was soon transformed into considerable respect and admiration – for some it even became adulation. Bion wanted to share his cultural interests, and maintained a reputation as a polymath. His skill at providing abundant and apt quotations was impressive. His status increased still further as he trained the swimming team to success. Invitations to Sunday afternoons at his home were much sought after. Despite this apparent success, Bion felt himself less and less suited to teaching. From the early 1920s onwards he and his old school friends had an annual Boxing Day reunion at Happisburgh. On New Year's Day they would swim in the North Sea. These reunions were of the mind as well as the body, and were occasions for stimulating intellectual discussions. It was on one of these occasions that Bion first read Freud in a book brought by one of his friends.

A surprising event concluded Bion's teaching career. He was friends with one of his students, an intelligent and athletic boy whom he had invited from time to time to have tea at his house. Bion thought this boy must have a very attractive mother or sister, and suggested that he might bring his mother with him to tea. The mother arrived by herself, and was far from being the beauty he had imagined. He found a large, gaunt, flushed, shifty and uncommunicative woman who seemed to be hostile towards him. Although tea was convivial enough, the next morning Bion was summoned by the headmaster, who had been notified by the mother that her son had been the victim of sexual advances from his teacher. Despite his protests, Bion was asked to resign on the spot. When the meeting was over he found it difficult to master the situation, and became preoccupied with the whole affair. He acknowledged that he had had enough of teaching, and wished he had the nerve to pack it all in. But that was a long way from the reality of being sacked. Bion knew also that he had never been at ease on the stormy seas of sexuality. All the guilty fantasies of his school days rose to the surface of his consciousness. This confusion prevented him from taking legal advice and undertaking an action for damages.

Bion left Bishop's Stortford School with the aim of starting a medical training and becoming a psychoanalyst. He was afraid that he might not be admitted, as his results from Oxford were mediocre. Sympathetic tutors attributed his 'blockhead' nature to the effects of war. In any case, his military and sporting track record was very much in his favour. He was offered a place at University College London, and passed his first-year preliminary exams without difficulty. Oxford had given him the opportunity to meet a range of people who changed his life and with whom he developed friendships. He felt at home at University College; he worked hard and achieved his personal ambitions. All his lecturers were competent and some of them were famous – such as Elliott-Smith, whose course on the physiology of the brain Bion

valued highly. He was fortunate enough to be invited by Sir Jack
Drummond to his club and to his home. Bion remembered
discussions and conversations between the famous people he met
there. His morale was revived.

Bion tended to judge himself and his life somewhat harshly,
motivated by a narcissistic preoccupation tinged with guilt. In the
early days he foresaw his future as doomed to frustration, with fate
against him. His sporting career, he felt, had been frustrated by a
torn cartilage the day before his team won a blue; his military career
has been spoiled because he had not been a fearless and blameless
officer; his university career had been botched by his failure to
obtain an honours degree. He did not appear to be a failure to his
old school friends (Anon., in Pines [ed.] 1985, p. 388). He was
remembered as a young man who had a successful higher
education, played rugby for the prestigious Harlequins team, and
topped this by winning the gold medal for surgery.

Bion began his housemanship at University College Hospital, and
was pleased to find himself working with 'a truly remarkable staff'.
One man, however, made a particular impression: Wilfred Trotter,
who became surgeon to King George V. Bion, one of his attendant
dressers, was happy to be able to work in close collaboration with
a man of such technical expertise and character. In Trotter's
maturity and integrity Bion found one of the father figures he was
to value throughout his life. Yet these father figures found it hard
not to become fallen idols, so critical was Bion's searching gaze.
Towards the end of his life Bion acknowledged that Trotter had
remained a role model for him throughout his professional career.
Even compared to another surgeon of greater renown, Trotter won
the young man's loyalty: 'Trotter, on the other hand, listened with
unassumed interest, as if the patient's contributions flowed from
the fount of knowledge itself . . . His undisturbed friendly interest
had the effect of eliciting further evidence from the patient; the
fount of knowledge did not dry up' (1985, p. 38). His ethical
superiority, based on personal integrity, had the added advantage
of greater professional efficiency. When other surgeons carried out
a skin graft, it might not take; Trotter's grafts, in contrast, were
never rejected by the body. (With this anecdote we should note the
importance that Bion accorded all matters concerning the 'psychic
envelope' of the skin, a preoccupation which led him eventually to
develop his theory of the psychic 'container'.)

Identifying with Trotter and his self-confidence helped Bion to modify his severe super-ego. He could tolerate making mistakes, as even a past master like Trotter could sometimes be wrong. Despite his temper, Trotter accepted his limitations, and those of others. Even though he was not as brilliant a lecturer as others, he 'spoke with an authority, a mastery of the subject which was unmistakable'. In his autobiography Bion does not mention that Trotter was the first to turn his mind to the problem of the psychology of group behaviour. From 1908 onwards he began to publish on the 'herd instinct', and his writings had introduced a wide readership to his concepts. His well-known book *Instincts of the Herd in Peace and War* was written during the First World War, and he had kept abreast of the advances in social psychology brought about by the war years. His book was studied by all who sought to prevent the outbreak of future wars, to find means of controlling the group instinct's tendency to find violent expression.

Bion had duped his friends and acquaintances. Despite success and social adaptation, he suffered from deep dissatisfaction. It was in the course of his medical studies, at around the age of thirty, that he suffered a serious emotional crisis and, for the first time, sought therapeutic help. He experienced moods of rage and despair following an encounter with a Miss Hall, the sister of a friend who had offered him hospitality after his resignation from Bishop's Stortford. Bion's autobiography dwells at some length on his immaturity. His experiences with his sister had left him with the conviction that all girls were 'selfish bitches', trying to create trouble by telling tales. He was still smarting from the episode with his pupil's mother, who had, as it seemed to him, been hypocritical enough to accept his hospitality and then immediately demanded his resignation from the headmaster. His medical studies had given him some knowledge of the female body, culled from anatomy texts. With difficulty he had acquired this knowledge by excluding the medium of pleasure: 'My intimidating conscience would not allow me to learn, or even allow an attractive young woman to teach me'. As a result, he had not thought about marriage for many years. Everything to do with sex he associated with 'ideas of temptation (nice feelings), madness, purity and high ideals'. It is not difficult to understand why such a romantic young man should have been so profoundly affected by receiving a box of freshly gathered wild roses by post: 'At that time they were inseparable from romance, innocence and love'.

Bion was ready to be consumed with passion. He wrote to the young woman. He saw her again often, as she had come to London to train as a physiotherapist. One evening in St James's Park Bion proposed to her, and she accepted his offer of marriage. He was overwhelmed with pride at the thought of having such an 'extremely beautiful' fiancée. None of her other characteristics is mentioned; we learn only that he was fascinated by such beauty. However, Bion was also anxious about his future. He had not finished his medical training, he had no money or possibilities of earning any in the near future. She had no money either, and her family was against the marriage. A few weeks later, when his fiancée wrote to break off their engagement, he went, literally, into shock.

Fifty years later, Bion had still not fully worked through the pain: 'It was not funny: it hurt. It still does' (1985, p. 26). His autobiography returns four times, in three brief chapters, to the memory of the wild roses. Although he must have gone over the events in his mind dozens of times, he still blamed the young woman, considering her to be an irresponsible seductress. He remained convinced that she had deliberately tried to poison the wound to prevent it from healing. He had heard of her comments about her engagement to him: 'Even from the first I felt my engagement to Wilfred was a mistake; even while I was engaged I was in love with Pat.' Later, during a weekend at the seaside, Bion met the couple unexpectedly. He chose to cut short his stay: 'If I had had my service revolver with me, I would have shot him. Then I would have shot her through the knee in such a way that the joint could not be repaired, and she would have had a rigid leg to explain to her future lovers' (1985, p. 30). He then reassures his readers that even in the unlikely event of having gun and ammunition, he would have been deterred at the last minute from enacting his murderous fantasies: it had been enough for him simply to fantasize about revenge. It would have been unworthy, shameful, to attack the unarmed couple, just as he found it intolerable that a British general massacred an unarmed Indian crowd with machine guns.

There was another person who proved to be of immense importance to Bion during the course of his medical studies: his psychotherapist. We are told even less about his identity than about that of the beautiful fiancée. Bion consulted him initially because of the anxiety he had suffered following what he had experienced as academic and sporting failures. His psychotherapist, whom he refers to as an 'analyst' in inverted commas, informed him that twelve sessions should be enough.

Initially Bion used an army gratuity to pay for his therapy, but the treatment did not end as predicted. He had to borrow £30 from a colleague who had been his teacher at one time. To his previous failures he had added his dismissal from his job and his fiancée's rejection. His analyst (in the autobiography the inverted commas are removed) kindly agreed to allow him credit, and Bion found himself £100 in debt – a considerable sum for an impoverished student at that time.

With his typical sense of humour, Bion explains the reasons for terminating his therapy: 'in contrast to my finances, the acquisition of a fund of failure seemed inexhaustible'. His therapist referred him a client, the son of a general. We deduce that his therapy must have lasted for seven or eight years, and was terminated only when Bion set up a private practice of his own.

Bion gained his medical and surgical qualifications in 1930. He added LRCP (Licentiate of the Royal College of Physicians) to the DSO and the BA after his name. He had taken six years, the average length of a medical training. Despite all these initials, so impressive to the layman, Bion did not aim to acquire any post-university qualifications. He launched himself straight into psychiatric practice.

Bion, somewhat ironically, dubs his analyst 'Mr Feel-it-in-the-past', because he seemed to use this phrase whenever his patient complained of some unpleasant occurrence. The theory was that there must have been some traumatic event in the patient's past that had been 'repressed'. Therefore, the unpleasantness experienced in the present was linked to past traumas, not to the present being lived. Bion did not appreciate this 'mad logic' (however psychoanalytic it actually was) when he told his analyst how his fiancée had run off with a rival. When he wrote his autobiography Bion was still settling scores with this psychotherapist, who is referred to as Mr FiP. The therapist, Bion felt, was trying to make him understand that after being abandoned by his fiancée it was time to 'fall back on myself'. Bion had little confidence in his self – even less than he had in God, who had also proved something of a disappointment. His adequacy as a human being was called into question as he had, until then, 'admired, adored and worshipped' people who were unable or unwilling to play the parts which he wanted to assign them. Bion concluded that he lacked the qualities required to enable him to make people play these parts, and also, no doubt, that his therapist had not been up to scratch.

Bion's only entry in the *Medical Dictionary* of the time is his home address in Nottingham Place. He was probably surviving on a small private practice and some hospital fees. He had been shocked to discover that fee-splitting was being practised, albeit in a covert way, while it was very much disapproved of on medical grounds. An established consultant would refer patients to a colleague in exchange for a percentage of the patient's fees. Bion rebelled against this lucrative practice, which meant that patients were being referred not to the practitioners most likely to be of the greatest help to them, but to those most likely to offer remuneration to the consultant. Bion was further shocked when Dr FiP calmly proposed to refer him patients on this basis. Naively and indiscreetly, Bion asked him whether or not this was the practice of fee-splitting. The therapist denied it and proceeded to explain that this was 'not so'. Bion probably needed only one such reason to break off a relationship which, from that point on, became increasingly awkward. He had severed his relationship with a psychotherapist who was far from unknown or unimportant.

The only person with a psychodynamic orientation working in a British university was at University College, where Bion studied medicine: Dr J.A. Hadfield. Hadfield's vocation was more academic than clinical. He was a great supporter of psychoanalytic psychotherapy, especially in his books, which included: *Psychology and Morals* (1923), *Psychology and Modern Problems* (1935), *Dreams* (1954), and *Childhood and Adolescence* (1962).[5]

Bion joined the staff of the Tavistock Clinic in 1932. He was employed initially as an assistant doctor, as he had not yet had sufficient experience in psychiatry or psychoanalysis. At this time Hadfield had considerable influence at the Tavistock Clinic. It had been set up in 1920 as one of the first out-patient clinics to make psychoanalytic psychotherapy available to people who could not pay the fees for private treatment. The clinic had been conceived of and set up by Hugh Crichton-Miller, its first director. Along with Crichton-Miller, Hadfield had been one of the seven doctors on the original staff. They wanted the public to benefit from the knowledge acquired in the First World War from the treatment of 'shell shock'. From the outset the clinic held an independent position halfway between official psychiatric medicine on the one hand and orthodox psychoanalysis on the other. The financial base was mostly private, helped by donations and public subscription, and with modest contributions from the patients.

In 1932 the clinic left the premises in Tavistock Square (from which it derived its name) for new, larger premises near the university in Malet Street. There was one powerful group within the clinic composed of those people who had been 'analytically' trained by Hadfield. Bion belonged to this group. The Tavistock grew rapidly between 1932 and 1939; research became a significant activity alongside treatment, training and being an information centre. Therapeutic technique became more systematic following Hadfield's influential views on training, backed by the influence of medical directors who had already been trained with him.

At this time, 'reductive' analysis was in vogue. The goal of treatment was to discover the dynamic links between a symptom and its origins in the past. Free association and dream analysis were used to bring to light what Hadfield called 'nuclear incidents'. These were not necessarily traumatic events but specific crises in the inner life of the child. Hadfield hypothesized the existence of a triad of drives: the sexual libido, the aggressive or self-preservative drive, and the drive towards dependence. Here we can note, in passing, the similarity between Hadfield's theory and the three 'basic assumption groups' proposed by Bion. The more advanced 'Hadfieldians' were critical of his 'deliberate and reasoned rejection of the significance of the transference'. Hadfield considered transference to be merely a transient phenomenon in the uncovering of infantile behaviour and material. This, according to patients, gave a slight unreality and artificiality to a procedure described by one as 'forced fantasy' (H.V. Dicks, 1970, p. 67). Several of his students, including Bion, ended by rejecting the process and went to complete their training at the Institute of Psycho-Analysis.

During these years Bion lived very much as the other doctors at the Tavistock did. The clinic could offer psychotherapy to people on low incomes only if its staff earned a living primarily through private practice. That was one motivation for finding a practice near central London, and if possible near Harley Street. Bion made up his income through part-time work. First he worked at the Maida Vale Hospital for Epilepsy and Paralysis (which was to become the Maida Vale Hospital for Nervous Diseases). In 1935 he concluded his neurological work at the hospital in order to work at the Institute for the Scientific Treatment of Delinquency. The Tavistock Clinic had begun to receive a growing number of clients with behavioural problems, including delinquency. It became clear that there was a need for a specialist treatment centre, and the Tavistock joined with the Institute of Psycho-Analysis to organize it. The new establishment was the Portman Clinic, set up under the aegis of the National Health Service. Bion was still working there when he was called up, once again, to join the armed forces in 1940.

The autobiography is discreetly silent on the two years Bion spent working with the man who was to be awarded the Nobel Prize for literature. Towards the end of 1933 Samuel Beckett, who had been suffering from recurrent health problems, had been persuaded by a doctor friend that his problems might be of psychosomatic origin. He managed to leave Ireland, and his mother, to live in London. He decided to leave both because of his physical symptoms and the anxiety they caused him, sapping his strength, and because the literary world had discovered psycho-analysis, partly through the Surrealist poets. On his friend's advice, Beckett went to the Tavistock Clinic early in 1934. As chance would have it, he began psychotherapy with a trainee who was to become one of the leading lights of psychoanalysis: Wilfred Bion. The experience was of great importance to both men, even though neither mentioned it in his publications. Each probably provided the other with the image of an 'imaginary twin', as Didier Anzieu (1986) suggested, on discovering a plausible series of analogies between the lives and problems of the two men. Their ancestors were French Huguenots who fled to Britain to escape religious persecution. They both had narcissistic and schizoid character-istics, and both had turned to culture to contain this psychotic part of themselves. Furthermore, Anzieu suggests that Beckett trans-posed the structure and experience of psychotherapy into his literature, although the writer himself considered that this suggestion was 'psychoanalytic fantasies'.

The therapy enabled Beckett to understand himself differently;

it pushed him to reveal more of himself in his writings of that period, although he was one of the most reserved writers of his time. He even acknowledged that his night-time panic attacks were caused by his 'neurosis'. His therapist soon had his work cut out, as he found himself faced with a negative therapeutic reaction. Beckett could not progress until he could acknowledge his 'addictive' relationship to his mother. Nine years older than Beckett, Bion, who was still in therapy with Hadfield, became, in the transference, the writer's older brother Frank (it was in his bed that 'Sam' sought refuge from his nocturnal panic attacks before coming to London). The two men shared many intellectual interests, especially literature. At times they discussed, even argued about, the nature of the creative process. According to Beckett, the 'analysis' was limping along. The patient suggested to his therapist that the cost–effect ratio was leaning towards termination, and that whatever his intellectual interests might be, he could not make a choice between Bion and his mother. His body somatized, producing boils, tremors and an anal abscess. Beckett announced his intention of stopping at the end of 1935.

Bion suggested to Beckett that he should go to the Tavistock Clinic to hear a lecture by Jung (the third in a series of five lectures). The clinic had a policy of building a public profile by inviting famous lecturers to speak. Beckett remained very impressed by Jung's ideas – he soon saw their relevance to his own work in progress. His therapy ended at Christmas. Bion had expressed reservations, as he doubted that the relationship to his mother would improve in the way his patient wished to believe. He was proved right in the long run. Nevertheless, Beckett finished his first novel, *Murphy*, not long afterwards.

Beckett was critical of his therapy in much the same way as Bion was to be critical of his analysis with Melanie Klein. Nevertheless, the writer maintained a lasting interest in psychiatry and psychoanalysis. In 1960 he questioned his nephew, a psychiatrist, on the differences between Freudian and Kleinian psychoanalysis. It is not impossible that he was aware of Bion's resounding success in his work. Bion, for his part, certainly remembered the person he had treated at the Tavistock who was nominated for the Nobel Prize each successive year from 1964. Beckett was awarded the Nobel Prize in 1969. It was in the 1970s that the inspirational flow was reversed. Bion, in the last period of his lifework, was oscillating between literature and psychoanalysis. He too wanted to transcend the literary style of James Joyce, in order to create a language in which to describe the reality of intrauterine life. Had he been asked 'Why are you writing?' he would no doubt have replied, like Beckett: 'Bon qu'à ça!' [loosely: 'The only thing I can do!'].

Bion's apprenticeship ended with an encounter with another memorable man: John Rickman. As he had felt the need to work on his tolerable but tormented inner life, Bion approached one of the most prominent psychoanalysts. As it turned out, like had been drawn to like. Rickman was only a few years older than Bion, but he had been practising medicine, then psychoanalysis, at least one generation earlier. He was a Quaker, descended from a long line of Quakers, and from an early age he demonstrated the intellectual and moral qualities characteristic of this community: altruism, social responsibility, organizational responsibility, and intellectual openness.

He finished his medical studies in 1916, in the middle of the First World War. He immediately volunteered to be part of an ambulance team to help the war wounded in Russia (his pacifism obliged him to pursue a non-military role). On his return from Russia, Rickman specialized in psychiatry, rapidly developing an interest in psychoanalysis. In 1920 he went to Vienna to to be analysed by Freud. When he returned in 1924 he joined the group of analysts led by Ernest Jones: the British Psycho-Analytical Society. He rapidly became a prominent member and a leading organizer of the Society. Rickman reserved part of his energy for editorial work on professional journals, writing articles (notably on groups and on psychoses) and reviewing books (he reviewed one of Hadfield's). He worked consistently to build the public status of the Institute of Psycho-Analysis, and to maintain links between psychoanalysis and other therapies. To this end he offered his services to the medical section of the British Psychological Society (later, in 1947, Bion was to become president of this same section).

Rickman was interested in the lectures on child analysis given by Melanie Klein in London in 1925. In 1928 he decided to undergo another analysis, this time with Sándor Ferenczi; he had to resign from his post at the Institute in order to complete this. In 1934 Rickman again undertook an analysis – with Melanie Klein. He remained in analysis with her until 1941. For many years he considered himself a Kleinian, although his allegiance remained dubious in the eyes of the leader herself, who seemed to demand total and unconditional adherence to her theories. And Rickman, writing a preface to Klein's article 'On weaning' in 1936, insisted on the fact that the father was crucial in children's lives. He had even gone so far as to write: 'In his fantasies, the child accords equal attention to the figures of the father and the mother'.

Bion met Rickman in 1937, and was analysed by him until September 1939. Although Rickman was convinced of the validity and importance of Klein's theories, he retained his independence of thought and his own convictions. Bion, having been part of a group of 'believing' officers in the Great War, had chosen a 'pi' analyst. At the International Psycho-Analytic Congress in 1938 Rickman gave a paper, 'The need for belief in God', in which he discussed Quaker faith in the light of Klein's concept of early object relations.

Bion slowly separated himself from Hadfield. Rickman's interpretations, rather than playing intellectual games, fanned the embers dormant in the ashes of the past. Bion was evidently as attached to Rickman as he became to Klein. In his autobiography he unburdens himself of his relationship to his analyst by attributing an overpositive countertransference to him: 'I thought Rickman liked me . . . But there was some kind of emotional turbulence, with its high and low pressure areas, which extinguished the analysis . . . It stopped; though not before it had also extinguished in me any spark of respect that might have been entertained for me by my pre-psychoanalytic colleagues, and before I had penetrated enough to be independent' (1985, p. 46). Bion's dense prose seems to indicate an extraordinary ambivalence on his part, but historical events led reality to bolster his ambivalence as the outbreak of the Second World War terminated this analysis prematurely, and brought patient and analyst together as colleagues in a pioneering clinical project. All things considered, Rickman had worked well with Bion, and his work enabled Bion to make use of a long analysis with Klein. Rickman lived long enough to witness the positive outcome of this work, and the second analysis, as he died only a few weeks after Bion's second marriage.

At times Bion writes with an intense dissociation which interrupts the reader's associative links. In the first volume of the autobiography he briefly alludes to the death of his mother. Eventually the reader, with some confusion, realizes that his mother died a few months before the outbreak of the Second World War, when Bion was still in analysis with Rickman. As the war interrupted this analysis, he was not able fully to work through this painful and difficult mourning. Her death is evoked in four poignant sentences, concluding a significant chapter in which Bion tells us of his own 'death' on 8 August 1918 (1982, p. 266).

PART 2:
THE GROUP PERIOD

In the narratives of myths we often come across the metamorphosis of deities into strange new forms. In biology we find that in some species the adult form is reached by a metamorphosis following an extended period of latency. An actor may completely alter his character and appearance in the course of a play. It is also said that love can work miracles. During the Second World War, when Klein's work was at its zenith, Bion underwent such a radical change that he seemed to have been through a metamorphosis. Yet this was not like the sudden changes wrought by actors and deities: Bion had been preparing himself for such a change throughout the previous decade.

We have chosen to call this the 'group period', as our focus is more on Bion's work than on his life, on the intellectual production rather than on biographical material. We present the work according to Bion's own classification:

- War research. During the war Bion identified with the British army, and worked to find solutions to some of the problems it encountered within its structure.
- Research into small groups. After the war Bion developed an original method of communicating the new clinical experience of working with groups.
- Retrospection, in which Bion recast his research into groups in terms of Kleinian concepts, and eventually left group work to become a full-time analyst.

5   The Army Psychiatrist

A TURNING POINT IN LIFE

Bion had enough time to organize the temporary suspension of his professional work before joining the army for a second time in 1940. He also allowed himself some rest and recreation time. He spent a few days with friends in the country, where he met an attractive actress whom he continued to meet. A little later he went by himself on a short but sunny holiday on the Côte d'Azur. Once this brief interlude was over, his life became like those of so many at that time: 'Frustration, futility, anger and humiliation'. Bion adds: 'hollow words, stupidity and bigoted hypocrisy' (1985, p. 46). The naive young man had become a lucid adult who was to be tormented by frustration in a tragedy of petty officialdom, bureaucracy and red tape. In his autobiography Bion sketches the vicissitudes of life as an army psychiatrist, remembering the emotional events rather than giving any chronological account.

It was in the Second World War that psychology and psychiatry began to be recognized as work of the utmost importance. The most frequent cause by far of soldiers invaliding out of the army was the significance of psychological problems. At the outset of war the army had only two psychiatrists, and half a dozen professional officers with some psychiatric or psychological skills; by the end of the war it employed over three hundred psychiatrists and psychologists. Besides taking on the clinical treatment of psychological troubles in the armed forces, the army psychiatrists were also expected to find ways of dealing with the proliferating urgent psychosocial problems that resulted from mass mobilization and total warfare. The army began to realize that clinical treatment should also be extended into research into preventive measures, and provision for demobilization and readaptation to civilian life. These problems were to be of immense significance for the reorganization of psychiatric care in postwar Britain.

One group from the Tavistock Clinic published an anthology of essays, *The Neuroses in War*, edited by Emmanuel Miller, which came out just before the war. Most of the authors, including Hadfield, wrote on their experiences of treating 'shell shock' in the Great War. Bion contributed an essay on the 'War of nerves', written in a rather dogmatic style. This essay bears interesting comparison with the first article he wrote for *The Lancet* in 1943. The two pieces are very different, and it is difficult to see evidence of the genius of the later works in the laboured lucubrations of the early essay. Bion never included his first published article in his listed writings, and his admirers and followers also (tactfully) forgot all about it.

Bion was quite well aware of the situation in which military psychiatrists would be working. It left much to be desired. He thus very much resented the obligation to go to Aldershot for military training, judging this training to be 'totally irrelevant'. The veteran of the First World War had not forgotten the Army Medical Corps, nor its reputation for incompetence. For a second time, Bion decided to devote himself wholeheartedly to the defence of his country, but whereas the first time he had been a young school leaver, this time he was a man in his forties, self-confident, well socialized, with years of professional practice. Having already experienced the 'glory' of war, and the heavy cost of such an illusion, he looked to his future with a realistic, mature eye.

Like the majority of his colleagues, once enlisted Bion began work at Craigmile Bottom Hospital by treating men who had been traumatized, suffering 'shell shock'. This concept had been much discussed during and after the First World War, and was still controversial. In a literal sense the term connotes an emotional shock caused by experiencing the explosion of a shell or missile. It was the way in which the symptoms of shell shock were repetitious that Freud considered significant, and these 'traumatic neuroses' led him to the concept of something that lay 'beyond the pleasure principle'. Bion was also moved by this psychological damage suffered by the victims of war. However, whereas Freud had had the opportunity and time to think about these symptoms at some remove from his patients, Bion felt constrained by his responsibilities as part of the Army Medical Corps. It was clear that something had to be done to understand and to treat these problems, which were threatening, in increasing numbers, to handicap further a nation at war.

At this time it was decided that the medical section of each command should have a psychiatrist attached to it. The 'Command Psychiatrist' was the specialist adviser to the other medical officers, and consultant for all the patients. In practice the specialist gave consultations wherever there were troops or military hospitals, and also made visits to various units set up to cater to their specific needs. Bion was assigned to Western Command at the David Hulme Military Hospital in Chester. This seems to have been one of the relatively peaceful times. His visits enabled him to meet acquaintances from the First World War again. He also socialized with the officers in Command. One reason why invitations were especially forthcoming was that the relationship with Betty Jardine, the actress he had met just before the outbreak of war, had led to mutual love, and marriage.

The event had finally occurred – the confirmed bachelor had tied the knot! Bion had admired the actress on stage as a spectator before meeting her at a friend's house. He found her less attractive and amusing in real life than on stage, but none the less she seemed 'likable'! In his autobiography Bion is rather silent about Betty, as if no other woman could compare with the beautiful fiancée of the wild roses, who had rejected him. One of the couple's close friends writes: 'She was very warm, attentive, very intelligent and very attractive in the way of a very poised and mature personality . . . they were an ideally matched couple' (E. Trist, personal communication, 3 June 1987).

There must have been a great number of men who would have liked to marry Betty Jardine. This young woman had started her acting career in 1926 in Manchester (her birthplace), working in repertory for seven years with the same company. She made her debut on the London stage in 1933, and continued to work in London until her death. In 1936 she went to New York with her company for a season, and the following year she began taking some small film roles. But it was in 1938 that she achieved her major success.

Along with large audiences, Bion applauded her performance in *The Corn is Green* at the Duchess Theatre. The 1938 edition of *Who's Who in Theatre* does not indicate Elizabeth McKritick Jardine's date of birth, but she was probably some ten years younger than her husband. There are many photographs of her in the journal *Theatre World* which show that she was very attractive.

Emlyn Williams's play *The Corn is Green* was loosely autobiographical. The title is an allegory for the development of the soul, brought to ripeness and maturity through experience. The role of the main protagonist was taken by the playwright himself, who was re-enacting, rather than acting, the dramatic narrative, and Bion probably found that he could identify with many of his predicaments. The protagonist is torn between the desire to take up his scholarship to study at Oxford, and wanting to help look after his illegitimate child. Betty played the role of the young woman who decides to become pregnant, and seems to have given an excellent performance. She was used to playing the role of the beguiling adolescent, but in this narrative the adolescent is transformed into a somewhat cynical, powerfully seductive young woman. The critics were unanimous in praising her ability to enact this transformation. Although Betty was not the star of the play, many critics (in *The Daily Telegraph*, *The Sphere* and *Theatre World*) were enthusiastic about her performance. Besides acting, Betty studied speech dialect and was interested in photography. As a sophisticated young woman she seems to have been an ideal partner for Bion, the proud young army officer of legendary heroism. Bion often noticed how, as an ideally suited couple, they could arouse the envy of their hosts.

SELECTION

Although married life held promise of a new dawn, the ominously dark clouds of army life loomed on the horizon. Bion was dismayed when he visited a therapy unit and found 'a balance in insecurity which was maintained by doctors and the medical institution as much as by the patients'. With Rickman he wrote a report for the army's psychiatric service, the Wharncliffe Memorandum, outlining a project aimed at treating neurosis through group therapy. Although both Bion and Rickman had hoped to be able to put the project into action fairly promptly, they had to wait three years before it became operational. Yet the Wharncliffe Memorandum was an important document which introduced their ideas to a wider constituency and was supported by many psychiatric colleagues.

Shortly after writing the Memorandum Bion was paid a visit by J.R. Rees, whom he considered a friend. Rees, a brigadier, was trusted as an authority by the army High Command. He had once been a director of the Tavistock Clinic and had been able, with his gifts of diplomacy, to make his way in the world. With good administrative skills and organizing abilities, he had become known as the 'founding father of British army psychiatry'. After this informal visit Bion became confident about his future, and was shattered when his 'old friend' ordered him to take quite a different posting.[6]

From December 1940 onwards it became clear that the Command psychiatrists could not meet the demands of the work generated by the war, so it was decided to divide the work up geographically and hierarchically. The Command psychiatrists were to remain at general headquarters to co-ordinate the work of regional area psychiatrists. Bion had assumed that he would be one of those based at headquarters. In the event he was posted to York as an area psychiatrist, and given only a week or two to leave his base at Chester. He took it badly: 'I was angry and hurt . . . I had got the sack'. His wife supported him, and was patiently tolerant throughout this difficult time.

Bion's disappointment left him so embittered that his autobiography omits any description of his success in implementing his project for officer selection. During World War One it had been possible to select officers from among those who had distinguished themselves in actual combat. With a few exceptions, it was no longer possible to use a similar method in the Second World War because of the frequent repatriation of British soldiers. Most of the foreign armies had established psychological testing for officer selection, and had been using such methods for some time. The British army began to use similar methods, although the tests took a long time to process and tended to be unreliable indicators of efficiency. The physical tests administered by medics were more or less satisfactory, but it was gradually recognized that the psychological testing was a real problem. The army needed a great many officers, but did not employ enough psychiatrists and psychologists to administer and process the tests. What was needed, then, was a method which would enable rapid and effective selection from a very large number of candidates.

Towards the summer of 1941 informal experiments were being conducted at High Command in Scotland. New psychological tests, taking only a few hours, produced results which correlated very closely to the results of tests entailing several weeks of training by professional officers. In the light of these encouraging results, a first experimental commission was set up in Edinburgh in early 1942. It was known as the No. 1 War Office Selection Board, and comprised six people, three of whom were to assess candidates for their military qualities and three of whom (one psychologist and two psychiatrists) were to give specialist advice. The Selection Board was to synthesize the two different – and sometimes divergent – sources of information from the military and psychiatric panels, with the help of a professional officer presiding over the group.

Bion was posted to the Selection Board, and worked there as a psychiatrist with John Sutherland and Eric Wittkower. It was in this context that he proposed his 'Leaderless Group Project', which was to replace the lengthy individual tests with one two-and-a-half-hour exercise that included several candidates simultaneously. Another advantage of his project was that the two panels of army professionals and medical officers could work together to pool a joint assessment of candidates. Bion suggested that a leaderless group be formed, and set a task which would enable observers to assess the attempts to organize or guide the group from within. For example, eight or nine candidates would be asked to build a bridge, and as they received no instruction on how to organize the work, nor on the function of leaders, they had to improvise among themselves. It was felt that this kind of exercise would provide an opportunity for observing how each man reconciled his ambitions, hopes and fears with the demands of the task assigned to the group.

Bion emphasized that the observers should attend to the real-life situation rather than the set task (such as the building of the bridge in the example). The set task acted as a device to account for the presence of the observers, and the latter were to evaluate each candidate's capacity to relate to the tensions produced, in himself and others, by desires for personal success and fears of group failure.

Later Bion described the 'revolutionary nature' of his method, which differed so radically from existing methods of psychological testing. The standard practice had consisted of two phases: the first of identifying specific qualities required by the particular functions and roles, the second a lengthy attempt to measure those specific qualities in individuals through a series of evaluative tests. With the leaderless group a selection team observes candidates in interaction. This process is in dramatic contrast to the fairly rigid hierarchy of power characteristic of the army – in effect, it introduced a democratic principle into the process of selection by focusing on communal relational aptitudes. Bion's project was accepted and adopted because it fairly accurately reproduced the types of conflicts and feelings engendered in officers in wartime conditions. He explained that an officer in action can be efficient only in so far as he is able to take account of interpersonal relations. Bion summarized the relational principle of his approach with characteristic wit: 'If a man cannot be the friend of his friends, he cannot be the enemy of his enemies' (1948, p. 88).

The origins of the Leaderless Group Project probably lay in Bion's experiences as an officer serving at the front in World War One. How could he have forgotten the experience of leading his team under enemy fire? The oldest of the NCOs had asked him to accept leadership, at which point Bion had had to reconcile his personal interests with those of the men, whom he had met for the first time, and for whom he was responsible. During the Second World War the officers proved more receptive to Bion than to other medical officers, because he had fought in the First World War and been decorated for his courage. This gave him incontestable prestige, because very few British soldiers had seen active service since 1939.

More selection boards were set up along the lines of the No. 1 Board in Edinburgh. During 1942 a Research and Training Centre was organized in London, near the War Office. The Edinburgh team expected Bion to be given leadership of the Research Centre, with the rank of lieutenant colonel. He too wanted to be responsible for training, so that personnel could be trained using the leaderless group method without it becoming too distorted or compromised. But it was a company officer who was assigned leadership of the

Research and Training Centre, and became head of the selection committees. Bion was not even promoted.

This disappointment angered him. He could not accept the post of deputy assistant, and asked to be transferred to Northfield military hospital in Birmingham. Although the army adopted Bion's method of selecting officers, it did not have the desired effect on military hierarchy.

From the outset the Selection Board psychiatrists had worked in a dual capacity: as experts administering the tests (in collaboration with psychologists) and also as medical specialists examining each candidate. The psychiatrists became increasingly relegated to the individual examination of 'problem' cases. The official version, described by Ahrenfeldt, cited the very large number of candidates and the lack of specialized staff. But in March 1943, a 'political' decision was made to limit the psychiatrists' intervention only to those cases referred to them by the president of the Board. Then, in August 1943, the War Office decided that psychiatrists would no longer take any part in the selection of officers. There was a growing movement in the army which was very hostile to psychiatry, and opposed it with great efficiency. There is no doubt that Bion's radically new methods of testing and selection suffered from this growing hostility.

In fact it was not only the army but a large section of British society that was afraid of the 'evil' of psychoanalysis. The psychiatrists of the experimental Board set up in Edinburgh were all analytically orientated. Most people were suspicious of what seemed to them to be unwarranted meddling with sexuality or religion.

Bion believed that a nation at war could do more than maintain the quality and quantity of its officers; it could also increase their number and value. The army had to be as careful in selecting officers as conservationists are in selecting trees for the development of forests. Selection should be the concern of the army as a whole, not just the Selection Boards. Trist recalls the spirit of this approach as being 'an experiment in Regimental Nomination'. As the Edinburgh Selection Board sometimes had no candidates for examination, Bion suggested that every 'good' regiment could nominate candidates for officer training, in addition to those men chosen by the regimental commander. This suggestion was accepted by Regional Command, permission was granted, and in some regiments candidates were chosen by a series of secret ballots. The experiment was successful: the quality of recruits was maintained, while the number of officers was greatly increased (Trist, in Pines [ed.] 1985, p. 12).

Some people, however, thought that the introduction of these democratic principles into army hierarchy was dangerous. Although they undoubtedly improved the efficiency of the selection process, Bion's methods were considered potentially subversive. Perhaps Bion was sensitive to the spirit of social change that Rickman had encountered in the Soviet Union which, at this time, was one of the Allies. Nobody concerned with social progress could remain utterly deaf to the 'songs of the Red Army'.[7] In the event, the question of officer selection was debated at the highest level by an Army Council, and a majority opposed Bion's regimental nomination project. By this time, however, Bion was already working on another project.

REHABILITATION

Psychoses were only a small fraction of the range of emotional disturbances treated by army psychiatrists in World War Two. It was soon evident that most of their work involved the treatment of neurosis and behavioural problems. These men were initially referred to specialist centres within the general emergency services, along with other medical emergency cases. The extent and depth of the problem, and the inadequacy of treatment provision, were eventually recognized. In April 1942 army hospitals were set up specifically for the treatment of 'war neuroses'. The largest of these was Northfield in Birmingham, which had two hundred beds in the hospital wing and four hundred beds in the training wing. Patients were initially given active psychiatric treatment in the hospital wing but were transferred, as soon as possible, to the training wing. Here the psychiatrists were called upon simply to supervise the rehabilitation process, which was administered by the rather severe rule of regimental officers. Ahrenfeldt notes that 'the two units were sharply delimited, and there were no nursing sisters or medical officers in the training wing, but military training officers who regarded psychiatrists with some degree of suspicion' (p. 151). The atmosphere of the hospital, especially in the early days, was intensely dismal, and general efficiency left much to be desired. Bion asked to be transferred to Northfield with the aim of making it an efficient and functional hospital for treating emotional and behavioural problems of war. He introduced group treatment, although the entire experiment lasted only six weeks. In the light of group interaction each individual's problem was comparable, and neurosis was found as much in the group as in the individual. Before this the majority of patients and nurses had known only one form of help: avoiding the problem.

In psychiatric hospitals neurosis has to be confronted as an enemy is confronted, instead of retreating from it. The staff as a group must realize that neurotic behaviour makes communal life difficult, and finally destroys any co-operation and efficiency.

Northfield Hospital treated only those men who were thought to be capable of returning to active service after rehabilitation. Rickman was in charge of treatment in the hospital wing. In each fifteen-bed ward he organized a group discussion every morning. After physical exercise the men could return to consult the psychiatrist and talk about the problems that had been raised for them as individuals in the group session. Rickman thought that neurotics contributed well in group discussion because of its structure of equality in interpersonal relationships.

The men knew that their next step was to move to new groups in the training wing. There Bion received them, to rehabilitate them to army life or to assess whether or not they were capable of returning to active service. In cases where rehabilitation was impossible, the psychiatrist judged whether the man should take up auxiliary employment or be discharged. Bion thus organized his wing as 'a framework enclosed within transparent walls' – the patient's behaviour signalled his competence and his aims, in much the same way as the leaderless group interactions signalled officer capacities in selection candidates. Bion managed to re-establish discipline, and to keep the men usefully occupied. He helped to build 'an unmistakable esprit-de-corps'. He added: 'anyone with a knowledge of good fighting regiments in a theatre of war would have been struck by certain similarities of outlook in the men of such a unit and the men of the training wing' (1961, pp. 21–2).

Bion fostered the initial stage of group life, in which the leader and the men hold one another in reciprocal idealization and set aside feelings of persecution and guilt. With his extraordinary aptitude for leadership, Bion managed to create a team which aspired to the best in army life. However, he and his men also had responsibility for facing up to matters of life and death. The idea of death generates extreme anxiety and deep feelings of guilt. If the leader knows about an officer's life on the battlefield he can 'be spared the hideous blunder of thinking that patients are potential cannon fodder, to be returned as such to their units'. Bion solved this problem by transcending his immediate role as an officer. His task as a psychiatrist was 'to produce self-respecting men socially adjusted to the community and therefore willing to accept its responsibilities whether in peace or war' (1961, p. 13). So far so good . . . if we overlook the reasons why this experimental treatment was brutally terminated after only six weeks.

With hindsight, Bion thought there were several reasons why this structure was prematurely closed down. 'Intra-group tensions in therapy', written in the thick of it in 1943, clearly states his view that the brief duration of the project in no way compromised its scientific principles, nor the results obtained. It was the local contingencies alone that prevented the long-term implementation of the method. His 1946 article 'The Leaderless Group Project' deals with 'the problem of the psychiatrist'. Bion acknowledges there that patients may feel a violent hatred towards a psychiatrist whose aim is to return them to the firing line: 'A psychiatrist attempting to use the group method to study internal tension is, in the situation of today's context, interrupting a withdrawal and so risks being in the firing line' (1946, p. 81). In 1947 Bion again chose to write about his experiment at Northfield, giving the impression that he had had a shock. He openly states that his superiors put an end to the experiment without giving any explanation. His experiment, he surmised, had provoked a 'powerful release of emotion which showed itself chiefly in heightened morale amongst the patients, acts of indiscipline by two warrant officers of the staff – ex officio stable personalities – and minor, but persistent obstruction of obscure origin' (1948, p. 81).

Bion observed that he had set off 'a chain reaction'. Trist recalls that Bion was very angry, and continued to be angry after he was again transferred. He thought about publicizing the events that had taken place at Northfield. He considered fighting his case through higher authorities. In the end, he thought it best to to keep silent about it. The only successful outcome would have led to displacing General Rees and his colleagues at the War Office, and Bion felt that he had neither the popular support nor the political acumen necessary for such action. Some thirty-five years later Bion returned, at length, to this episode when he wrote his autobiography. The passage of time had barely changed his feeling of betrayal. He tried to moderate his bitter resentment towards his superiors in the military hierarchy, but it was still simmering. He added his thoughts that his superiors had considered it dangerous to have people as 'intelligent as Rickman' and himself around because 'we would blow up the Military Training Scheme, and the whole of Army Psychiatry'. He thought his immediate superiors were afraid of being punished for permitting them to carry out their experiment.[8] Bion had good reason to feel bitterly critical of the army. The army had greatly benefited from his skills and his commitment, but had never recognized them. In his autobiography he notes that he was the only psychiatrist he knew who left the army at the same rank as he had entered. Bion ended his military career as a major, whereas both Trist and Sutherland finished the war as lieutenant colonels. His record of service in the Great War should have given him a significant advantage over his colleagues – he had ended that war on his way to becoming a general.

It is worth asking whether or not Bion colluded in his fate. According to Sutherland, he tended to take a somewhat uncompromising attitude on issues such as the Northfield affair. He was reluctant to expand on the implications of his ideas, so that the administrators often did not know how they could be implemented. Sutherland considered that Bion had 'a rather uncommunicative attitude' (in Pines [ed.] 1985, pp. 50–51), remembering him as a rather self-contained man, making mostly brief and incisive remarks. Moreover, Bion was 'totally uninterested in, if not actively hostile to, playing politics'. Bridger, who was posted to Northfield as his replacement, confirms this: 'It must be said that he made few concessions and I do not recall him ever bartering or negotiating' (p. 88).

How was it that despite his constant and concerted efforts, his method was never properly recognized? Melanie Klein, who was to become his next analyst, offers a possible explanation. Towards the end of her life Klein became interested in envy. She found that some people defend themselves against situations in which they feel envious by inverting them. In this way the disturbing feelings are activated in others, while those thus defended can validate their own qualities and behaviour.

Bion joined the army psychiatrists with a history of legendary heroism. With his powerful physique and his self-confidence, he made a strong first impression. In addition, the army must have seen him as someone with strange projects, a messianic spirit, unafraid of difficulty. Trist remembers that he was very easily mythologized. But people who deny their own envy often become targets of persecution by others. Klein notes that the defence against envy is often manifested as a devaluation of the object, as in a manic defence, because a devalued object need no longer be envied. Throughout his autobiography Bion expresses regrets that he had to deal with so many mean, narrow-minded and even contemptible individuals. Could there be echoes of a Céline in this predicament? Furthermore, according to Klein, the devaluing of the self may also be part of a defence against envy. Bion was quite capable of systematically devaluing each of his qualities as he presented them in his autobiography. Francesca, his widow, then wanted to reveal, equally systematically, 'the other side of genius'.

What are we, with hindsight, to make of the experiment that Bion and Rickman set up at Northfield? It was undeniably a manifestation of creative genius. From November 1944 S.H. Foulkes and T.F. Main went to Northfield, and set up the famous 'Northfield Experiment II'. It very often happens that real innovation is prematurely terminated; but the environment may slowly become more receptive to the initial idea, and the innovation then gives way to more permanent changes and influences. Northfield Hospital became the birthplace of the 'therapeutic community' which was to lead psychiatric practice in hospitals after the war, first in Britain and then in the United States.

Under Foulkes and Main the hospital was entirely devoted to care and rehabilitation. In the special issue of the *Bulletin of the Menninger Clinic* devoted to the Northfield experiment, Bion's 'Leaderless Group Project' figures prominently as the precursor of the therapeutic community.

THE YEARS OF TRAGEDY AND SURVIVAL

After Birmingham, Bion was posted to Winchester. He liked the commander of the Selhurst unit, who helped him to overcome his psychiatric 'pyrexia'. At this stage he was far from being unhappy. His wife was working in London again, after a tour with her company. Betty was living with old friends in London, and could visit her husband once or twice a week. She was soothing and supportive after each disappointment. Her own acting career was going from strength to strength, and Bion was justifiably proud of his wife. During the Great War he had wished that his mother might think of him as a hero; now it was for Betty that he wished to do well. We find this hope in his poignant remark 'I still cannot help hoping that she was not deprived of the comforting lie that he [her husband] was really a man and a hero' (1985, p. 60).

For six months, between March and August 1943, Bion was at Selhurst interviewing officers who had been prisoners of war before liberation following the surrender at Tobruk. He interviewed some four hundred officers who needed to be rehabilitated to everyday life. Still ahead of his time, Bion was already raising questions that would be recognized after the war.

Betty became pregnant. Bion stopped being so preoccupied by his professional frustrations, and the couple looked forward to the birth of their child. The end of the war was within sight, and a kind of optimism began to emerge. Despite – or perhaps because of – the pregnancy, Bion accepted a posting for a final mission. In North Africa the army had discovered that men with emotional disturbances became worse when they were evacuated from the front; so a new aim was to offer the soldiers treatment as close to their unit as possible. The need for a closer link between military action and the psychiatric team was first recognized during the Allied landing in Normandy. The 21st Army Corps was formed. According to Trist, it was Bion who was Montgomery's first choice as military psychiatrist. With his wife's agreement, he joined this new project.

Bion found himself in Normandy, hoping to use his group methods of treatment for soldiers near their units. There he heard the news that the birth had gone well – he had a baby daughter. Three days later, by telephone, he received the tragic news that

Betty was dead. It seems to have been a pulmonary embolism, for which there was no treatment at the time. Bion was devastated. He returned to London immediately. Thirty-five years later, writing his autobiography, he was still tormented by lacerating self-doubt: 'What killed Betty and nearly killed her baby? Physical malformation? Incompetent obstetrics? Callous or indifferent authorities? Or the revelations of the hollow drum that was being so loudly beaten by her husband's departure?' (1985, p. 62).

Bion was outraged that Betty's parents thought he might want to have the baby adopted. His partner had left him with a baby and £8,000, a sum they had saved from his pay 'for a rainy day' . . . He entrusted the baby to the same woman, in Slough, who had taken good care of Betty. The war was over.

Bion did not return abroad; he was posted to Surrey. Although the autobiography might lead one to believe that he withdrew from his work and was submerged by grief, Trist informs us that he was as active and circumspect as before. He successfully completed the final task demanded of army psychiatrists at the end of the war. The Selection Boards were no longer required for selecting officers, but for rehabilitation and redeployment. Bion's influence spread further afield than the situation in which he was working. Some officers had been inspired by his leaderless groups and his rehabilitation therapy in groups, and they came to learn from him. Bion held to two simple principles: first, the duration of rehabilitation should not be prescribed; rather, each man should leave when he felt that he was ready to do so; secondly, tasks should be not under medical control but ordinary regulation.

These principles were adopted by Lieutenant Colonel Trist, a psychologist who had become a staunch supporter of Bion since the Edinburgh days, and Colonel Wilson, a close colleague from the Tavistock before the war. Wilson was important in the history of British military psychiatry, and his plans for the rehabilitation of prisoners of war were taken up by the War Office. Trist thought that the staff selected for work on the famous Civil Resettlement Units were posted there largely because of their sympathy with Bion's ideas. At the same time, his ideas were central to the second Northfield Experiment. Bion was neither promoted nor decorated, but he could be certain that he had made a magnificent contribution to the army psychiatric service throughout the Second World War.[9]

6   THE EXPERIMENTAL THERAPIST

No sooner was the war over than Bion emerged relieved, disenchanted, devastated and worried. He was relieved to be free of the war and the army that had taken so many of his working years, disenchanted because there had never been any official recognition of his work and ideas, devastated by the loss of his Eurydice during his quest for recognition, worried because he was now left with a young child and no money.

He took one day at a time. With his savings from the marriage he was able to buy a cottage in the country at an auction. He settled in Iver Heath with the family that was looking after the baby. This domestic arrangement brought him some peace of mind, but he still had to worry about earning a living. He rented a consulting room in Harley Street. Concerned about his reputation, he was aware of the prestige of a Harley Street address. He was so short of money that he had to work long hours – not only throughout weekdays but also on Saturday and Sunday mornings. Whenever he had spare time, he spent it with his young daughter. He bought a bicycle, added a baby seat to it, and every Saturday afternoon took her for a bike ride. Parthenope soon became very attached to her father. Parthenope was the unusual name that Betty and he had decided to give the child, should it be a daughter.[10] As soon as she could walk, the toddler would come to meet her father at the bus stop. This event is one of the very few recorded in the autobiography at which Bion expresses a real feeling of joy and gratification.

Eventually the problems of work began to invade the peace of his domestic family life. He found it impossible to ignore them, even when he was gardening or preparing home-grown apples for bottling.

In 1945 Bion started analysis with Melanie Klein and resumed his training at the Institute of Psycho-Analysis. This proved a time of extraordinary desire for intellectual work, and Kleinian concepts became his 'base camp' from which he began the solitary ascent of his life's work.

ACTIVE RESEARCH

As soon as he was demobilized, Bion returned to part-time work at the Tavistock Clinic. He found that in only a few hours per week he could research into institutional dynamics. He approached groups as he had always done, as an arena for active research. He was not simply making objective observations but actively facilitating change. It was not always clear whether he was aiming at changes in the institution, in the therapeutic process, or in training methods, but in every context Bion was impressively efficient and original. Sutherland gives a good description of the atmosphere in the early stages of a training group. Bion wanted to be able to compare group dynamics from a range of contexts, and to compare the results derived from different groups. At this time he was interested in people working from positions of power, and he organized a group at the Tavistock for ten people working in senior management in industry. He hoped that through this initiative his methods would be used in industry. Rickman and Sutherland participated in the study group, and worked with Bion for many months. Sutherland notes how impressed they were by Bion's sensitivity and intelligence, but he admits: 'His role was stressful much of the time, and Rickman and I were not sufficiently on his wavelength to take the pressure off . . . despite the denial mechanisms in the group, the impact was profound; two members developed duodenal ulcer symptoms before the group finished, and three decided to have personal analysis subsequently' (in Pines [ed.] 1985, p. 52).

A little later Bion organized regular meetings in his consulting room for analysts who had worked with groups. Each person could talk about their experiences and their projects, and everyone was on an equal footing. It was a kind of 'self-help' group, but Bion did not find that it provided the kind of help he was looking for, nor did his colleagues find it useful. Rickman jokingly dubbed it the 'Pentecostal' group. The meetings drew to a close. Trist, who had been an observer at the Tavistock therapy group, paints a – by now familiar – picture:

> He was detached yet warm, utterly imperturbable and inexhaustibly patient. He gave rise to feelings of immense security . . . His interventions were on the sparse side and tended to be terse. They could be kept so because he always waited until the evidence for what he would say was abundant. He expressed himself in direct, concise language that everyone could understand. If a patient made an intervention before he did, so much the better; there was no need for him to make it. He seemed to want to make the group as self-interpretative as possible and to facilitate its learning to become so (in Pines [ed.] 1985, pp. 30–31)

Before leaving the clinic Bion proposed a final project: a therapy group for the staff. The committee accepted the proposal and the 'staff group', open to all, met at first once and then twice a week. The clinic's working process with fears of possible staff redundancies and demotions had created much acrimony, divisiveness, tension, anxiety and guilt. Bion's group offered a collection of very disparate people, with different roles, aims and institutional relationships, the only occasion on which they could meet one another on equal terms. The group worked well for about a year. During this time the committee responsible for reorganization managed to find satisfactory solutions for most of the staff problems. As people began to find satisfactory solutions to their work problems they stopped attending the group, and it eventually stopped meeting because there were no more participants.

THEORETICAL INNOVATIONS

After the war, the Tavistock Clinic was brought into the new National Health Service. Bion gave up most of his sessions there; he wanted independence. He also wanted to approach psychological problems on an individual basis. He resigned from most of his commitments at the Tavistock, but despite his withdrawal he had managed to develop a method of group therapy that was to have a tremendous influence there, and he had done so in the space of only a few years. His 'bequest' arrived at just the right time. While psychiatry was almost exclusively devoted to treating hospitalized patients, Bion developed a group technique that could, in some cases, replace psychotherapy.

Bion had organized the groups in early 1948. He had worked under the aegis of an institution that allowed him complete freedom. He had developed concepts that were foreign to psychoanalysis in two ways:

- first, the material observed was different;
- secondly, setting aside analytic theories of group formation, he could decide whether or not his own ideas were complementary to or in contradiction with existing theories.

He aimed to: 'try to persuade groups composed of patients to make the study of group tensions a group task' (1961, p. 29). The psychiatrist neither formulated rules nor presented any agenda. With no other task before them, the group had time to participate in something akin to free association. The participants often turned to him, waiting for him to do something. As in psychoanalysis, Bion would respond to this demand with an interpretation. Having been placed at the centre of the group, he communicated his feelings to the other members.

This dynamic enabled verbal exchanges to take place between psychoanalyst and participants. Whenever he felt it appropriate, Bion would make an interpretation; he would try to express concisely the group's attitude towards him. He based his interpretations on this concept of the group's attitude towards an individual because people are influenced by: 'what we feel to be the attitude of a group to ourselves, and [how we] are consciously or unconsciously swayed by our idea of it'. Bion extended the scope of his interpretations when he considered that the same process was taking place in another member of the group. The emotional dynamic that is usually focused on the leader may also become displaced on to another member of the group. But before extending his theoretical concept of interpretation, Bion developed an entirely new concept of group dynamics.

GROUP MENTALITY

Throughout his work Bion employs many visual and optical metaphors. Accounting for the emotional dynamic described above, he invokes his experience as a student of medicine observing a specimen under a microscope. On one focus setting one structure can be seen; by changing focus an entirely new formation can be discovered. Bion transposes this metaphor to the observation of emotional dynamics through a 'mental microscope'. A group mentality can be perceived, and the image of people meeting in order to resolve their emotional problems can also, at times, be perceived as a group mobilizing its hostility and contempt towards patients, and especially towards those patients who seriously wish to tackle the problem. But each individual member may deny any feeling of hostility, because the group facilitates anonymous expression of hostility. Every group has a mentality which is in contradiction to its conscious aims, and in contradiction to the conscious aims of the individuals that constitute it. The group's uniformity contrasts with the diversity of individuals' thoughts. 'Once he had identified this concept he was in possession of a referent for the group setting analogous to the unconscious in the individual setting' (Trist, in Pines [ed.] 1985, p. 32).

When individuals come together as a group, they create a 'basic assumption' by contributing selectively unconscious elements. This anonymous collaboration creates a group mentality which expresses the unanimous but unspoken aims and beliefs of the group. But this group mentality destroys any possibility of any individual privacy. Group mentality, typically, will not tolerate the fact that an individual member may derive satisfaction from anything other than what the group makes available to its members. This is what Bion calls group culture. Group culture is a function of the conflict between the individual's needs and the group mentality. As an example of group culture, Bion describes the creation of a 'miniature theocracy' in which a leader is turned into a supreme being (the group mentality of children in a school playground), and another where all participants, including the leader, are deemed equal. The role of the therapist is to throw some light on to the emotional dynamic suffusing the group, usually one of tension and confusion. In order to describe the nature of the tensions Bion introduces a triad of concepts: individual, mentality and culture.

'BASIC ASSUMPTION' AND 'WORK' GROUP

Working with the emotional life of groups, Bion was amazed at the futility of group conversations: 'If judged by ordinary standards of social intercourse the performance of the group is almost devoid of intellectual content' (1961, p. 39). So he focused on the emotional charges underlying verbal exchanges rather than their 'contents'.

Drawing his hypothesis closer to his experience, Bion substitutes 'desires' for the 'needs' of his original formulation of group culture as a function of the conflict between individual and group mentality: 'In the group mentality the individual finds a means of expressing the contributions which he wishes to make anonymously, and at the same time his greatest obstacle to the fulfilment of the aims he wishes to achieve by membership of the group' (1961, pp. 52–3). Bion discovers that the 'aims' of group interaction can be categorized into three types of 'basic assumption', and an individual who contributes to the group mentality will feel uneasy whenever he thinks or acts in a way that does not accord with the basic assumption in play. Bion focused on identifying the types of basic assumptions to be found in groups. The new concepts derived partly from his previous experiences. Maintaining a tripartite structure, he extends its theoretical profile. By the end of his research Bion was convinced that in all groups there is an interaction between two levels of emotional activity. One of these he calls the work group; the other he calls the basic assumption group.

The category 'work group' describes only one aspect of mental activity (it does not describe the individuals constituting the group). Even a random collection of individuals may come together to complete a task of some sort. All individual members of the group voluntarily co-operate with the necessary activities. All activity presupposes a contact with reality which requires respect for reality. As a consequence, the work group is characterized by its awareness of the dimension of time, and the need for progress. Characteristic of the work group are those features which Freud describes as characteristic of the ego.

Bion was concerned to identify those mental activities which impede, corrupt or sometimes support the rational group process. They derive from powerful emotional states which push the faculty of judgement into second place. At first sight these activities seem rather chaotic, but they acquire a certain coherence when they are understood as manifestations of the basic assumption held in common by all members of the group. It is not that members of the group create a basic assumption and all else follows from this; rather that 'The emotional state exists first and the assumption follows from this'. The work group requires an aptitude for collaboration with other participants. The basic assumption group, by contrast, is held together by an automatic and involuntary participation of its members. To account for this Bion uses the concept of 'valency' as a description of an individual's readiness to enter into combination with a group in making and acting on basic assumptions. An individual without valency would no longer be human.

The 'basic assumption group' does not recognize the passage of time, and understands little of whatever relates to time. It therefore rejects all processes of growth and development, which depend on changes in time, and in place of growth it offers the alternative of a feeling of increased vitality: 'This longed for alternative to the group procedure is really something like arriving fully equipped as an adult fitted by instinct to know, without training or development, exactly how to live and move and have his being in a group' (1961, p. 89).

Bion identifies three types of basic assumption group that may underlie the work group: the basic assumption may be one of dependence, pairing, or fight–flight.

In a group where the basic assumption is of dependence, the group seeks the support of a leader from whom it hopes to receive spiritual and material guidance, protection and nurture. It believes that all its needs can be satisfied by one person, on whom it develops total dependence. Bion asks us to take this in a literal, not a metaphorical, sense. At first members of the group try to reinforce the idea that the group comprises a doctor and his patients. They insist that the doctor is the leader, and the only important person there. They feel cared for only when they are directly relating to the leader. If they are not relating, they feel frustrated and trapped in their need and hunger. For this type of group, power is something that is magical rather than scientific: the ideal leader is something of a sorcerer.

The second type of basic assumption concerns the group's aims in uniting. Bion was drawn to recognition of this problem by a recurring situation. The discussion would become monopolized by two people who would seem more or less to ignore the presence of other members of the group. From time to time the couple would exchange glances in such a way as to suggest an amorous relationship. In the meantime, their conversation was not very different, in its content, from other conversational exchanges in the group. While neurotics are usually very impatient with any activity that does not refer to their own problems, members of the group may accept this monopolization of the conversation by the couple with apparent ease.

Bion noticed that the gender of the individuals is of little significance to the basic assumption of the pairing in the group. Every time this relationship emerges, it seems to be a kind of sexual relationship. During this time a mood of irrational hope contrasts with the usual feelings of boredom and frustration, and the group develops a belief that a person or an idea will save it by making all difficulties disappear: 'For the feeling of hope to be sustained it is essential that the "leader" of the group, unlike the leader of the dependent group or the fight–flight group, should be unborn. It is a person or an idea that will save the group – in fact from feelings of hatred, destructiveness and despair, of its own or another group – but in order to be able to do this, obviously, the Messianic hope must never be fulfilled' (1961, p. 151).

In the third type of basic assumption, group members unite in order to fight against or escape from a threat. The group can opt for either activity with apparent indifference – hence the name 'fight–flight'. Group members accept a leader whose demands offer them opportunities for fighting or for evasion. In this type of situation a therapist will quickly realize that the group unites easily around any proposition that expresses violent rejection of all psychological difficulty, or offers means of avoiding difficulty by creating an external enemy.

THE PROTO-MENTAL SYSTEM

Bion was preoccupied with two questions concerning basic assumption groups.

The emotions associated with basic assumptions can be described in familiar terms, such as anxiety, fear, hatred, love. But these emotions affect one another when they are combined in a basic assumption. This means that anxiety, for example, as it is expressed in the dependence group, is different from its expression in the pairing group. The same holds true for other emotions and their combination: 'In a word, the important thing is not the presence of such and such a feeling, such as security for example, but the way in which it combines with others.' The first question concerns the nature and origin of psychological combinations. Bion wonders why it is that emotions can combine with a tenacity and exclusivity characteristic of chemical reactions.

There are no conflicts between the basic assumptions, and they can alternate easily within the same group. Conflict arises from the relationship between the basic assumption group and the rational (work) group. However, the emotional state associated with each of the basic assumptions excludes the emotions characteristic of the other basic assumptions. This leads Bion to his second question: What happens to the latent affects, the emotions belonging to the basic assumptions that are inactive in a group?

When a person joins a group, they try to identify themselves entirely with either the basic assumption or the rational structure. If a member identifies themselves with the basic assumption, they feel persecuted by what seems to them to be the arid intellectualism of the group (and especially interpretations). If the member identifies with the rationality of the group, they feel persecuted by internal objects. The emotional state of the group's basic assumption cannot be acceptable to all concerned. The group process can support individuals only in detaching themselves from everything they find 'bad'. The feelings which an individual seeks in a group exist only in combination with other feelings which may be less desirable to them, or even strongly disliked by them. The group therapist should allow himself to see all situations in a double psychological perspective. Bion illustrates this concept of the double perspective with the help of the diagram, first made by the Swiss crystallographer Wecker in 1832, showing an ambiguous cubic structure. Perception of the figure can oscillate between a receding and a projecting perspective. According to the traditional perspective of cubic forms, the side closest to the spectator will be larger than the side farthest away. With a reversible cube, the spectator can focus on either of two squares as closest or farthest, because their size is identical. The spectator interprets the diagram in two ways simultaneously without being able to settle definitively on either.

Bion was not entirely satisfied with analogies from the psychology of perception; he was seeking a method analogous to mathematical formulae. Eventually he turned increasingly to mathematical models of psychic processes. At this stage he uses the mathematical 'principle of duality': 'a system that proves the relationship in space of points, lines and planes, appears equally to prove the relationship of its dual in terms of planes, lines and points. In the group the psychiatrist should consider from time to time what is the dual of any emotional situation that he has observed' (1961, p. 87). The basic assumptions no longer appear to the psychiatrist to be separate states of mind. Each of these states of mind, even when it can be fairly clearly differentiated from the other two, has a quality which makes it the 'dual' of one of the other two, or is an aspect of what he might have taken for another basic assumption.

Explaining the relationship of emotions to the basic assumption, Bion postulates the existence of a 'proto-mental' system: 'the proto-mental system I visualize as one in which physical and psychological or mental are undifferentiated'. This system contains the prototypes of the three basic assumptions. 'It is from this matrix that emotions proper to the basic assumption flow to reinforce, pervade and on occasion to dominate the mental life of the group' (1961, p. 102). If the work group is infiltrated by emotions associated with the basic assumption dependence group, then the emotions characteristic of the other two (pairing and fight–flight) inoperative groups are confined to the proto-mental system. In this situation, only the proto-mental stage of the dependent group will have been allowed to develop into the differentiated state where its operation as a basic assumption can be observed by a therapist.

THE SPECIALIZED WORK GROUP

Following Freud, Bion was interested in the group structure of the army and the Church. He conceived of these as specialized work groups. Some groups work with a task that is particularly likely to stimulate a basic assumption. However, the state of mind founded on a basic assumption cannot be expressed through action, as action requires maintaining contact with reality. Basic assumptions become dangerous in so far as an attempt is made to translate them into action. The specialized work group understands this threat as it attempts to invert the process; it attempts to translate action into terms of a basic assumption mentality.

The Church is usually susceptible to interferences from dependent group phenomena, and the army to those of the fight–flight phenomena. To maintain their rational functioning, they have to prevent their respective basic assumption group from being too active or exercising too much influence. A flourishing Church should strengthen itself with religious faith, while not becoming a basis of action. An efficient army must convey the message that its strength is invincible, while not trying to make use of it.

Bion suggests that the aristocracy performs the same function for the basic assumption pairing group as the army and the Church do for the other basic assumption groups. This subgroup connotes birth and breeding, and so provides expression of the desires of the basic assumption pairing group, without negating the rational activity of the group as a whole.

Changes in group mentality are not limited to moments at which one basic assumption replaces another; they may also take 'aberrant' forms. Sometimes the therapist's interpretations do not satisfy the group. The group therefore begins to treat him as a child whose fantasies must be indulged. When the therapist no longer protests but nourishes the group, the group will nourish him and keep him alive.

The dependence group has as urgent a need for a dependent member as for a member on whom to depend. It has to recognize that its leader is mad, but is at the same time to be respected. The group can maintain this logic by oscillating between the two points of view. As the distance between the two points of view increases, the oscillations are increased and amplified. Sometimes the group loses control over the situation. With an explosive violence it extends itself to other groups until it has absorbed enough elements that are foreign to its own emotional atmosphere to decrease the tension of ambivalence.

Another form of aberration is splitting and schism. Schisms are the result of the group's resistance to the need for growth. Depending on temperament, each member will adhere to one or other of the subgroups created by a schism. When one of the subgroups refuses to go any further, it appeals to the loyalty of the leader of the dependence basic assumption group. Another substitute for the leader may be found in turning to the group's history; minutes are taken, forming a sort of 'bible' which protects the group in its struggle against the threat of having to accept an idea which might require individual progress. Members of the subgroups invoke tradition, the Word of God or a deified person. They try to manipulate the leader so that being a member of the group requires no painful effort, and is a guarantee of popularity. By the exclusion of all feelings of discomfort, thought becomes stabilized at a level that tends towards platitude and dogma. The subgroup comprises converts to the new idea, but they become so dogmatic and so exacting in their demands that they cease to recruit new members. The two subgroups reach the same level, and conflict between them disappears: 'Schematically, the numerous schismatics are opposed by the numerically negligible schismatics, and both groups avoid the painful bringing together of the primitive and the sophisticated that is the essence of the developmental conflict' (1961, p. 159).

RESPONSIBLE AND HISTORICAL THINKING

In January 1947 Bion read a paper to the Medical Section of the British Psychological Society as its president. His theme was the question of what psychiatry might have to offer Western society at a time of crisis. Although he was speaking of a world-view, Bion was mainly thinking about the British situation. Churchill had been beaten in the 1945 general election by a popular Labour victory. The ensuing social progress included the nationalization of a number of industries, the setting up of the National Health Service, a welfare state and a policy of voluntary decolonization of the British Empire. Bion's beloved India officially became independent in June 1947, the British Empire was disappearing, and the battle for world supremacy was divided between the USA and the USSR.

The lecture, published in 1948, was not included in the 1961 collection of papers entitled *Experiences in Groups*, although it does contain the beginnings of the theory of groups he was to develop later. Bion describes the contemporary crisis in Western society, and discusses the solutions that he saw as confronting all intellectuals. From the beginning of the twentieth century mankind enjoyed the benefit of great technological progress which vastly improved the quality of daily life. However, the effect of technological advance on personal happiness remains debatable. Mankind has more or less succeeded in regulating external relations by means of law, but fails every time he tries to systematize a way of tackling the emotional tensions that underlie human relations.

Psychiatrists have made progress in the treatment of neurosis. Unfortunately, no therapeutic method has ever considered the group in the way that psychoanalysis considers the individual. The problem almost certainly lies in emotional factors. Bion suggests that the capacity for the acquisition of technical skills is to be considered separately from the capacity for full self-realization through emotion and intellect. Technical skills are easily communicated: a man of outstanding scientific creativity can convey a new technological capacity to thousands of colleagues very quickly. On the other hand, nobody has managed to communicate anything other than limited means of assuring man's emotional development. Imitation, in this sphere, is not of much use, and may even be dangerous if it creates false or imitative development. Hopes must rest on the development of a technique capable of facilitating emotional development, and it is this that psychological institutions should offer a society in crisis.

It is not only technological changes that affect emotional development – some forms of social organization also disturb many people. If they are to develop fully, people must have the scope for building personal relationships. The Greek metropolis allowed its inhabitants to participate fully in social life. Our perspective on Greek metropolitan life is perhaps an idealization rather than a historical reality, but it may none the less enable us to establish a criterion of the psychological health of a community: 'In the small community, it is possible for men to exercise their special talents without being condemned to the frustration and the atrophy of their other desires' (1948, p. 85).

Bion had started the gestation of these thoughts during his experiences in the Second World War. As a psychiatrist he had been able to recognize that the majority of patients belonged to the category of 'psychologically underprivileged' people. Of course it might be that these were people who deprived themselves of a wide range of personal relationships, but it might also be that the type of education they received at home and at school was largely responsible for this systematic deprivation. When a state of deprivation arises, a certain satisfaction can be found in renouncing the satisfaction of the frustrated desire, but this kind of renunciation can never really be successful, because the repressed desire will return in some form or other.

Bion's general thinking in this period, with the theory of group formation and the themes of social and historical issues, was influenced by the work of Arnold Toynbee.[11] As soon as he began to think seriously about group dynamics, Bion was influenced by Toynbee, who had posited the concept of an unknown factor, apparently of a psychological nature, operating in the growth of civilizations. Bion considered that he had been able to identify this unknown factor: it consists in the individual's capacity to form personal relationships, and in the quality of those relationships. When a community exists within a context of generosity, it will be able to recognize that leisure is important. Leisure in no way connotes a pleasant absence of work but a 'dynamic state of personal relationships which, properly produced and used, is one of the most potent forces in psychiatric investigation' (1948, p. 87).

Bion illustrates this with an example from his leaderless group technique. He cites the moment at which the group waits, without having any specific task to which it must apply itself, for consciousness of personal relations to enter into the mind of each member. In this situation, when the survival of the community is not imposing any particular task on the group, the unknown quality characteristic of groups and civilizations can be found. This idea that the threat to contemporary civilization is something that emerges from unconscious emotional drives, rather than from the environment, is one that had been proposed earlier by Freud, Jung, Adler and their followers.

As a historian Toynbee was searching for a quality that was self-sufficient 'and which consequently remains more or less intelligible when isolated from the rest of history'. In contrast to the contemporary convention of historical writing, according to which the nation was taken as the historical unit, Toynbee chose to work with a structure rather more inclusive than the nation-state, and used the term 'civilization'.

The nineteenth-century study of neurosis had foundered on the fact that neurosis tended to be studied simply as the suffering of the individual. When Freud began to formulate an explanation derived from an interpersonal as well as an intrapersonal dynamic, he discovered the perspective from which many of the problems raised by neurosis became intelligible and could be deciphered. Bion followed the same intellectual trajectory – looking for solutions for neurotic distress, as Freud did, but substituting the group dynamic for the two-person interpersonal relationship.

In order to reach a general view of history, Toynbee had to relinquish contemporary historical method, in which all historical causality is structured by the perspective of the historian who is writing. He could not accept the apparent 'givens' of history, but had to rethink their conditions of existence. To compare several concurrent series of events requires a synoptic perspective, which can be derived only from a comparative method of study. In order to make comparisons, Toynbee needed to identify categories and types of civilization. It was to this end that he introduced the concept of the 'external model'. In order to classify his historical material, Toynbee identified twenty-one civilizations at the start of his study, and thirty-one by its conclusion, which could be categorized in terms of three external models: the Hellenic, the Chinese and the Judaic. Bion adopted this comparative method, and the concept of the external model was – in a different form – to play an important part in the epistemological period of his work. Although Bion never cites Toynbee as an influence, he seems to have duplicated his structure in his theory of the three models of the basic assumption group underlying all group structure.

From the earliest days, Hellenic civilization was divided by tensions between political pluralism and cultural unity. Although they shared a similar culture, many sovereign states were at war with one another. In Graeco-Roman civilizations, mankind sought the potential creativity of a system of great independence and great regional diversity. But the cost of such a system is permanent conflict – when such conflict becomes too intense, society seeks peace in unity. According to Bion, the group characterized by the fight–flight basic assumption tries to resolve its problems by fighting. Historically, this predicament is ended only when each national group is absorbed by an element which is foreign to their indigenous emotional structure, such as the Roman Empire.

As the historical dynamic of classical Antiquity does not provide a model for all civilizations, Toynbee also proposed the Chinese model. Chinese history comprises a succession of historical eras in which the ideal is the universal State, punctuated by intermediate stages of disorder and discord. Within the Chinese model the so-called 'civilized' man strives to maintain a social unity, and to rebuild it whenever it is fragmented or ruptured. This rebuilding avoids the struggle and disruption caused by fragmentation. When a group is dominated by the basic assumption of dependence, it seeks security and hopes to protect its members from the emotional experiences characteristic of other basic assumption groups. The establishment of a universal State usually erases the identity of the other states it incorporates.

Despite having no state and no territory, the Jewish community maintained its unity and its historical continuity. Since Jewish history is not the only civilization in diaspora to have responded in this way, Toynbee calls this type of civilization the Jewish model. A community of this type conserves its identity despite diaspora and deracination. The Jewish community achieved this by strict adherence to religious ritual. It did not seek to merge into the surrounding majority, believing itself to be in possession of a unique religious revelation. Finally, it always made every effort to gather the economic resources necessary for survival. In the Jewish model, culture seeks to protect the faith of the 'chosen people' while the rest of society resigns itself to the fusion of national identities in ecumenical unity. The basic assumption of pairing is always accompanied by feelings of hope: a person or an idea will come to save the group. But to fulfil this role, the messianic hope must never be actualized; it must remain a potential.

7 THE KLEINIAN
PSYCHOANALYST

Apart from his theories of group structure, Bion always maintained a psychoanalytic frame of reference. It is not surprising that he finally entered the analytic fold. However, he entered it in two stages. In the last essay of *Experiences in Groups* (first published in *Human Relations*, vols I–VII, 1948–51) he starts by setting out his own theories in relation to Freud, then demonstrates how the discoveries of Melanie Klein allowed him to find new solutions to the problems.

THE FREUDIAN

It is extraordinary that Bion, who was still unknown in psychoanalytic circles, treated Freud's work on group behaviour with such 'familiarity'. He addressed Freud as if he were an equal, as if he were in discussion with a colleague from the Tavistock Clinic. Bion did not avoid direct criticism of Freud's theories if he considered it necessary.

With his analytic experience Freud had tried, in 1921, to cast some light on the more obscure points in the work of Le Bon, McDougall and others who had written on group psychology. They suggested that group psychology was a specific response to the situation in which a number of people are brought together at the same time and in the same place. Bion, on the other hand, thought that the external situation is not necessary except in so far as it permits the observation of the phenomena manifested in group behaviour. The situation is of interest because it is the framework within which group dynamics, expressed as relations between individuals, can be observed. The members of a group should be close enough to the therapist for the latter to make an interpretation without raising his voice. If all participants are to be able to observe the interactions on which the therapist is basing his interpretations, spatial dispersal must be limited. Similarly, all participants must be present at the same time. However, the assembling of individuals does not in itself create group formation, nor does it add anything to the structure of individual psychology. For Bion, the idea that the assembling of a group is what creates the phenomena of group formation is erroneous. The error issues from the belief that something begins only when its existence can be demonstrated.

In fact, no individual, however isolated, can exist outside a group, nor be free from the effects of group behaviour. An individual cannot be understood except in terms of the group and the society in which he lives. Yet few mistakes are made in psychoanalysis when group phenomena are not explicitly taken into account, as analyst and patient share many group dynamics between them.

For Bion, group analysis allows a greater understanding of the analytic situation. Psychoanalysis can be thought of as a work group with a predisposition to a basic assumption of coupling. Also, psychoanalysis has a tendency to accord sexuality a determining role in human imagination and thought. Naturally, it is assumed that two people can meet only for sexual reasons. Freud assumed that the link uniting the couple is libidinal in nature; but Bion suggests that even if this is true of the basic assumption pairing group, it is not so evidently true of the basic assumption dependence and fight–flight groups.

Therefore, Bion felt that it was necessary to use more neutral terms to describe the links between individuals and groups. We have shown that two types of mental processes can be found here. In the work group, which operates through rational processes, the term co-operation seems most appropriate for describing the nature of these links. As we have seen, Bion uses the term 'valency' to describe individuals' instinctive capacity to unite according to the basic assumptions. Freud revolutionized the treatment of neurosis by acknowledging its origins in the individuals' object relations rather than in the idea of the individual as an entity in itself; but according to Bion, he was not fully able to apply this

Intrapsychic phenomena

revolutionary approach to the theory of group psychology. By observing a group, the focus of study is simply widened to include phenomena other than intrapsychic processes. In other words, the difference between group psychology and individual psychology is only illusory. The group provides a focus of study in which certain aspects of individual, intrapsychic phenomena are made more distinct.

In many cases Bion felt that a correct interpretation has the effect of bringing the behaviour of a group closer to the reactions found in a family situation. In other words, Freud's idea that the family group is the basic prototype of all groups seemed to him to have some basic validity, but it seemed inadequate in that it left obscure the origins of some of the most powerful emotional forces in a group.

The more stable the group, the more it reflects the Freudian view. The more disturbed the group, the closer it approaches the mechanisms and primitive phantasies described by Melanie Klein. Freud considered group psychology from the starting point of whole-object relations and neurotic defences, whereas Bion considered the group in terms of part-objects and more psychotic defences. It seems that although he wanted to liberate himself from being constrained by existing theories, Bion was hesitant to begin a Copernican revolution in which family life and psychoanalysis would be specific examples of a more generalized group dynamic.

KLEIN'S STUDENT

By publishing his article 'Group dynamics: a review' in the issue of the *International Journal of Psycho-Analysis* dedicated to Melanie Klein in 1952, Bion participated in a celebrated event.[12] From the outset he states his theoretical position: 'In this article I shall briefly summarize some theories at which I have arrived by applying to groups, in which I was participating, the intuitions developed by present day psychoanalytic training' (1952, p. 253). By the time the article was republished in *Experiences in Groups*, Bion had become even more explicit about his theoretical direction: 'I propose to discuss the bearing of modern developments of psycho-analysis, in particular those associated with the work of Melanie Klein' (1961, p. 141).

The problem in question was that of the aspects of group psychology that had not been fully analysed by Freud. Bion's tone and attitude towards Freud had undergone a great change since his previous article. As a result of his official affiliation with Melanie Klein, he seemed to be revisiting his true ancestry. Now, Bion identified himself as a descendant of Klein who, in turn, saw herself as extending the work of the founder of psychoanalysis.

An individual seeking to join the emotional life of a group makes efforts as formidable as an infant seeking the mother's breast. If these efforts are frustrated, they regress: 'The belief that a group exists, as distinct from an aggregate of individuals, is an essential part of this regression, as are the characteristics with which the supposed group is endowed by the individual' (1961, p. 142).

The individual constructs a fantasy of the existence of the group as they lose the sense of 'individual distinctiveness' and experience something indistinguishable from depersonalization. In order for a group to exist, the members must have experienced this regression, which prevents them from seeing it as a collection of individuals. When the individuals constituting the group are threatened with being made aware of their individuality, the group enters a state of panic. Bion agreed with Freud that the phenomenon of a group, crowd or mass is not in itself capable of creating a new instinct in human psychology. He counters all theories which suggest that the group is larger than the sum of its parts. It is easier to demonstrate and observe group behaviour when the individuals are united: 'I think it is this increased ease of observation and demonstration that is responsible for the idea of a herd instinct, such as Trotter postulates' (1961, p. 169).[13] Whereas the work group can apply itself to various tasks, the basic assumption group must essentially be explored by an analytic method. Since the basic assumptions are interconnected, and even seem to represent different facets of one another, psychoanalysis should be able to understand them in terms of a yet more fundamental structure. The phenomena associated with basic assumptions are analogous to defences against psychotic anxiety. At a certain point we find that the characteristics of the three basic assumptions are analogous to the three positions of a person in an oedipal predicament: for example, the leader of the fight–flight group sometimes resembles the dangerous father. But the analogy is not complete: 'The relationship appears to be between the individual and the group. But the group is felt as one fragmented individual with another, hidden, in attendance' (1961, p. 161). When the analyst suggests that the group itself should become the object of investigation, he provokes primitive anxieties. In the minds of group members these anxieties are close to the earliest phantasies of the contents of the mother's body: 'It will be seen from this description that the basic assumptions now emerge as formations secondary to an extremely early primal scene' (1961, p. 164).[14] The concept of the primal scene used by classical psychoanalysis does not seem to account entirely for group dynamics. In groups the scene seems bizarre; it 'seems to be that a part of one parent, the breast or the mother's body, contains among other objects a part of the father' (1961, p. 164). Seen as a link between part-objects, this version of the primal scene is associated with psychotic anxiety, and the primitive defences of splitting and projective identification as described by Melanie Klein.

The more powerful the group's basic assumption, the less it makes rational use of verbal communication. Klein underlines the significance of symbol formation in individual development, analysing the way certain individuals become unable to make or use symbols. Influenced by a basic assumption, all group members behave as if they are unable to use symbols. The group will be unaware of the fact that symbols are used for communication: 'Instead of developing language as a method of thought, the group uses an existing language as a mode of action' (1961, p. 186).

Bion's concept of the leader is different from that of Freud and his predecessors. Because Freud considered identification only as a form of introjection, he conceived of the leader as someone whose personality marks and influences the group. He compares the leader to a hypnotist. Bion, however, considers the leader as a creation of the basic assumption, as are all the other members of the group. He could not exist otherwise, as the members' identification with the leader is created not only through introjection but also through projection. The leader does not influence the group through a strong will and dominance, but tends to efface his own personality to satisfy the demands of the basic assumption group. The description of the leader seems to be a mixture of basic assumption and work group phenomena. It may happen that one person can simultaneously satisfy the demands of the basic assumption and retain contact with external reality, but it can also happen that an individual is endowed with all the prestige of being a work group leader simply because he is a vehicle for the emotions of the basic assumption group. This accounts for some of the disasters into which groups have been led by leaders whose qualities seem to be devoid of substance once the emotion prevalent at their prime dies down.

Bion states that 'In group treatment many interpretations, and amongst them the most important, have to be made on the strength of the analyst's own emotional reactions' (1961, p. 149). The analyst functions, in effect, as the recipient of the projective identification described by Klein in 1946 (Klein, 1946). This defence mechanism, which plays such an important part in group dynamics, provokes emotional reactions in the analyst. Bion was part of the group which, in the 1950s, encouraged the use of the countertransference as the starting point of interpretations.[15] An experienced analyst recognizes when he is the object of projective identification. He senses that the patient is trying to manipulate him to make him enact a role in his fantasies. At that point he feels violent emotions, while he is convinced that they are objectively justified by the situation. The analyst manages to transcend this impasse by unburdening himself of the paralysing feelings of reality. If he achieves this, he perceives the relationship with the preceding interpretation whose validity he had been led to doubt.

By this time Bion seemed to have come a very long way from the optimism he had expressed at the outset of his group projects. With hindsight, his experiences confirmed that there could be no scientific justification for calling his group treatment psycho-analysis. A person engaged in group therapy must be able to hope that their initiative will bring about some healing or progressive change. Almost all patients in groups are convinced that the group is of no value as treatment, then their participation convinces them that their prejudices are justified. In the group they discover a total and real indifference towards – even hatred of – each other. Bion considered Ernest Jones's idea that 'group psychoanalysis' might even be no more than an ingenious form of resistance to the unconscious. He wondered whether it would be possible to test this idea in a group composed of people who had either been psychoanalysed or were being analysed as individuals. He was aware that he was a group therapist who had been trained on the job, and that he had never had a training in group therapy himself.

He nevertheless maintained the illusion that the group process would be different in groups of individuals who had previously been psychoanalysed as individuals. Bion finally allowed the matter to rest in the judgement of the individual who might test their ideas and theories in the groups encountered in everyday life.

WITH HINDSIGHT

Bion was interested in group dynamics throughout his life, even though he did not use his direct experiences in groups as a basis for theory and writing after the 1940s. In a letter written on 17 October 1977, he confirmed: 'I have not abandoned groups but the urgency of work to be done with individual analyses leaves me no time for anything else'. In 1961 he allowed his articles on groups to be reprinted in their original form. By this time he was intensely preoccupied with disturbances of thought, and was completing the work of theorizing psychosis. Also at this time he was preparing the publication of the first of the books that we have classified as belonging to the 'epistemological period' of his work. In retrospect, there were to be no further writings on the themes of the 'group period'. We can see, however, that Bion brought to his subsequent work the perspectives developed in this period of working with groups. The conceptual wealth and fertility of the group period consist in its theoretical synthesis; concepts such as the basic assumption, the proto-mental system, span the differences between the work of historians such as Toynbee and psychoanalysts such as Klein. Beyond his interest in therapeutic groups, Bion had discovered a consuming interest in the theory of knowledge and philosophy. He began a synthesis of all these aspects of his intellect, later publishing an book subtitled 'The scientific approach to intuitive understanding in psychoanalysis and in groups' (1970).

When his early papers were published under the title *Experiences in Groups* in 1961, Bion added a preface. He was now writing as a psychoanalyst, and in his analytic work he had been struck by the feeling that individual analysis and group analysis are tackling different facets of the same phenomenon. By this he meant that it is in the nature of the analytically orientated person to identify with different aspects of those situations in which interpersonal relationships are activated.

The phenomena observed in such situations can be understood in two ways, depending on the observer's perspective. In the first view, what is foregrounded is the oedipal relation of the 'pairing group' basic assumption; in the second, it is the problem of self-knowledge, as symbolized by the mythical figure of the Sphinx. Bion refers to the figure of the Sphinx when he sets out the principles of basic assumption groups, identifying the predicament in which the work group, and its leader, are feared as being enigmatic and sinister, and all spirit of enquiry manifested in the group unleashes feelings of terror, like the terror of Thebes before the Sphinx in the Oedipus myth.

In the 'group period' Bion writes in an open and accessible style, reflecting his direct access to fundamental human experience and his desire to share it. Problems arise when he tries to evoke for his readers the atmosphere of a particular group, often immersing them in the group's feelings of frustration, exasperation, humiliation, rage and, especially, boredom. The reader, in turn, follows the same solitary and thankless path as the author. The only way out of the impasse with the group is to identify oneself with the author, from whose perspective the interaction is described. Bion's prose style often reflects a highly unusual turn of mind. It is hardly surprising to find that participants in his groups often felt as if they were faced with a sphinx. Even when the enigma is not that of human mortality, illness and anxiety can become the price to be paid for avoiding intellectual constriction. As readers our source of guidance is the author, who remains as inaccessible, enigmatic and mysterious as the Sphinx. In this respect we are in much the same position as the participants in the groups, being 'led' by someone who seems to be wanting to extract the maximum amount of personal effort from them.

Bion often plays with ambiguity, and the reader may remain in a state of uncertainty, or begin to think for himself, while awaiting the author's enlightenment. Bion's readers are subjected to this textual process from his very first article, where he considers the question of the kind of discipline needed by neurotics. He decides that it must depend on the presence of (1) an experienced officer without fear or blame; and (2) a common enemy. Bion's readers are then left to speculate on the meaning of this until the following page, where he explains that even hospitalized soldiers remain under attack from 'the common enemy, which is the existence of neurosis as a disability of the community' (1961, p. 13).

Another textual strategy much employed by Bion in his epistemological period is borrowing a technical term from another discipline, so that the word used in a psychoanalytic context remains surrounded by the 'associative penumbra' of its original context. As we have seen, for example, he uses the term 'valency' to describe the type of relationship which accounts for the pull of the basic assumption group. Valency was originally taken from chemistry, where it is used to describe the number of bonds that an atom or molecule may make with other elements in a chemical change. This kind of thinking manages to convey the stranger aspects of reality, but it may also create a sense of uneasiness and suspicion. In the opening sentence of the first of the articles to be printed in *Human Relations*, for example, Bion writes: 'It was disconcerting to find that the committee [the Professional Committee of the Tavistock Clinic] seemed to believe that patients could be cured in such groups as these. It made me think at the outset that their expectations of what happens in groups of which I was a member were very different from mine. Indeed, the only cure of which I could speak with certainty was related to a comparatively minor symptom of my own – a belief that groups might take kindly to my efforts' (1961, p. 29). According to Freud, humour is pleasurable in so far as it saves us from emotional work. Humour is not only liberating, like other forms of wit; it also has something of the sublime. The sublime in humour is a product of the way in which humour brings about a triumph of narcissism.

At his age, Bion was coming to terms with the inevitability of death, having witnessed the death of so many of his fellow soldiers and of his wife. The introduction of death into his psychological work gives his writing, from the very beginning, a tragic and philosophical element. His concentration of thought and his capacity for working through enabled Bion to transform a private preoccupation into an intellectual project, through years of silent work. It is difficult, and perhaps impossible, to reconstruct the threads of his systematic yet audacious thought: it is a thinking which frequently retraces its path to transform the thread of continuity, which then may re-emerge suddenly at a further point.

PART 3:
UNDERSTANDING
PSYCHOSIS

As soon as he was able to return to the solitude of the consulting room and private practice, Bion began a study of the psychotic personality. Between 1950 ('The imaginary twin') and 1958b ('Attacks on linking'), Bion wrote a series of extraordinarily original papers, which he presented at international congresses and published in the *International Journal of Psycho-Analysis*. His originality lay in the emphasis he placed on the relationship between thought and language in psychosis, and his new ideas in the analytic study of psychoses earned him lasting recognition as a pioneer in the field. With hindsight, these papers might be considered the starting point of his theory of thinking and thus of the third, 'epistemological', period of his work. 'A theory of thinking' (1962a) indeed marks the beginning of the epistemological period rather than the closure of the period during which he explores psychosis.

During this decade Bion considered himself first and foremost a Kleinian: 'Even when I do not make specific acknowledgement of the fact, Melanie Klein's work occupies a central position in my view of the psychoanalytic theory of schizophrenia' (1953/4, p. 23; 1967a, p. 23). Here Bion tackles the problems of thought disturbances which are connected to instinctual activity. Over and above Klein's work, his was securely anchored in Freud's theory of the psychic apparatus as organized by the reality principle. Freud had identified the hatred of reality as a characteristic of psychosis, and Klein links this to phantasies of attacks against the breast. Bion adds that the sadistic disequilibrium described here cannot help but affect the thought processes of the psychotic.

It would be incorrect to think of the psychotic period of Bion's work as simply a preparatory stage. Bion was no less creative in his work on psychosis than in his later project on psychoanalytic epistemology. He simply had a different perspective in these earlier writings. Far from feeling oppressed by the history of psychoanalysis, Bion made good use of Freud's legacy, especially as augmented by Klein, to facilitate his own new departure. Eventually he formulated a theory of schizophrenic psychosis which is still used by most Kleinians today. In the next period he was to develop a model for explaining psychoanalytic understanding itself.

8   WITH MELANIE KLEIN

In 1945 Bion began an analysis with Melanie Klein which was to last until 1953. In the course of these eight years a number of important changes took place in his life. Once he was accepted by the British Psycho-Analytical Society as a member, he began to be identified, through his writing and his presentations, as a brilliant student of Klein. He found a new psychic equilibrium – he married for a second time, and flourished in the presence of a very understanding partner. He was able to find Parthenope again, and to father two more children. It was during this time that Bion prepared to publish his work on group dynamics, as well as his first articles on psychosis. Psychoanalysis had awakened in him a deep creativity which was to stay with him until the end of his life.

CHOOSING A GROUP

Bion went for analysis to the leader of one of the three major analytic groups of the British Society: Melanie Klein. Before leaving Austria, Klein had been analysed by two of the leading analysts of that generation: Sándor Ferenczi and Karl Abraham. Both had encouraged her to specialize in the analysis of children, and it was her pioneering work in this field that led to her election as a member of the Hungarian Society at the end of the First World War. At this time Bion was just embarking on his studies at Oxford, where he was to read history. A few years after settling in Berlin, Klein had developed a technique of analysing children through play. It was because of these innovations that Jones invited her, in 1926, to settle in London.

Her book *The Psycho-Analysis of Children* was widely recognized as the work of an original mind (Klein, 1932). It was the first systematic account of her understanding of early childhood, and engendered as much curiosity as criticism from analysts, who welcomed the rich and intuitive description of infantile fantasy. Klein had located the onset of the Oedipus complex at an early age; thus she tended to find this structure in almost every stage of a child's development. In this, she proved herself almost more 'Freudian' than the founder of psychoanalysis himself. The idea of infantile sexuality was no longer quite as shocking as it had been, but Klein's work caused controversy because of her emphasis on the role of the death instinct in mental life and development. With her views on the phase of sadism at its height, readers could begin to intuit the central place that she was to accord the death instinct in her work. The first Kleinian system in fact contains the seeds of the concepts that were to surpass it. At this time there seemed to be a parallel between the development of the British Psycho-Analytical Society and that of Melanie Klein and her ideas; she felt at home in this organization, which stimulated her work and co-operated with her.[16]

Until the point at which Klein read her paper on the psychogenesis of manic-depressive states, there was a 'British School of psychoanalysis' which was not so very different from the Vienna and Berlin schools. Within this school the members were more or less in agreement with some – or all – of Klein's theories to date. In her paper written in 1935 Klein introduced the concept of the depressive position, and it was this paper which can be seen, retrospectively, to have initiated a historical split. By 1940, when Klein further elaborated this concept in relation to mourning, reparation and creativity, the split was even more pronounced. Klein thought of herself as a faithful follower of Freud – perhaps, even, his most faithful follower – yet she had developed a theory and a technique of analysis that were quite different from his. Not only did she claim to describe the unconscious life of very young children; she also claimed that there was psychosis in all of us.

The tension grew, owing to the historical events of the Nazi persecution, which brought many analysts from Vienna and Berlin over to London. Now the Controversial Discussions between Anna

Freud and Melanie Klein began to dominate the British Society. Faced with uncompromising partisans, many analysts became unequivocally opposed to Klein's ideas, but the outbreak of the Second World War cast a different perspective on the controversies. If Klein had broken away from Freud by distorting rather than developing his work, then she – like Adler, Jung and Rank – should be excluded from the British Society.

The famous Controversial Discussions which took place in 1943 and 1944 eventually gave rise to the formation of a Kleinian School within the British Society. This series of discussions meant that Klein and her followers had to formulate their ideas much more rigorously. At the time when Bion was looking for an analyst, the British Psycho-Analytical Society comprised three groups – one following the work of Anna Freud, one led by Melanie Klein, and a third comprising the majority of analysts who could accept only part of Klein's discoveries. The training regulations had been altered to allow students to follow specific groups and affiliations of their choice. This reorganization proved a positive change for Klein. She was surrounded by a group of loyal followers, and she had a forum within which to present her research.

Bion started his analysis when Kleinian analysis was reaching its definitive state. In one of her most important papers, 'Notes on some schizoid mechanisms' (1946), Klein had described the development of the phase preceding the depressive position, calling it the paranoid-schizoid phase. It predominates in the first three or four months of life, and may emerge again in childhood and in the regression of adults with paranoid or schizophrenic psychoses. The discovery of a concomitant defence mechanism, named projective identification, was to enable Kleinians to understand the pathology of schizophrenia and borderline disorders. The play therapy developed with young children had also helped to extend the terms of the analysis of adults. Bion made an excellent choice in selecting Melanie Klein as his training analyst. Not only could she appreciate the suffering of his infantile self, because of her extensive experience with children, but she was also unlikely to be hampered by his narcissistic and schizoid defences, as these were the areas of her own research.

In 1952 Klein and her close collaborators published an anthology of their research, *Developments in Psycho-Analysis*,[17] in which they set out a general theory of the early development of the mind in the first years of life, and the pathological forms of such development. The theory of drives accounted for the dynamics of anxiety, and object relations and defence mechanisms were explained in terms of fantasy. It was just before Bion terminated his analysis with Klein that she made the clearest, most systematic and comprehensive account of her theory of the developmental positions. The centrality of the depressive position remained her most fundamental principle. The structure of the personality depends on the way in which object relations become integrated into this position.

Do training candidates avoid the real issues at stake in the termination of their analysis by the act of becoming a member of the same society themselves? The question was a serious one for Bion. In the same year as he finished his psychoanalysis with Klein, his article 'Group dynamics: a review' was given a prominent place in the issue of the *International Journal of Psycho-Analysis* dedicated to her. He remained a loyal follower for many years, declaring his allegiance in his international papers and talks.

As soon as Kleinian thought had developed a systematic theory, Kleinians began to apply this to cultural, social and intellectual phenomena. They considered that a theory could be tested only by being applied. Bion set out to test the 'scientific theory' that Klein had derived from research into infant development in the field of group dynamics. He confirmed that the way in which a baby manages to master the life-and-death struggle between conflicting drives is an illustration of collective unconscious life. He discovered that the basic assumptions arise as secondary manifestations of an archaic fantasy of the primal scene: 'Basic assumption phenomena are characteristic of defences against psychotic anxiety, which is not so much a contradiction of Freud's ideas but rather an extension of them' (1961, p. 130).

PERSONAL COMMITMENT

Bion did not only choose a leader of a school of thought, he became involved with a person. He had read some of Klein's work before asking her for an interview, and had soon realized that they shared deep concerns, even though his interests had initially been explored from a different direction. In history, literature and group dynamics he had been searching for elemental and primitive emotions, underlying psychotic structures, the anguish of early childhood. These intellectual affinities were fuelled by irrational sympathies and antipathies. Bion had the opportunity to see and hear Klein speak before deciding on a training analyst. She seemed to be 'a handsome, dignified and somewhat intimidating woman' (Bion, 1985, pp. 66–7). Nobody would deny that Melanie Klein was an unusual person. Nevertheless, it is still difficult to perceive the person herself, because of the aura of fragmented contradictions that surrounds her name, an aura created by both her disciples and her opponents. Bion had a better opportunity than most to experience her person and her aura, as he visited her often after his long analysis with her. But the dynamic between them was so intense that he seems even more subjective in his judgements than others who retained a greater distance.

It would have taken a woman of Melanie Klein's calibre to embark on an eight-year analysis with a man so burdened with resentment of the opposite sex: 'My experience of association with women had not been encouraging or conducive to the growth of any belief in a successful outcome' (1985, p. 67). We can see why Bion often contested interpretations from a woman. He dedicates only one of fourteen chapters in the second part of his autobiography to an account of his training analysis with Klein, and his account breaks off just before the conclusion of this analysis.

Bion was wondering whether it was now time to find another wife. With an unusual mastery of style, he writes of a screen memory. Despite the apparent insignificance of the anecdote, this memory condenses strongly infantile elements and expresses an unconscious phantasy. He leaves us to speculate about the secret thoughts and feelings that led him to put it into writing.

At this point Bion still felt very 'numbed and insensitive'. The fact that there was something wrong with him was brought home to him through an incident with his baby daughter. He was sitting on the lawn near the house while Parthenope was crawling on the other side of the lawn. The baby began to call out to him – she wanted her daddy to come to her. Her father remained seated. She began to crawl towards him, calling to him to fetch her. He remained seated. As she crawled, her cries became more distressed. The space that lay between her and her only parent must have seemed vast to her. Her daddy did not move, but simply watched her.

Bion recalls feeling bitter, angry and resentful. He wondered why she was doing this to him. But an inner voice replied by inverting the question: 'Why are you doing this to her?':

> The nurse could not stand it and got up to fetch the child. 'No,' I said, 'let her crawl, it won't do her any harm.' We watched the child crawl painfully. She was weeping bitterly now, but sticking stoutly to her attempt to cover the distance.
>
> I felt as if I were gripped in a vice. No. I would *not* go. At last the nurse, having glanced at me with astonishment, got up ignoring my prohibition, and fetched her. The spell snapped. I was released. The baby stopped weeping and was being comforted by maternal arms. But I, I had lost my child. (Bion, 1985, p. 70)

If Bion started an analysis immediately after being demobilized it was, no doubt, because he felt he needed it urgently. His first analysis had confirmed in him his desire to become a psychoanalyst, but this time there were other, more urgent difficulties. He had returned from the war devastated by the death of his wife, worried about his double – paternal and 'maternal' – responsibility for his child, worried about earning a living, with the extra expense of a nurse. Bion never forgave himself for being absent at the birth of his child, even if his presence could not have altered the course of events: 'I had begged Betty to agree to have a baby: her agreement to do so had cost her her life' (Bion, 1985, p. 70). This sentence, following immediately after the screen memory, expresses the feeling of fundamental failure. Bion punished himself with his memories: 'And again I felt I had killed her by not staying with her when her pregnancy was nearing term' (ibid., p. 26). Is this not the greatest of 'all the sins remembered' in the autobiography?

Bion could only conceive of himself as guilty before the severe judge of his conscience; he seems to have been unable to acknowledge any negative feelings about someone whose life was so cruelly cut short. Moreover, Betty's death had reinforced, and literally enacted, his conviction that attachment to a woman always rests on a fundamental deception, and always ends in irreversible separation. He experienced his wife's death as an emotional abandonment, and felt betrayed. This reawakened the wounded narcissism of the blow caused by the beautiful fiancée who had broken off their engagement. These associative links are expressed with terrible clear-sightedness in the autobiography: Bion, in imaginary dialogue with the reader, makes a link between the beautiful fiancée and Betty: 'In short, you mean her love had died? No, you are mixing it up with Betty – and it was not her love that had died. *She* had died' (Bion, 1985, p. 26).

His unconscious turmoil had also fused the image of Victoria Station, where his fiancée had come to bid him farewell, vowing eternal fidelity, with the image of Waterloo Station, from which he had left for the front, alone, during World War One. An hour earlier he had said goodbye to a 'chalk-complexioned mother' who had sworn fidelity to him even as she was taking him so far away from home during his childhood. This final image of his pale mother prefigures his last sight of his wife – he was saying goodbye to Betty before leaving for France: 'At the time I thought she was being very brave, although she looked deadly pale' (Bion, 1985, p. 27).

The meeting between Melanie Klein and Wilfred Bion was fundamentally an encounter between a feminine universe and a masculine world. The candidate arrived hoping to be valued for his masculine achievements, the very qualities that had gained him entry to Oxford and London universities: sporting victories, military decorations. Bion was something of a victim of a rather Spartan educational system which separates children from their parents at a very early age in order to create a ruling class. The boys' separate lives create a homosexual experience which, in Bion's case, was exacerbated by his very great distance from his family, his intense attachment to team sports, and his years in the army. His hopes of being valued for this masculinity were doomed to frustration. He was faced with a woman who had been considered a beauty in her youth, whose stylishness remained evident in her clothing and appearance. Her marriage had not been happy, and she was now flourishing through female friendships.

Bion considered that his analysis followed a 'normal course: I retailed a variety of preoccupations, worries about the child, the household, financial anxieties – particularly how I was to find the money for such psycho-analytic fees and provide a home and care for the baby' (Bion, 1985, p. 67). He was upset that Klein seemed to remain unmoved by his material difficulties. In his autobiography he uses the metaphor of a mendicant friar to sum up his predicament. Klein certainly understood that he needed something other than money from her. Bion was relieved that she did not capitulate to this emotional pressure, but this did not stop him from resenting her correct technique. After thoroughly criticizing himself, he was able to criticize the analyst, whose insensitivity seemed to him to border on inhumanity. She made him pay for sessions, even when he fell ill with jaundice. Bion had to return to his normal schedule, even though his doctor did not consider that he was cured.

Despite his grievances, Bion went regularly to his sessions. His state of mind meant that he rarely found an interpretation correct. He acknowledges that some of the interpretations he had at first misunderstood or ignored seemed to him to be true in hindsight, but: 'As time passed I became more reconciled to the fact that not even she could be a substitute for my own senses, interpretations of what my senses told me, and choice between contradictories' (Bion, 1985, p. 68). Time did not make him any less intransigent, only more aware of his disagreement. Mysteriously, something in these series of experiences made him grateful to his analyst, although he also wished to be free of the burden of analysis.

Shortly before leaving England in 1968, Bion told Sutherland that 'During his analysis and subsequently, he had felt Mrs. Klein to be out of sympathy with, if not actively hostile to, his work with groups. She thought that he was being diverted from more important psychoanalytic work' (Sutherland, in Pines [ed.] 1985, p. 55).

Bion was in analysis almost throughout the duration of his writing on work with groups. Can his analyst be criticized for not colluding in the countertransference he tried to set up for her, albeit in the guise of independence of mind? We should note that an unspoken conceptual break had its origins in this period. The more deeply Bion felt fascinated by Klein's specifically feminine genius, the more the partisan loyalty she demanded of her followers began to bring about a claustrophobic rejection in him.

He emphasized the things that divided them. He claimed to work with society as a whole, whereas Klein limited herself to the society of psychoanalysis. He stated his public concern – responsibility, even – for the future of Britain, whereas she seemed unconcerned by social problems. (Klein had lived through the end of the Austro-Hungarian Empire, whereas Bion was still living through the end of the British Empire.) He proposed a general sociopsychology, whereas she preferred to keep psychoanalysis as a limited unchanging framework for personal growth and individual development. Finally, he sought to be as open to all things as she sought to focus on a single issue to be explored and understood in depth. All in all, they might have complemented each other quite well, but the predicament in which Bion found himself remained thus, give or take a few compromises, until Klein's death.

Klein and Bion had both started creative intellectual work after a mid-life crisis. Their creativity should have displayed more depressive than paranoid-schizoid traits. In fact, each found opposite resolutions to their crisis. It is interesting to compare the autobiographies that each wrote towards the end of a long life. Whereas Klein's thoughts keep returning to the centrality of her love for her mother and a nostalgia for a happy childhood, Bion grants his parents a very brief mention during part of his childhood, whereupon they vanish completely. But was Klein's childhood really such a happy one, and did she really love her mother so much, and was Bion's childhood really so unhappy, and his internal parents really so absent, as all that?

9 ⋁ Late Maturity

With characteristic wisdom, Freud suggested that an analysis could be said to be complete when the patient had gained or regained the capacities for work and for love. Before starting his analysis, Bion had published only two papers. In the course of his analysis he published the series of articles, later collected as *Experiences in Groups*, on which his reputation was based. The capacity to love arrived a little later. His father had been living with him since being widowed, and was encouraging him to consider finding another wife. But could there be a relationship that would not remind him of Betty's absence, or of his first fiancée's rejection? The Harley Street practice was beginning to bring in an income. He could now afford proper meals which, under his acerbic pen, became 'the pleasures of gluttony' to which he refers to in his autobiography. But were there no other pleasures?

In March 1951 Bion met a woman, also widowed, who was rather younger than himself. She worked as a research assistant at the Tavistock Institute. She had been trained as a singer, and had considerable musical talent. They met often, and as soon as the relationship grew serious he started writing to her regularly. His correspondence, later collected and published by Francesca, leaves us in no doubt about the 'renaissance' she had brought about in his life. Francesca and Wilfred announced their engagement in April.

The couple moved rapidly from their engagement to marriage. Their wedding was planned for 9 June. In his letters Bion allowed his love, joy, pride and relief full expression. He was delighted that she had spoken of a 'nursery': 'The mere thought of *our* children is inexpressibly sweet to me'. But he was also thinking about his daughter, and was immensely grateful for what Francesca had managed to give her: 'You have given Parthenope back to me and made me feel what it is like to have a child. You cannot think how terrible it has been to feel all the time that every day she was becoming more lost to me till at times she hardly seemed my child at all' (Bion, 1985, p. 85). Before the wedding he recalled his years of suffering: 'Six years of anxiety centring on the life of a small daughter and how she develops have made me get into a groove of anxiety – trying to be father and mother in one' (ibid., p. 97).

At the end of May Bion sold the house he had bought with the savings from his first marriage. He bought another, Redcourt, bigger and more beautiful. On the morning of his wedding he again felt the need to write to his fiancée, making another declaration of his love and his pride. The couple had planned a honeymoon, but they waited seven years before they were able to spend a week on holiday together away from home. A month later Francesca and Parthenope went on a seaside holiday together, while Wilfred stayed behind to work. He was making a new start in both his life and his work. He wrote about Rickman, who had died suddenly a few weeks after their marriage. The previous year Bion had presented his paper 'The imaginary twin' to the British Psycho-Analytical Society as his membership paper. These two commitments, of work and of marriage, lasted until the end of his life. They were the mainstay of his years of maturity.

It is said that happy people have no story to tell, and this proved true enough of Bion after his second marriage. The story of his life began, slowly, to be eclipsed by his work. His wife gave birth to a boy, Julian, on 30 July 1952. While she was in hospital, Bion stayed at home, making use of the free time to write his articles. He was in the process of leaving behind his preoccupation with groups to work on psychosis. The following year, he terminated his analysis. On 13 June 1955 his wife gave birth to a little girl, Nicola. Bion celebrated his fifty-eighth birthday some months later – he was becoming a father at an age when many other men become grandfathers.

These years, during which Bion's intellectual activity was at its height, comprise the period of his work on psychosis. In June 1955 he went to the International Psycho-Analytic Congress in Geneva. He kept close to his family in his thoughts – the birth of the little girl must have made him fear a repetition of Betty's tragedy. He wrote long, detailed letters to Francesca. These letters are a mine of information about his perceptions, his state of mind, his tastes and his relation to his 'head of school'.

Of especial interest is the account of his complicated and close relationship with 'Melanie', or 'M.K.'. The Kleinian School was at its apogee, and most of the eminent Kleinians spoke at that Congress. Bion, along with Elliott Jaques, had the privilege of being always in the company of the 'boss'. The great intimacy that had been established during a long analysis allowed Melanie Klein to demonstrate her real empathy. She intuited whenever he was thinking about Francesca, and sympathized with his regrets about her absence. They tacitly understood how important a part she played in his life.

As soon as he was awake, Bion had to concoct ruses in order to escape from his mother substitute: 'I have to find a way of explaining to M.K. that I need sleep and then to use the time for writing!' He wrote to his wife, protesting about the invasive presence of the analyst whom he had maintained as a third party in his relationship with Francesca, and about whom he wrote constantly. Bion was honoured by being so actively sought after, but it was about the negative aspects of the relationship above all that he wrote to Francesca: 'Melanie is extremely demanding. I suppose it is because she has had so many attacks and so little genuine happiness in her life, but I always feel sucked dry' (Bion, 1985, p. 116). It was not only Klein's exhausting presence in his life that made Bion nervous. He appeared nonchalant, but was concerned about the reception of his paper 'The development of schizophrenic thought'.

Although he joined the British Psycho-Analytical Society relatively late, Bion's career progressed quickly. By 1956 he was Director of the London Clinic of Psycho-Analysis. He remained there until 1962, and every year he wrote an original paper; all these papers have proved of lasting value to psychoanalysts all over the world. He was equally generous in his attempts to be a perfect husband and an attentive father to three children. Nevertheless, he was overworking. He was rushed to hospital in February 1959 – he had continued to work in his private practice despite having flu. One day he fainted on the Underground, and was detained in hospital for tests. He stayed there for almost two weeks. The tests ruled out heart disease and diabetes. He was advised to follow a diet in order to lose weight, a deprivation which he accepted with bad grace. Bion often returned to the depression that continued to haunt him.

Despite his concern about his health and his tendency to depression, Bion did not give up his desire for professional advancement. He made good use of this time of illness and convalescence away from the demands of practice, thinking of it as a sort of summer holiday during which he could produce his own work. He turned his attention to an article that proved central to his theoretical development, 'Attacks on linking'. He had doubts about the value of his work: 'I am at the moment feeling a bit depressed about my paper, wondering if it's all just working round stalking a most majestic mare's nest; a horrid feeling' (Bion, 1985, p. 129).

The approach of his sixtieth birthday increased the demands for creative production made on him by his rather grandiose ego-ideal. It was in the calmness and solitude of his home that he felt he could work. However, he felt that his worries about money and his social responsibilities were 'destroying my ability to work'. His evenings were taken up by the Melanie Klein Trust and the Psycho-Analytical Society. It was for these same reasons that, ten years later, he proposed to move to California. It must be said that he did not try to free himself from these obligations; in fact he tended to add to his responsibilities.

10 THE ANALYTIC CONTEXT

Freud's pessimism about the ability of psychoanalysis to treat psychosis was a burden to psychotic patients for a long time. Only in the 1930s did a certain curiosity about this kind of treatment emerge, and not until the 1950s was there any real interest in the psychoanalysis of psychotic patients. The American analysts, sparked by the concepts of Harry Stack Sullivan, were the first to publish on the subject. They held that a psychotic patient may be analysed, provided the classic technique is modified.

A little later, British analysts were inspired by the work of Melanie Klein. Her three most eminent students – Hanna Segal, Herbert Rosenfeld and Bion – all spoke to the international analytic community. They claimed to have analysed psychotic patients successfully with little or no modification of the classic technique. Hanna Segal was the first to publish an article putting forward this view, in 1950. Bion did not take long to catch up – he presented his theory of schizophrenia in 1953. Melanie Klein considered that his theory adhered to the basic principles of scientific method, which consisted of formulating hypotheses and proving or disproving them through material and data furnished by clinical practice. Bion had adopted this definition of scientific method, which was in vogue at that time. In the same spirit, throughout this period he maintained notions of 'diagnosis' and 'cure', as these notions had been transposed on to psychoanalysis from a medical model.

At that time Bion, close to the attempts to exclude Melanie Klein and her followers from the Society, took care to establish the scientific basis of his work, stipulating that the diagnoses had been officially made by other psychiatrists. Bion was not analysing only schizophrenics. The clinical material he used as case studies came half from cases of schizophrenia and half from cases of severe neurosis and addiction. Similarly, he was determined to prove the 'cure':

> I am not yet prepared to offer any opinion about the prospects of treatment except to say that two of the three schizophrenics of whom I am speaking are now earning their living. I believe that if the course I have indicated above is followed, there is reason to anticipate that the schizophrenic may achieve his own form of adjustment to reality, which may be no less worthy of the title of 'cure' because it is not of the same kind as that which is achieved by less disordered patients. (Bion, 1967a, p. 34)

In any case, Bion maintained that the results achieved by psychoanalysis should not be mistaken for the phenomenon of spontaneous remission known to psychiatrists. He was aiming to establish the existence of lasting improvements which were beyond doubt because they had been brought about using a coherent analytic theory. Bion also wanted to stress the fact that he, like Segal and Rosenfeld, had employed the same method as for the treatment of neuroses: the analysis of the positive and negative aspects of the transference through interpretation. He had simply added data drawn from behaviour and from the counter-transference to those drawn from free association.

We have seen that Bion based a large number of the interpretations given in group therapy on the analyst's emotional responses. Similarly, he affirmed that an analyst faced with psychosis will often be able to interpret only from the basis of his emotional response to the patient. Klein carefully avoided the notion of countertransference, and Bion was emphatic in his statements that he was not in favour of such a notion. He thought of it more as an expedient concept necessitated by the limitations of the contemporary state of knowledge. The objection that the analyst simply misrecognizes the projection of his own conflicts and fantasies could not be easily overruled. Bion replied that there was a safeguard in the psychotic's tendency to indicate promptly to the analyst that he was the victim of the latter's projections. Finally, Bion, ever pragmatic, observed that 'the process works'.

Unlike Klein's other students, Bion broached the analysis of psychotics with an original intellectual endowment, forged through years of experience with therapeutic groups. When the concept of countertransference began to appear in the psychoanalytic literature of the 1950s, Bion had encountered the phenomenon a good ten years earlier. His writings on psychosis, in their originality and their density, are immediately distinctive. If the experiences of groups extended beyond the sphere of psychoanalysis, they had nevertheless given him a system of intuition, a form of thinking, and style of writing.

11 THE PSYCHOANALYST'S DEBUT

At the end of 1950, after five years of psychoanalysis with Klein, Bion read his membership paper to the British Psycho-Analytical Society. This paper, 'The imaginary twin', did not evoke much discussion. Bion did not publish it until 1967, in the anthology *Second Thoughts*. However, it offers us insight into the analyst's thought processes.

Bion chose to present the treatment of a difficult case. The symptoms were essentially severely obsessional, and of such gravity that a leucotomy had even been suggested by a previous psychotherapist. The patient made particularly ambiguous statements in an intonation drained of emotion, which made the analyst unable to judge the validity of his interpretations. There were numerous occasions to interpret oedipal material, which he 'duly' did, but elicited only 'perfunctory' responses, or none at all.

The analyst then became aware, over three months, of a change in the analysis. He felt like a parent addressing ineffectual exhortations to a refractory child. As this was communicated to the patient, a gradual change occurred. Even if the associations were still dreary and monotonous, something in their rhythm changed: 'It was as if two quite separate co-existent scansions of his material were possible. One imparted an overpowering sense of boredom and depression, the other, dependent on the fact that he introduced regularly spaced pauses in the stream of his associations, an almost jocular effect, as if he were saying "go on; it's your turn"' (Bion, 1967a, p. 5). A further examination brought him to the realization that the associations were stale, and invited well-worn interpretations. If the analyst broke the rhythm, the patient showed signs of anxiety or irritation, but if he continued to offer the same old interpretations – which the patient invited, and seemed to desire – the process seemed to reach a dead end.

The patient felt that the treatment was not going anywhere, and was doing no good. He asked his analyst if he felt it was worth continuing. If by treatment he meant psychoanalysis as such, then Bion agreed that some other method of approach to his problems might well be better. If it was psychoanalysis as practised by himself, then the solution might be to change analysts rather than methods. Bion had to call upon a range of subtle responses in order to find the meaning of his patient's ambiguous paradoxes.

Sometimes symptoms may be alleviated by factors which are inseparable from analysis itself, such as the sense of security derived from the fact that somebody is there to go to. Maybe the patient was referring to some factor of this kind. In reporting the case, Bion employed a perspectival shift and gave these associative links a central rather than peripheral role. Before presenting them to the reader, Bion first gives more relevant information. The patient often made statements such as 'I was thinking of speaking to Mr X'. Some of these statements referred to completely imaginary conversations – but not all of them. It was as if the patient could not differentiate the real from the imaginary. Discovering this, Bion reconsidered everything he knew about the various people his patient had spoken of. It is notable that they were all male, as was his analyst. Bion stressed his patient's extraordinary 'ability to convey a lot of information, too much information, in a concise way', although he does not seem to have noticed that this was also a striking characteristic of his own style of writing.

Bion returns to his patient's silence following the various interpretations made by his analyst on the eventual termination of treatment. He asked him what he was thinking about. The patient replied that he was thinking about a woman who suffered from rheumatic pain: '"She's always complaining about something or other and I thought that she's very neurotic. I advised her to buy some amytal and packed her off"' (Bion, 1967a, p. 7). Bion replied that he was probably offering him a compact description of the treatment he was having from his analyst, about which he had doubts. The patient felt interpretations as vague complaints to which he paid little attention. His associations were very stale, and were used more for their soporific effect – as a barbiturate – than as ways of conveying information. They kept the analyst employed without bothering the patient.

Bion therefore decided to make an interpretation on the particular rhythm of the 'association–interpretation–association' sequence, which indicated that the analyst was the twin of the patient, supporting him in jocular evasion of the 'complaints' of interpretations and softening his resentment. The patient could identify with any one of these roles. The analyst was impressed by the patient's response. He confided, in a depressed tone, that he felt dirty and tired. It was as if, in a moment, he had before him the patient as he had seen him at the very first interview. It was as if – and the *as if's* abound in this paper – he had swallowed the twin and the complaining parent. The session drew to a close. Bion then remembered that the patient often gave the impression that he had a poisonous family inside him, but that this was the first time he had seen such a dramatic example of introjection.

Why was the imaginary twin so significant for this patient? Because this psychic creation went back to the earliest object relation, and to his inability to tolerate the fact that an object might not be under his complete control: 'The function of the imaginary twin is to deny a reality different from himself' (Bion, 1967a, p. 19). The denial of external reality was a correlate of the inability to tolerate internal psychic reality. To the extent that the analyst managed to allay this fear of his psychic mechanisms, the patient could allow them to take a more central place in his stream of associations: 'Only when I had been able to demonstrate how bad I was on all levels of his mind did it become possible for him first to recognize his mechanisms of splitting and personification and then to employ them, as it were, in reverse, to establish the contact they had originally been used to break' (ibid., p. 20). In this sentence we find that since 1950, Bion had almost formulated a personal definition of psychosis. The verb *demonstrate* emphasizes the the intellectual connotation that Bion had continued to give interpretation since the group period. He located the origin of pathology in an excess of aggression, resulting in the introjection of bad objects.

Less interested than Klein was in the moral and emotional consequences of hatred, Bion conceived of the problem in a more intellectual way. This aggression is a problem because it prevents reality-testing. The defence mechanisms are used to sever contact with reality, whereas they should be used to establish such contact. Bion substitutes the notion of reversibility for that of reparation. The analyst gives the patient new ways of exploring his inner world. This new power serves to resolve a problem that already exists, but it also reveals other problems which require other solutions, notably the Oedipus complex.

This patient seemed preoccupied with the problems incurred by the presence of a damaged internal object. However, his newly acquired analytic capacities led him immediately to the relationship between a father and a daughter (one of his pupils).

In this paper Bion aims to show that he has correctly learned his trade as an analyst. How could it be otherwise in a paper which is first and foremost a membership paper, aimed at gaining membership of the British Psycho-Analytical Society? The demonstration of the imaginary twin proved a real turning point, allowing the analyst to exist as a real person rather than being an object created by the patient. It was followed by a period in which the patient became more integrated. He was less afraid when his attention was drawn to what was happening inside his psyche. He developed the ability to personify the split-off parts of his personality.

It would be a mistake to reduce this paper to a reworking of the theme that was so popular in the nineteenth century – the theme of the split personality. Taking Klein's concepts of splitting and personification, Bion transformed the hysteric's doubling into the schizoid dissociation. He was also able to renew the genre by his own inimitable narrative style, which literally re-creates the twinning interactions between analyst and patient for the reader. Bion could have followed Klein more closely and discussed the origins of splitting at the breast. He might have considered the more nurturing rhythm of 'interpretation–association–interpretation', for example, rather than the more intellectual scansion of 'association–interpretation–association'. But from this paper onwards, Bion decided to follow his own path. Being returned to contact with external reality made him confront an oedipal situation directly. Far from presenting himself simply as a good student, Bion established the first outline of his future theory of psychosis.

Bion followed his analysis on the imaginary twin with a discussion of the role of vision in psychic development. He combined the material on the imaginary twin with brief extracts from cases of two other patients who had great difficulties in making contact with reality. In order to grow, the patient had to gain mastery over his visual function as it became more powerful, along with a more powerful intellectual capacity. Similarly, the growth of the psychic apparatus implies the growth of the oedipal predicament. The problems that emerge in the course of development because of the oedipal predicament might be linked to the development of control over the visual faculty, just as oral aggression is linked to the development of teeth. These conclusions give a biological basis to the concept of the early Oedipus complex described by Klein.

The paper on the imaginary twin is not generally cited in Kleinian texts, as if it were an 'early' work. However, one of the only references that Klein made to Bion's work was to this paper. Reflecting on the feeling of solitude, she wrote:

> The longing to understand oneself is also bound up with the need to be understood by the internalized good object. One expression of this longing is the universal phantasy of having a twin – a phantasy to which Bion drew attention in an unpublished paper. This twin figure, as he suggested, represents those un-understood and split-off parts which the individual is longing to regain, in the hope of achieving wholeness and complete understanding; they are sometimes felt to be the ideal parts. At other times the twin also represents an entirely reliable, in fact idealized internal object. (Klein, 1963, p. 302)

12 THE FIRST THEORETICAL REFERENCE POINTS

Almost all Bion's reference points were taken from Melanie Klein or Sigmund Freud. But whereas he refers to the Kleinian *oeuvre* in its entirety, he refers only to certain, carefully selected passages from Freud. Meanwhile, his originality is evident from his theoretical references. Rosenfeld and Segal conceived a psycho-analysis of the psychoses through a fundamental adherence to the work of Klein and her reworking of Freud's theories. Bion, on the other hand, turned to Freud's works directly, and made use of some of his fundamental concepts. Once these concepts had been selected, Bion used them throughout the psychotic period and the epistemological period.

Like all Klein's students Bion used the concept of infantile psychosis, although he had to integrate the fragments of the theory, as Klein herself had not presented her thoughts in a systematic manner. Bion used three fundamental Kleinian concepts:

- *The early Oedipus complex.* The mother's body is conceived as the context for all the sexual phantasies. The infant imagines that it contains the father's penis, faeces and babies. Anxiety and more violent attacks are directed against the imago of the combined parents. We have seen that Bion had already made use of this concept in his theory of group dynamics.
- *Instinctual conflict.* According to Klein, defences are first employed in relation to the destructive instincts in the course of the early oedipal conflict. Bion thought it was impossible to understand schizophrenia without taking into account the conflict between the life and death instincts.

- *The close connection between epistemophilia (the drive to knowledge) and sadism.* Epistemophilia is stimulated by the onset of the oedipal drives and the sexual curiosity that accompanies them. The infant conceives of its first questions before the development of language. Its limited intellectual faculty cannot assimilate all the problems confronting it.

Bion was completely convinced of the 'importance of symbol formation in the development of the ego'. Anxiety leads the child to direct its aggression outside itself, and to endow it with symbolic meaning. In significant quantities anxiety leads to the formation of extensive fantasies and symbols. Inversely, when the ego sets up a premature and excessive defence against sadism, the relation to reality cannot be established and the development of fantasy life is stifled. Bion also adapted Klein's account of intellectual inhibition, developed in the 1930s. At that time Klein accorded as much importance to paranoia as to schizophrenia. She had formulated an original concept of obsessional neurosis. Her almost exclusive preoccupation with obsessional neurosis was echoed in the essentially obsessional symptoms of the patient with the imaginary twin. Klein had demonstrated that some structures of intellectual inhibition are identical to those of obsessional neurosis. Starting from this point, Bion suggested that in adult psychosis there is an oscillation between neurosis and psychosis, analogous to the equilibrium of infantile neurosis.

Bion's first works are contemporaneous with the introduction of the paranoid-schizoid position, and he was almost exclusively concerned with this, giving the impression that he accorded it a central role in psychic development. In his view, the outcome of the depressive position depends mostly on the way in which its elements are broached in the earlier position.

In effect, Bion makes no explicit reference to the developments of Kleinian theory between 1932 and 1945, which are largely given over to developments of the notion of the depressive position. He therefore did not employ the concept of reparation (he uses the verb *to repair* on only one occasion, and in relation to the ego rather than a damaged object). For this reason Bion accords fundamental significance to the concept of *projective identification.* Initially he held the Kleinian view that paranoid-schizoid pathology derives from excessive projective identification, but he soon recognized that this mechanism can be pathogenic, in quality as well as quantity. As a corollary to this, he seems to have supposed the infant to be schizophrenic at the outset, whereas Klein repeatedly maintained that most babies are not psychotic even if they all experience insanely anxiogenic situations. One passage from a letter written by Bion during this period is unambiguous on the subject: 'How people can think of childhood as "happy" I do not know. A horrible, bogey-ridden demon-haunted time it was to me, and then one has not the fortitude, or callosities perhaps, to deal with it' (Bion, 1985, p. 76). He maintained that psychotics have never managed adequately to come to terms with the reality principle. Here he was referring to Freud's paper 'Neurosis and psychosis' (1924), in which he differentiates between neurosis and psychosis in relation to the second topography. Stressing the psychotic's hatred of reality, and the conflict that results from this, Freud enabled a fundamental aspect of intrapsychic conflict to be understood. We have noted that Bion had already been interested in the reality principle when he formulated a psychoanalytic approach to group dynamics. He had always used Freud's text 'Formulations on the two principles of mental functioning' (1911) as a founding theory of his explanations. According to Freud, in order to come to terms with the reality principle the ego must develop functions of consciousness (attention, judgement, memory), to replace motor discharge of the drives and inaugurate the faculty of thought. According to Bion, verbal thought represents the essential element of the functions developed by the ego in order to enter into contact with reality. For the psychotic, an attack on the rudiments of verbal thought is equivalent to an attack on all the other ego functions.

Bion formulated a theory of schizophrenia starting from the language use characteristic of schizophrenic patients.[18] He was aware that language was becoming a major theme in Anglo-Saxon philosophy. The philosophy of language was emerging at the same time as linguistics was also coming into its own. The 1953 article which proposed a theory of schizophrenia gave rise to another article in 1955, a chapter in the anthology *New Directions in Psycho-Analysis*. Bion had altered parts of it and retitled it 'Language and the schizophrenic'. He refers to Wittgenstein's *Philosophical Investigations*, which had been published in 1953. Instead of working on scientific language, as Wittgenstein had done in the *Tractatus Logico-Philosophicus*, he discussed the use of ordinary speech. Bion admired this philosopher who, rather than aiming to formulate theses, had aimed to clarify thinking in relation to the traps of language. Wittgenstein was also a linchpin for the theories of Freud, Klein and Bion. The *Tractatus* had contributed to the Neo-Positivist theories of Moritz Schlick and the Viennese circle.[19] In Britain Roger Money-Kyrle was one of the few analysts to apply Melanie Klein's ideas to philosophy.

Bion maintained close connections with Klein's work while returning directly to Freud. He constructed a new theory of psychosis by connecting the intellectual elements of one with the other, respecting the difference between the strengths of each. Moreover, the construction of Bion's 'theory of thinking' could be seen as the creation stemming from their union.

13 Psychotic Thinking and Psychotic Personality

Bion maintained that the schizophrenic cannot find a way of resolving his psychological difficulties, as he has compromised his mental development through the severe inhibition of his fantasies and dreams. His difficulty in thinking and communicating stems from massive use of the defence of splitting, which prevents him from either creating or using symbols, or using words themselves. It is the analyst's task to show him these difficulties as and when they emerge. Since verbal thinking is based on the capacity for integration, the appearance of speech is closely linked to the depressive position, which facilitates integration and synthesis. Verbal thought stimulates awareness of psychic reality and, consequently, awareness of depressive experience associated with the destruction and loss of the good object. At the same time this consciousness leads to a greater understanding of the internal persecutors. Thus the patient feels the relationship between verbal thought and the depressive position as one of cause and effect. This amplifies the hatred he has of analysis because it is, after all, 'a treatment which employs verbal thought in order to resolve psychic problems'.

At this stage of analysis the patient becomes very anxious, as he cannot do anything with this embryonic capacity to think with words. He prefers to leave this to the analyst, who seems to him to offer protection from catastrophe. Bion envisaged the possible outcome of the schizophrenic who would be capable of uniting split objects and ego, leaving his original state of mind and entering the depressive position. In such cases the development of verbal thought is an immensely important turning point in the analysis.

However, treatment does not progress in straight lines. As he gains awareness of psychic reality, the patient begins to realize that he has hallucinations and is delirious, begins to realize that he is or has been insane; and may not feel able to feed himself or to sleep. His violent hatred will be directed against the analyst. He will affirm with conviction that he has been insane, and with intense conviction that it is the analyst's fault. The analyst should expect that the patient's family will become concerned and try to intervene. He should be prepared to explain the situation to them. The patient has spent his entire life trying to avoid any emotional realization of certain facts. The analyst will try to maintain the patient's consciousness of his insanity, and his hatred of the analyst who brought him to such a realization.

Before describing the mechanisms of psychosis, Bion took care to outline their 'preconditions'. Following Melanie Klein, he considered schizophrenia to be the result of the interaction between an environment and a personality. In the beginning he located the the main cause of the illness in an innate characteristic of the child. There are four essential preconditions for a person to be prone to psychosis:

- strong predominance of destructive drives, to the extent that they suffuse the impulse to love and transform it into sadism;
- a hatred of internal and external realities, extended to all that makes for awareness of them;
- a dread of imminent annihilation;
- premature and precipitate formation of object relations. These reflect the endlessly unstable conflict between the life and death drives.

The schizophrenic forms a transference which is thin but extremely tenacious, revealing his profound dependence. Throughout the analysis the transference relationship moves between restriction and expansion. When the patient, under pressure from the drives, expands the relationship, two types of phenomena emerge simultaneously. First, projective identification on to the analyst is dramatically intensified, resulting in painful confusional states, as Rosenfeld has described in his 'Notes on the psychopathology of confusional states in chronic schizophrenia' (1950).[20] Secondly, whatever action the dominant drive takes to express itself – be it the life or death drive – is immediately mutilated by the drive that has been temporarily subordinated. Driven to avoid confusional states and tormented by mutilations, the patient seeks to return to a restricted relationship. This oscillation between restriction and expansion thus characterizes the entire analysis.

Bion was led to speak of 'psychotic personality' rather than a schizophrenic character. To his mind, the adjective 'psychotic' seemed to have been more or less synonymous with 'schizophrenic'. Contemporary British psychiatry saw an enlargement of the definition of schizophrenia, and was perhaps open to such conceptualization. However, it derived, above all, from the Kleinian view that most of the phenomena observed during the paranoid-schizoid position can be found later in schizophrenia. Bion deduced that a schizophrenic's progression through the positions must be radically different from that of the neurotic or the manic-depressive. The main difference is that the schizophrenic makes massive use of projective identification. This is where Bion made an original contribution: he saw that this excessive use of projective identification is not only in relation to the object but also defends the psychic apparatus overwhelmed by the demands of the reality principle.

Bion evolved a theory to explain how the psychic apparatus becomes schizophrenic.[21] His starting point was the content of the framework of Klein's paranoid-schizoid position. He starts with the sadistic phantasies that the infant directs against the breast, deducing that the infant who becomes schizophrenic makes similar attacks on its perceptual apparatus. The future psychotic thus manages to remove one part of his personality, to split it into small pieces and to expel these fragments outside himself. By getting rid of the apparatus which facilitates the awareness of internal and external realities, 'the patient reaches a state which is felt to be neither life nor death'. Bion considered that the apparatus which facilitates awareness of reality was closely connected to verbal thought. Thus he could differentiate between the 'psychotic personality' and the 'non-psychotic personality': the former uses projective identification excessively as a defence against consciousness of reality, and against the rudiments of verbal thought. This process is active from the outset of life. It explains why the gap between the psychotic and non-psychotic parts of the personality grows wider, and eventually becomes unbridgeable.

The schizophrenic feels that he is a prisoner of his state of mind.

He feels unable to escape from it, as he lacks the apparatus for acknowledging reality. This apparatus represents the key to escape and the freedom sought through escape. The feeling of being imprisoned is reinforced by the threatening presence of the expelled fragments of the ego. The patient imagines that these expelled parts of himself have a completely autonomous existence outside himself. He feels as if the process has simply increased the number of split-off parts of the self, and provoked their hostility towards the psyche which expelled them.

The patient then feels that he is surrounded by 'bizarre objects'. For him, each object consists of a fragment of external reality 'encapsulated' by the part of the personality which has engulfed it. The character of this complex particle depends as much on the nature of the real object as on the nature of the part of the personality which has engulfed it. In the patient's animistic world the object is angry at being engulfed; it reacts by swelling, suffusing and controlling the part of the personality that engulfed it. In this way the patient feels that the particle of personality has become a thing. From the moment when he uses these particles as prototypes of ideas (from which, later, words will spring), this suffusion of part of the personality by the contained but controlling object means that, for the patient, words become the actual things they name. Bion employs the distinction, which had just been proposed by Segal, between symbol and symbolic equation, but he had located the genesis of this type of intellectual deficiency in a much earlier stage.[22] 'The patient now moves not in a world of dreams but in a world of objects which are ordinarily the furniture of dreams' (Bion, 1967a, p. 51). Although these objects are primitive, they are not less complex than others. A non-psychotic person, such as the analyst, would attribute to them characteristics proper to the psyche as well as to matter. When the patient confuses objects from the outside world with primitive ideas, he is confused to find that they obey the laws of natural science rather than the laws of mental functioning. But unfortunately, this is not all. If he feels that one of these objects is penetrating him, the patient feels attacked, and that makes him believe that the object is seeking revenge, according to talion law, for having been violently penetrated itself.

Furthermore, whenever the patient wishes to internalize an interpretation or to bring back a bizarre object in an attempt at restitution of the ego, he has to bring it back by the route by which it was expelled – 'projective identification in reverse'. Bion illustrates this proposition using the material of one of his patients, who explained that he used his intestines as brains. If the analyst told him he had swallowed something, the patient replied: 'The intestine doesn't swallow'. This projection of rudimentary thought on to the digestive apparatus provided the framework of what eventually became Bion's theory of thinking.

In reaching this new milestone Bion was, in a way, returning to the Freudian problem of the unconscious. Why does the schizophrenic treat word representations as if they were thing representations? Bion replied that the psychotic personality employs splitting and projective identification where the non-psychotic personality would use repression. Having expelled the mechanism by which the psyche represses, the schizophrenic replaces what should have been his unconscious by 'the world of dream furniture'. This description remains a poetic metaphor until the point in the epistemological period when Bion proposes the concepts of alpha (α) function and beta (β) elements to describe these forms of thought.

14 THE PSYCHOTIC AND NON-PSYCHOTIC PARTS OF THE PERSONALITY

Bion had initiated a break from the theoretical orientation of his predecessors. The concept of bizarre objects could have no place in the paranoid-schizoid position if this was considered to be a normal stage of psychic development. Klein considered only excessive projective identification to be pathological. Bion demonstrated that this defence mechanism can be pathological in its very structure. He was also to discover the correlative to this: that projective identification also constitutes a primitive method of communication.

Bion always employed a Freudian concept of the mental apparatus as called into activity by the demands of the reality principle, and in particular that part of it which is concerned with the consciousness attached to the sense organs. However, he modified this in two ways in order to make it appropriate to discoveries encountered in analysing schizophrenics. First, the ego never completely withdraws from reality, at least not in those patients who come for psychoanalysis. The patient's contact with reality is overridden by the predominance, in thought and behaviour, of an omnipotent phantasy which 'aims to bring about a state which is neither life nor death'. Since contact with reality is never completely lost, the so-called neurotic phenomena are never completely absent; they can be found within psychotic material when the patient has made some progress. The fact that the ego always maintains some contact with reality implies the corollary, the existence of a non-psychotic part of the personality in schizophrenics.

Bion's second modification was that the withdrawal from reality is an illusion, not a fact – but, appreciating the almost paradoxical nature of this structure, he added: 'The predominance of this phantasy is such that, to all intents, it does not seem to the patient to be a phantasy but a fact; the latter acts as if his consciousness could be split into little pieces and projected into objects' (Bion, 1957a, p. 46).

To understand how a phantasy can destroy awareness of reality, we start with the work of Melanie Klein. In her view, what might be described by an observer as a defence mechanism is experienced, by the person concerned, as a particular phantasy. She discovered that the ego cannot split the object without a corresponding splitting taking place within the ego. In phantasy the baby splits its objects and splits itself: 'But the effect of this phantasy is a very real one, as it leads to feelings and relations (and later on thought processes) being in fact cut off from one another' (Klein, 1946, p. 101). Bion extended the effect of the illusion to the phantasy underlying the projective identification. Clinical practice had shown that this mechanism was not limited to psychic reality. The schizophrenic exerts pressure within an interpersonal relationship in order that his analyst will experience emotions related to this projective identification. This is why Bion made intensive use of the analysis of his countertransference. Projective identification has an effect on analyst and patient. These modifications of classic Freudianism were necessitated by the discovery that a part of the personality maintains contact with external reality, even in those patients certified as psychotic.

Bion started by stressing the significance of verbal thought for awareness of psychic reality within the depressive position. Although chaotic thought is more apparent in the depressive position, it does, in fact, originate in the paranoid-schizoid position. The foundations of primitive thought should be laid down at this time, but this will not take place where there is intense splitting and massive projective identification.

Analysing schizophrenics led Bion to hypothesize the existence of rudimentary forms of thought in the paranoid-schizoid position. He considered that this primitive thought was closer to 'ideographs and sight rather than words and hearing'. Primitive thought rests on the capacity for establishing an equilibrium between the introjection and projection of objects and, above all, in awareness of them. Introjection leads to the formation of unconscious thought 'turned towards the relations between object-impressions', in Freud's terms. Bion considered that this unconscious thought was linked to the 'consciousness attached to' sense impressions. This primitive mode of thought is a precursor of verbal thought, which is bound up with awareness of psychic reality. So Bion expected the deployment of projective identification to be particularly severe against whatever kind of thought was turned towards the relations between object impressions. If this link could be severed – or, better still, if it could have been prevented from becoming established in the first place – then consciousness of reality could be destroyed, even if reality itself could not.

Psychotic attacks destroy not only the links between consciousness and the sensory impressions of reality, but also the links within the thought processes themselves. The primitive matrix of ideographs from which thought springs contains within itself links between one ideograph and another. All these are now attacked, until finally two objects cannot be brought together in a way which leaves each object with its intrinsic qualities intact, yet able, by their conjunction, to produce a new mental object. Symbol formation becomes difficult, because it depends on the capacity to unite two objects by perceiving resemblance while preserving their difference. At a later stage the result of these attacks can be seen in the denial of articulation as the principle of combining words.

Bion concluded that the psychotic part of the personality is distinguished from the non-psychotic part essentially by its tendency to fragment the ego and its expulsion into and around its objects. This process is active from the earliest days of life. The objects projectively invaded by sensory functions react when the patient aims to use them in his ideographic thinking. This can lead to a confusion of real objects with primitive thoughts.

In analysis a patient is obliged to try to reintegrate his ego by bringing back one or other of these objects. But he must bring them back in the same way as they were originally expelled – by inverting the projective identification. Every attempted reintegration can become dangerous, owing to the extreme splitting of the ego and of its objects. The schizophrenic can fuse, but cannot articulate; he can compress, but cannot unite. His capacity for synthesis remains faulty, because he has unburdened himself of 'that which links'. Bion thus announced the thesis of his final work: psychosis is the result of attacks on linking.

To conclude, Bion emphasized the increasing divergence
between the development of psychotic and non-psychotic personalities. He located the essential difference in the substitution of
projective identification for repression. He was not altogether clear
as to whether the psychotic part exists only in people with serious
mental illness, or if it is to be found in us all. The enumeration of
factors that are preconditions for schizophrenic illness seems to
indicate the former, but Bion also maintained that the psychotic
part of the personality which is concealed within neurosis should
be revealed and treated.

15   HALLUCINATIONS AND DREAMS

Expulsion makes internal objects malevolent. When they return, they make the subject feel as if he is being tortured and attacked. Perceptual elements comprise some of the ego parts that are expelled; consequently, they return painfully compressed, causing agonizing hallucinations. Bion decided to concentrate on the hallucinations induced by the attempt to think, which is inherent in all analyses. When a psychotic patient reaches this stage the analyst can make him aware that he moves easily between 'depression' and 'schizophrenia' and vice versa. (Bion later gives diagrammatic representation of this oscillation with the formula PS↔D.) Far from belonging to the past, the dreaded depression emerges repeatedly. To escape it, the schizophrenic flees into the paranoid-schizoid position by attacking his verbal thought – but then he is often prone to hallucinations. The schizophrenic feels that he can use his sense organs for ejecting as well as receiving.

With such a view of psychosis, Bion managed to change traditional attitudes towards schizophrenia. He maintained that at times the schizophrenic can use mental processes in a creative way rather than binding them completely to destructive wishes: 'Splitting, evacuatory use of the senses, and hallucinations were all being employed in the service of an ambition to be cured, and may therefore be supposed to be creative activities' (Bion, 1967a, p. 68).

During this period the patient complains that he cannot tell the difference between real and unreal, and cannot tell whether he is hallucinating or not. That goes without saying, since schizophrenia is, basically, excessive projective identification directed against the self, and especially against those parts of the personality that are called into being by the dominance of the reality principle. The capacity for judgement is one such part of the personality. The patient can no longer differentiate between the real and the unreal because he has expelled his capacity for judgement from his psyche by the mechanism of projective identification. Following his theory, Bion then supposed that among the bizarre objects it should be possible to trace something analogous to the capacity for judgement. His experience had led him to believe that these particular bizarre objects, with traces of the capacity for judgement, are to be found in what are usually described as the patient's 'delusions'.

The theory of hallucination rests on the distinction between two types of hallucinatory activity: one psychotic, one hysterical. It differentiates between

- psychotic personality – splitting – paranoid-schizoid position;
- non-psychotic personality – dissociation – depressive position.

At first, splitting is something like what Klein described as a separation between good and bad, between love and hate. When he tries prematurely to bring together his objects, the psychotic makes the union with such violence that it results in a fusion of nuclear intensity. After many years of analysis the same patient may create a split with such a degree of gentleness, such a regard for psychic structure and function, that the term 'splitting' could be questioned and the process described as a creative one.

Bion suggested that the term 'splitting' should be reserved for phenomena first observed in severely disturbed patients. These violent processes aim to produce minute fragmentation, and to effect 'separations which run directly counter to any natural lines of demarcation between one part of the psyche and another' (Bion, 1967a, p. 69). Dissociation, on the other hand, appears to be gentler and to have respect for natural lines of demarcation between whole objects, which it uses to effect separation. It appears to depend on the pre-existence of elementary verbal thought and the capacity for depression. The psychotic personality splits; the non-psychotic personality dissociates.

The psychotic patient may use two types of hallucination. Psychotic hallucinations comprise elements analogous to part-objects, and are found in the early stages of the analysis of a schizophrenic. Hysterical hallucinations, in contrast, are directly connected to the onset of the depressive position, and comprise whole objects.[23] Bion does not refer to Karl Abraham's 1908 paper on 'The psycho-sexual differences between hysteria and dementia praecox'. With fifty years' hindsight, however, his work on psychosis can seem to offer a reply to the questions raised at the outset of psychoanalysis. Freud had used this paper in his analysis of paranoia in the Schreber case, from which he evolved his hypotheses on schizophrenia. Similarly, it was with reference to this paper that Klein reinterpreted Freud's Schreber case. Stipulating the existence of a paranoid-schizoid position, she adhered to the specific emphasis with which Fairbairn had 'demonstrated the intrinsic relation between hysteria and schizophrenia'. Bion was as concerned as Freud not to separate theory from clinical practice – he had accepted the challenge of schizophrenia cases. But whereas Freud had founded psychoanalysis on the theory of hysteria, Bion had extended the field of psychoanalysis by developing a theory of schizophrenia.

The appearance of whole objects in dreams is a sign of progress and a forerunner of depression, which may become dangerous if its origin is not elucidated. The 'peculiarity' of the dream, for the psychotic, is not its irrationality or incoherence or fragmentation, but its revelation of whole objects, which are connected with the powerful feelings of guilt and depression to be found at the start of the depressive position as described by Klein. Their presence in dreams is felt to be evidence that the real, valued objects have been destroyed. The immediate oscillation to fragmentation simply replaces the feared depression with an unbearable persecutory anxiety. The schizophrenic's dream life oscillates between this Scylla and Charybdis.

This kind of situation can be very dangerous. If the psychotic patient assembles fragments in order to create an object, and then finds that he cannot bear the new cohesion, the whole object may be followed by an explosion and further fragmentation. Bion thought that the descriptive aspect of his theory of schizophrenia was very similar to one stage of analysis also characterized by an oscillation between two states, which is no less dangerous even if it is less explosive. The return to the paranoid-schizoid position adds a secondary fragmentation which is imposed on the already

severe primary fragmentation which is characteristic of this
position: 'It seems as if the patient, regressing from the depressive
position, turns with increased hatred and anxiety against the
fragments that have shown their power to coalesce and splits them
with great thoroughness; as a result we have a danger of
fragmentation so minute that reparation of the ego becomes
impossible and the prospects of the patient correspondingly
hopeless' (Bion, 1967a, p. 81).

The analyst has to counteract the patient's need to avoid the
emotional recognition of what he has been trying to evade all his
life, but this involves taking risks, notably the risk of the patient's
suicide. If the analyst allows himself to become shaken by the risk
of suicide, he may misrecognize the relapse into the paranoid-
schizoid position. This can definitively compromise the chances of
recovery, as extreme fragmentation produces definitive deterioration, blocking the restoration of the ego. Here we find an
explanation *a posteriori* for the old name for schizophrenia:
'dementia praecox'.

Bion upheld his concept of the pre-eminence of vision in the
development of psychosis from the earliest to the last articles on
the subject of psychosis. He began by suggesting that the
development of visual capacity implies the appearance of the
oedipal situation, and confirmed that verbal thought, indissolubly
linked to the appearance of psychic reality, brings us to a
perception of the links between the parents in external reality. Bion
provided further elucidations on hallucinatory phenomena and
psychotic dreams when, later, he was able to formulate his theory
of 'attacks on linking'. The psychotic does not appear to dream, or
at least does not bring accounts of dreams to analysis until a
relatively advanced stage. Bion maintained that 'this apparently
dreamless period is a phenomenon analogous to the invisible–
visual hallucination' (Bion, 1958a, p. 98). This means that the
dreams consist of material so minutely fragmented that they are
devoid of any visual component.

The patient may bring a dream when it contains visual objects.
He then seems to attribute the same relationship between the
dream objects and the objects of his invisible–visual hallucinations
as that between faeces and urine. The patient feels that the objects
found in dreams are solid. He opposes these to the content of
psychotic dreams formed by a continuum of fragments rendered

invisible through diminution. This model of the psychotic dream and the invisible–visual hallucination becomes the basis of Bion's conceptualization of the psychoanalytic 'intuition' as a non-sensuous phenomenon, of the 'invisible–visual' nature of intuition, in the next period of his psychoanalytic work.

16 The Intellectual Oedipus

At first Kleinian theory comprised a systematic way of linking defence mechanisms and instinctual drives to an early Oedipus complex, a much elaborated and extended version of the Freudian concept. Bion had largely employed this genetic theory of psychosexuality, in so far as he had applied the Kleinian theory of infantile psychosis to schizophrenia in adults. But the Kleinian theory rather condensed the evolutionary schema. Not only was the phallic phase included in the pregenital organization, but the development of genitality itself was thought to emerge at a stage when oral drives predominate. Klein agreed with Bion, and one of her two references to his work includes the following note: 'I have reason to believe that this premature genitalization is often a feature in strong schizophrenic traits or in full-blown schizophrenia.' She explains that excessive envy interferes with adequate oral gratification, and so acts as a stimulus towards the intensification of early genital desires and trends. She adds that the premature onset of genitality may be bound up with the early occurrence of guilt (Klein, 1957, pp. 195-6).

In 1957 Klein put forward the concept of envy. Kleinian intuition seems to have revealed something potentially, but ubiquitously, present in Bion's mental universe. The concept enabled him to make its presence explicit. He agreed that envy might be a manifestation of the death instinct in terms of oral and anal stages, and that it was operative from the earliest days of life in the conflict between love and hate, giving projective identification a destructive aspect. He could even be considered to have thought of schizophrenia as a cancerous culture of envy. But Bion's perspective was so individual that he could not adopt the concept of envy as it stood. He subjected it to several alterations.

In the same way as he had substituted the reconstitution of the ego for reparation of an object, Bion found the antithesis of envy in *creativity* rather than gratitude. Klein, it is true, had described how the good feeding breast is experienced as the first manifestation of creativity. It is this that most fundamentally triggers envy. More than wealth, prestige or power, the envious individual is preoccupied with the capacity to give and maintain life. Klein accorded envy a fundamental role in disturbances of artistic creativity. Attacking the primordial source of goodness transforms the good object into an object that is hostile, critical and ultimately envious. Envy is projected into a super-ego figure which impedes the process of thinking, all productive activities and, ultimately, creativity. However, Klein continued to think of the depressive position as central to psychic development. Consequently, the central problem was that a very intense envy might prevent the object from being fully enjoyed, and thus prevent the subject from experiencing gratitude for what the object brings. Like a schizophrenic, Bion remained within a narcissistic perspective. Rather than aiming at the experience of recognition of a helpful object, he sought to redeploy the mental mechanisms that had been made destructive through envy back towards creativity. Envy impedes all positive resolution of problems by destroying the capacity for thought. In so far as thinking depends on the capacity to make links between two objects, Bion turned his interest to the envious attacks which are unleashed against the parental, procreative and sexual couple. He was finally induced to rewrite the oedipal myth, relocating the sexual crime as peripheral and identifying the central crime as the arrogance with which Oedipus seeks to lay bare the truth at any cost. In the new version, the central features of the myth are identified as the following: the Sphinx, who asks a riddle and destroys herself when it is answered; Tiresias, the blind man who possesses knowledge and deplores the king's resolve to search for it; the oracle that provokes the search; and, finally, the king whose search concludes in blindness and exile. The analyst's business is to be able to discern the scattered references to the elements of this intellectual Oedipus complex amid the ruins of the schizoid psyche.

Starting with the concept of envy, Bion, like Klein, was particularly interested in neuroses and in borderline cases of patients with some psychotic mechanisms, who were not overtly schizophrenic. In clinical practice the analysis of such patients seemed to follow patterns usually found in the treatment of neuroses, but improvement in the patient's condition is not commensurate with the analytic work that is done. The analyst comes up against a negative therapeutic reaction, then he comes across scattered references to curiosity, arrogance and stupidity. These should be considered as evidence of a psychological catastrophe with which he will have to deal. The analyst should treat reference to any of these three elements as a significant event demanding investigation.[24]

Unfortunately, the problem is complicated by the fact that curiosity, an integral component of disaster, is also an integral part of the analytic process. As a consequence, the very act of analysing the patient makes the analyst an accessory in precipitating regression and turning the analysis itself into a piece of acting out. From the point of view of successful analysis, this is a development which should be avoided, yet Bion is at a loss to see how. Therefore, regression and acting out should be accepted as inevitable, and detailed interpretation of events that are taking place in the session should be given. During this phase of the analysis the transference, besides manifesting the traits already mentioned, is characterized by its reference to the analyst as analyst. Thus he appears as 'blind, stupid, suicidal, curious and arrogant'. The patient is convinced that the analyst, in response to his curiosity, is attacking his capacity for projective identification, and his creativity. The patient seems to have no problems except that of the analyst's existence. Reworking Freud's famous analogy, Bion compares the analyst to an archaeologist discovering traces – not so much of an ancient civilization as of a primitive catastrophe. The catastrophe which was triggered by attacks on the primitive link connecting mother and infant is transferred on to the analyst. The analyst hopes that the investigations will lead to a reconstitution of the ego, but this aim is obscured by the fact that this analytic procedure is transformed into an acting out of destructive attacks launched against the ego.

Bion wondered what it was that could be so hateful in reality that a patient could be led to destroy the ego which leads him into contact with such a reality. He found his solution in the sexual dimension of the oedipal situation. When reconstitution of the ego has proceeded sufficiently to bring the oedipal situation into sight, it is quite common to find that it precipitates further attacks on the ego. Arrogance also plays a significant part in the unleashing of this aggression. In practice, it is a matter of the assumption, by patient or analyst, of the qualities required to pursue the truth. In analysis, this assumption is particularly concerned with the capacity to tolerate the stresses associated with the introjection of another person's projective identifications. In other words, an analyst who pursues the truth, no matter what the cost, is felt to be synonymous with a capacity for containing the discarded, split-off aspects of other personalities while retaining a balanced outlook.

Following the myth of the intellectual Oedipus, Bion's name becomes the root of a new adjective: the subsequent works are Bionian rather than Kleinian. Bion had decided to narrate the discovery of the imaginary twin starting from his inability to interpret the oedipal situation according to classical technique. He finished by replacing the game of the imaginary twin with the unbearable vision of the parental couple. Bion then maintained that schizophrenia originates with the destruction of that part of the psychic apparatus which creates awareness of external reality. A patient may deny the existence of the intolerable couple as soon as he becomes unable to acknowledge them.

While Klein elaborated the concept of envy, Bion used this notion to account for the premature presence of genital desire in schizophrenics and schizoid mechanisms. Whereas Klein is preoccupied with the relationship to the breast, Bion generalizes oral envy by 'oedipalizing' it. At the same time he transforms the budding Oedipus into someone who is more intellectual than libidinal. Bion's little Oedipus has a very different experience from Freud's. Whereas the latter feels sexual desire towards his mother and death wishes towards his father, the former becomes the intractable enemy of an envied couple and an arrogant investigator. The latter was the royal hero of a family tragedy involving three people; the former is a solitary incarnation of an intellectual odyssey. Arguing that analysis provides an intellectual method of resolving psychological problems, Bion inverts the values of the Oedipus complex: the arrogance of seeking to lay bare the truth at any cost overrides murderous sexuality. The epistemological period was to reveal that psychoanalysis, more than any other discipline, is devoted to the search for truth.

17   The General Theory of Psychosis

In his final conceptualization, Bion reduces the evil genius of psychosis to 'attacks on linking'. In the last analysis he defines the psychotic part of the personality as a tendency to aim at the destruction of all functions of unification, linking or joining of two objects. He located the origin of these attacks against linking in the paranoid-schizoid phase, and conceived their basis as fantasized attacks on the breast. The part-object relationships predominate, and the patient has fragmented relations as much with himself as with others. Since he uses concrete images as units of thought, we may be misled into thinking of the part-object as analogous to an anatomical structure. The part-object relationship is not with anatomical structures but with physiological functions. The infant relates not only to the breast but to feeding, poisoning, loving, hating.

The analyst is well placed to observe the attacks against links between two objects, as he must establish a link between the patient and himself. Their relationship will be creative in so far as it uses verbal communication. The analyst is in a position to see the attacks made on linking through verbal communication. Thanks to Klein, Bion had discovered that the introjection of a good object is a prerequisite of normal development. His personal contribution was the realization that no successful mental development can occur without the existence of 'normal' projective identification (without defining the limits of this normality). Bion had come to this realization in the course of analysing a patient who persistently used projective identification to show that the early use of this communication mechanism had failed him. In his analysis he made full use of a mechanism of which he had been cheated.

Little by little, Bion made a reconstruction of the patient's early childhood. (Uses of reconstruction such as this enable us to refute the criticisms made of Kleinians that they overemphasize the significance of transference at the expense of historical construction.) In his early childhood the patient had a mother who dutifully responded to the infant's emotional displays. This dutiful response had in it something of an element of an impatient 'I don't know what's the matter with the child'. This mother could not understand the infant's cry as anything other than a demand for her presence. From the infant's point of view she should have taken into her, and thus experienced, its fear that it was dying. It was this fear that the infant could not contain. It strove to split it off and unburden itself by projecting it into the mother. An understanding mother is capable of experiencing a feeling of terror, while maintaining her own equilibrium. The patient must have had a mother who was unable to tolerate the experience of such feelings, as she reacted either by denying them ingress or by becoming prey to the anxiety which resulted from the introjection of the infant's feelings. Overall, denial was the predominant feature.[25]

A situation that is yet more complex can be observed. The patient feels that the analyst offers him an opportunity that has always been withheld. This aggravates his resentment of the privation he has suffered. The patient blames the analyst, as he imagines that he is someone who does not understand him and refuses him the use of the sole means of communication he has to make himself understood. But he connects himself to the analyst by projective identification, as the infant does to the mother's breast. He locates the origin of the destructive attacks on linking in an external source.

Bion reaffirms that the main cause of psychosis is to be found in the infant's innate disposition. The death instinct and envy push the infant to attack everything that links it to the mother's breast. If the mother does not receive these projections, the intensity of the attacks increases. If the mother manages to introject the projected feelings, while maintaining her own equilibrium, the intensity of the attacks diminishes. The psychotic infant's predicament remains critical because it is overwhelmed by the hate and envy provoked by this maternal capacity. The same situation reappears in analysis. The patient clamours for the analyst's understanding, but is overcome with hatred when he realizes that the latter can be understanding without breaking down. To him, the analyst's peace of mind seems like hostile indifference. The patient is prepared to use anything to destroy this enviable equilibrium, whether it be acting out, delinquent behaviour or suicide threats.

Bion gives a clue to the significance of the term 'attacks on linking' when he emphasizes that he conceives of it as a description of the patient's relationship to a function rather than to the object fulfilling that function. The interest of the breast and the penis lies in their capacity to make a link between two objects. Bion draws a comparison between the link created by breast or penis, and the linking within verbal thought. Freud, Abraham and Klein had conceived of the concept of the part-object as an unconscious fantasy, of an essentially visual nature. Bion formulated another system of representation of the part-object, characterized by its power to create or destroy links. Meltzer makes much use of Bion's extended system, as well as its repercussions for the Oedipus complex. In the darkness of our first mental life all the links are still indistinct, and the infant's relationship to the breast is equivalent to the relationship between penis and vagina. Since orality is predominant, it pervades the connections between masculine and feminine, and genitality is introduced into the infant's feeding relationship. The infant conceives the relationship between its part-parents in terms of its relationship to the breast.

When functions excite his curiosity, the patient tries to discover their nature through projective identification. Since he is unable to tolerate his own feelings, they are disposed of among the functions. Thanks to analysis, the patient is offered the opportunity to study his experience, despite the limitations of a personality which cannot contain the feelings it experiences. The psychotic cannot make use of this process – either because the mother refused to act as receptacle, or because the infant's envy prevented the mother from playing her part. The link between the small child and the breast is damaged or destroyed, and this deprives him of the only way he has of dealing with emotions that are too intense. Then all emotions, and the external reality which evokes them, are hated.

The future psychotic has introjected an external breast which refused to introject, harbour, and so modify emotions. This internalized object is felt, by a weak immature ego, to intensify the strength of the emotions, as it is even less able to bear them. Since the emotions have a linking function, the psychotic part of the personality, paradoxically, finds itself invaded by an over-abundance of links: 'These attacks on the linking function of emotion lead to an overprominence in the psychotic part of the personality of links which appear to be logical, almost mathematical, but never emotionally reasonable. Consequently, the links surviving are perverse, cruel, and sterile' (Bion, 1958b, p. 109).[26]

Mental development is seriously threatened. Curiosity can no longer fulfil its role, as the infant employs projective identification to explore the nature of the functions which excite its curiosity. However, all learning depends on the drive for knowledge. The incapacity for introjection makes the external object appear to be radically hostile towards curiosity and all the means of satisfying it – in other words, projective identification. Envy transforms the breast into an avid object which devours projective identifications. Instead of introjecting an understanding breast, the psychotic infant has internalized an object which functions as a super-ego intent on destroying the ego. During the paranoid-schizoid phase there is no whole object, and the bizarre objects composed partially of elements of a persecutory super-ego are predominant.

When analysis successfully brings the patient back on to the normal course of development, a further difficulty comes to the fore. The patient is preoccupied with one function or another, and is aware of this function despite being unable to grasp the totality of which the function is but a part. The problem is that the question 'What is it?' cannot be resolved without questioning the why and how. The patient cannot tackle the problems that are entailed by the question 'why?'. In fact the feelings of guilt which were prematurely activated by envy obliterated the 'why?' by means of an extreme splitting. A patient who is unable to understand causality suffers from painful states of mind, while pursuing lines of action that are deliberately aimed at creating such states of mind. Such a patient is unable to formulate questions that might be articulated, if not resolved, in a more sophisticated language capable of questioning causality. To wonder why is to consider accepting one's own responsibility and the possibility of feeling guilty. This focus on disturbances of thought gives great homogeneity to the works of the psychotic period. While it proposed a structural dialectic between the basic assumption group and the work group, the group period was based on an act of faith: that the work group will win out because it is turned towards reality and reaches a rudimentary level of scientific method. Learning from experience, which is characteristic of the work group exclusively, is what creates psychic growth: 'The whole point about civilized speech is that it greatly simplifies the thinker's or speaker's task. With that tool problems can be solved because at least they can be stated, whereas without it certain questions, no matter how important, cannot even be posed' (Bion, 1967a, p. 62). Bion continued to study the problems raised by the relationship between the basic assumption group and the work group, seeing this in terms of the psychotic and non-psychotic parts of the personality. The psychotic part, which attacks all linking activities, prevents the development of verbal thought. It prohibits the non-psychotic part from making use of a therapeutic method to move from rationality to responsibility and the concept of causality.

PART 4a:

THE EPISTEMOLOGICAL PERIOD: THE IDEAL OF A SCIENTIFIC PSYCHOANALYSIS

From the 1960s onwards Bion no longer worried about whether or not he was a Kleinian. The esteem in which he was held by his colleagues was made manifest in his election to president of the British Society in 1962. He remained president for the statutory three years.

Bion made more time for his family. When Parthenope went to Italy to study, he wrote to her often. As soon as she reached the age of seventeen, he shared his cultural discoveries with her. His letters to the two younger children were often decorated with humorous and talented drawings. When he was in hospital, for example, he sent them a drawing of the fat lady with the vacuum cleaner. Later he drew animals from thumbprints made with ink. He was interested in scenes of animal life, especially birdlife. Lastly, he told them about his professional engagements.

From 1966 to 1968, Bion was a member of the training committee and the publications committee of the British Psycho-Analytical Society. At the same time he was also president of the Melanie Klein Trust, which protected the interests of the late Mrs Klein. Bion's social success could not be doubted. It must be said that he had distanced himself from the Establishment of which he was part. He had entered his epistemological period, and adopted other value systems. If creativity is evaluated in terms of its originality and its depth, there can be no doubt that Bion's creativity was at its zenith at this time. It has been noted that it started shortly after Klein's death. We would add that it started at the threshold of old age. It was when he was midway into his sixties that Bion amazed the psychoanalytic community: he published several books, disheartening in their hermetic sophistication and awkward in their extreme ambition. In search of a theory of knowledge, Bion pursued his ideal of a psychoanalysis constructed on a mathematical model, but the pursuit of this ideal came up against psychoanalysts' modes of knowledge: they observe and communicate an experience which is not derived from the senses. The result was a new conception which was also inspired by mystical Gnosticism. Bion's ambition was to reach the ultimate reality unveiled by the analytic experience by means of 'psychic' mathematics.

Bion clearly describes the ambitious project that motivated him at the outset of the epistemological period: to write a genesis of the psyche, while establishing the foundations of a scientific psychoanalysis. This project was realized in the almost simultaneous publication of two books. The first, *Learning from Experience*, shows how thought evolves towards abstraction and complexity, starting from basic experimental origins. Thought finally takes itself as object of study. With this first book, Bion introduces the cornerstone of a new intellectual system: the alpha function. This mysterious expression designates a symbolic function that is essential for the reception, elaboration and communication of experiences favourable to growth.

A second advance consisted of a new solution for the problem of recording analytic sessions, a new 'system of scientific notation' for psychic phenomena.

The desire for an abstract system of notation was further developed in the next book, *The Elements of Psycho-Analysis*. Bion set out a method that would enable the practising analyst to sharpen his powers of observation and clarify his thinking in his day-to-day work. To this end he isolated abstractions which were 'capable, in combinations, of representing all psychoanalytic theories and situations'. This was achieved in the construction of a grid, the written convention for reconstructing psychoanalytic phenomena.

The rupture between the psychotic and epistemological periods was not only a matter of their respective themes; it was also manifest on the level of a complete transformation in their respective modes of writing. The writings of the psychotic period had been communicated in the 'classical' way, in the form of articles in the official organ of psychoanalysis, after they had been read out to specialist learned societies. In the epistemological period the theory appears in the form of a book which touches on the totality of selected problems. Although the book was aimed at psychoanalysts, it was also hoped that it would be read by a wider public.

The style of writing was inspired by analytic technique to the extent that the reader was invited to privilege the processes of association and elaboration evoked and maintained by the text. The latter functions as an intellectual container, allowing the reader to introject a state of mind conducive to the search for truth.

18   THE THEORY OF THINKING

In 1962 Bion effected the transition by formulating a 'theory of thinking'. We can note the similarities between his formulation and philosophy, as philosophers have dealt with the same subject. At the same time his theory differs from philosophy inasmuch as it has a practical application as its goal. Bion hoped that his theory would be reformulated by practitioners in terms of 'empirically verifiable data', and that it would withstand such empirical testing. We may note the strangeness of this epistemological synthesis. Bion implies that analytic theories refer to ideal objects, such as mathematical objects, according to the Platonic tradition. At the same time he accords psychoanalytic practice the status of an experimental science. Eventually, some time later, when he was writing the commentary for his collected papers, *Second Thoughts*, Bion became aware of the dualistic nature of this position. Reconsidering his theory, he specified 'to achieve a feeling of security to offset and neutralize the sense of insecurity following on the discovery' (1967a, p. 166). Indeed, that discovery has exposed further vistas of problems to be solved.

Bion always organized his thinking from the starting point of the changes undergone by the psyche when the reality principle presides over its functioning. According to Freud, motor function discharge can rid the psychic apparatus of the increased tension of excitation during the domination of the pleasure principle. This excitation is transformed into action when it receives the instruction adequately to modify reality. Whereas motor functioning can bring about an instantaneous discharge of tension, the actions have little chance of bringing about effective change in the immediate future. Motor discharge can be transformed into effective action only if the psychic apparatus is capable of tolerating the accumulation of tension produced by the delay of discharge. In one sense, thought is a substitute for motor discharge. The capacity to think facilitates deferment and the toleration of the waiting time between the moment at which a desire is experienced and the moment when appropriate action can bring satisfaction.

Bion considered that thinking originates in this process of unburdening the psyche of accumulating tension. Consequently, he assimilated this activity to the projective identification described by Klein. In Klein's terms, it is possible to rid oneself temporarily of undesired parts of the personality by splitting and locating them elsewhere. Analytic experience shows that a patient motivated by such a fantasy of omnipotence may be able to give a certain amount of reality to the fantasy. Bion maintained that the reality principle always worked alongside the pleasure principle. As and when the psyche reaches reality, thinking takes the place of motor functions and is used to modify the environment. Bion simplified the problem by considering thoughts as epistemological precedents of the activity of thinking. He was well aware of the fact that he was contradicting common sense, which maintains that it is thinking that produces thoughts.[27] Bion suggests that the psyche is obliged to think because it comes across thoughts that pre-exist it.

From this first article onwards the concept of development becomes a leitmotiv. Thus Bion began by classifying thoughts according to their presence in chronological development. He placed preconception at the beginning. As an example he cites the infant's innate capacity to find a breast – or at least, the satisfaction given by what a more developed person would identify as a breast. When a preconception meets a similar realization, it becomes a conception. In other words, preconception (which corresponds to an *a priori* knowledge of the breast) is transformed into a conception when the infant comes into contact with the breast. The awareness of realization is accompanied by a conceptual development. Therefore, all conceptions will be connected to an emotional experience of satisfaction.

Bion reserved the term 'thought' for the linking of a preconception with a frustration. Thinking results from the encounter with a negative realization. Bion suggests a model for the formation of thought, referring once again to the prototype of early infancy –

an infant awaiting the breast realizes the absence of the breast that might satisfy the waiting: 'this linking is experienced as a non-breast or a breast that is internally absent' (Bion, 1962a, p. 111). As a result of this frustration, the personality thus confronted with the need to think may follow one of two diametrically opposed paths: either it can tolerate frustration, and so develop its non-psychotic part and its psychic creativity, or it cannot tolerate frustration, and founders in psychosis and emotional self-destruction.

If the personality manages to tolerate frustration adequately, the absent internal breast becomes a thought and develops a structure for thinking. It engages in a creative spiral, as a psyche which is capable of tolerating frustration generates thoughts which make frustration even more tolerable. The linking of preconceptions and realizations, be they negative or positive, engenders a process which leads to 'learning from experience', the name of the first book in Bion's epistemological period. He hypothesizes a generic series of thinking, from preconceptions to concepts, via conceptions or thoughts. The emergence of the mechanism for thinking within this development of thoughts is not yet understood. At this time Bion offers an elliptical metaphor: 'The failure to bring about this conjunction of sense data, and therefore of a common sense view, induces a mental state of debility in the patient as if starvation of truth was somehow analogous to alimentary starvation' (Bion, 1962a, p. 119).

If the psyche cannot tolerate frustration, it will try to evade it. The process that should have created a thought (through the juxtaposition of a preconception and a negative realization) becomes a bad object which must be voided. The thinking mechanism does not emerge, and in its place there is an excessive use of the mechanism of projective identification. For this psychotic psyche, voiding a bad breast is the same as maintaining a good breast. All thoughts end up by being treated as if they could not be distinguished from bad internal objects. This results in the creation of a mechanism not for thinking thoughts, but for disencumbering the psyche of its surplus 'badness'.

In order to survive, the infant's personality should be managed by the mother (or her substitute). If all goes well, mother and child adjust to one another. Projective identification plays a part in this process of adapting, as this usually omnipotent fantasy can also function realistically. The child who wants to unburden himself of certain feelings behaves in a way which will create these feelings in the mother. An infant who feels that it is dying can arouse fears that it is dying in the mother: 'A well-balanced mother can accept this fear and respond therapeutically' (Bion, 1962a, p. 11).

The mother must manage to give the infant the feeling that its fear is returning in a form which the infant personality can tolerate. If the mother cannot tolerate these projections, the infant is reduced to continued use of projective identification with more increasing force and frequency: 'The increased force seems to denude the projection of its penumbra of meaning' (Bion, 1962a, p. 115). The infant ends up by reintrojecting 'a terror without a name'. Bion hypothesizes an infantile prototype for the pathological process observed in psychotic patients. The infant behaves as if it felt that an internal object had been built up, one with the characteristics of a 'greedy vagina-like "breast"' which strips the goodness from everything the infant receives or gives. Only 'degenerate objects' remain. Such an internal object starves its host of all the understanding that is made available. This in turn results in a precocious development of consciousness.

Bion was no longer satisfied with the binary oppositions of the psychotic period. He now recognized an intermediary state between psychotic and non-psychotic personalities. He conceived of cases in which the inability to tolerate frustration is not strong enough to motivate escape, but is strong enough to prevent the reality principle from being accepted. In this case the personality substitutes omnipotence for the linking of a preconception to a negative realization. As a result, omniscience is substituted for learning from experience. Therefore there are no thoughts, nor is there a process of thinking that might differentiate between the true and the false. Instead of separating truth from error, the psyche simply asserts that such and such is morally right and such and such is wrong. The distinction between true and false is a product of the non-psychotic part of the personality, whereas psychosis creates this pseudo-morality which denies reality.

19 EXPERIMENTAL KNOWLEDGE

The psychotic period ended with the rediscovery of a traditional intellectual project: the theory of knowledge. Philosophy had studied rational thought for a long time. Where fundamental personality troubles are manifested in disturbances of thought, however, the philosopher lacks the psychoanalyst's experience. Bion was exceptionally fortunate in this respect. His undergraduate studies had given him a grounding in philosophy and epistemology; then two training analyses had enabled him to treat psychotic patients successfully through psychoanalysis, something which many analysts would not have attempted. This new experience had cast some light on the nature and origins of thought, as it demonstrated that cognitive development takes place alongside the genesis of the personality. Finally, Bion aimed to rewrite the theory of knowledge from the perspective of object relations, and the analysis of disturbances of thought.

THE THEORY OF FUNCTIONS

why?

The basic principle from the group period was still valid: the analyst's strength is his ability to comprehend all experimental findings in terms of the minimum number of theories, rather than to use the greatest number of theories. Bion created something of a minor intellectual revolution when he put forward his theory of functions. Despite its name, this new tool was not part of analytic theory – it was as different from the Kleinian and Freudian theories Bion had used as it was from his earlier theory of psychosis.

Bion introduces the concept of function in relation to action. It is usual to define an action in terms of the name of the person of whom it is thought to be typical. Dadaism, for example, was created by adding the suffix -ism to the name Dada; it refers to the activities of an early-twentieth-century avant-garde art movement (Don Quixotism would not be an inappropriate term for the group period). Bion gives the following example of functions: 'X's relationship with his associates is typical of a personality in which envy is a factor'. Certain factors (in this case transference and envy) are combined to give a function of this personality. These factors are not deduced directly, but by observation of a function. The matter is further complicated by virtue of the fact that a function may seem to be transformed into a factor, or vice versa, depending on whether levels of psychic integrity increase or diminish.

Bion deliberately chose the terms 'factor' and 'function' because of their association with mathematics. He wanted to maintain a certain semantic ambiguity so that readers would think as much about mathematics as about other disciplines in which these terms are used. He states clearly that his use of these terms is not one which carries the obligation to adhere to their exact usage in other disciplines: 'In psycho-analytic methodology the criterion cannot be whether a particular usage is right or wrong, meaningful or verifiable, but whether it does or does not promote development' (Bion, 1962b, Introduction). In the same way, during the group period, Bion had simply noted, with satisfaction, that his method 'worked'.

Bion considered that the thinking process was a function of the personality. When he spoke of the alpha function he deliberately avoided using a term such as 'mental faculty', which conveys a set of specific associations and meanings derived from an intellectual tradition. The term 'alpha function' was deliberately 'devoid of meaning' in order to provide psychoanalytic research with an equivalent to the concept of a variable in mathematics. The alpha function represents an unknown. A realization must satisfy it, as in mathematics an element satisfies the terms of an equation. When the value of the alpha function has been determined, it may be hoped that thinking will acquire a new, more precise meaning. An incidental problem was that the fact of using the term 'alpha function' in an investigation inevitably led to its reinstatement with meanings associated with the field of research. Bion was insistent

Alpha function — unknown

on the need to counteract such a tendency to prevent this analytic tool from being impaired from the outset, by being prematurely endowed with irrelevant meanings.

Bion gives detailed specification of the field of investigation into the alpha function, but he does so almost without reference to other theoretical texts. He seems to consider that the fundamental issues are still those described by Freud in 1911 in his paper on the two principles of mental functioning. These mental functions, linked to the acceptance of the reality principle, served as the boundaries of the investigation.[28] Bion's first aim is the under-standing of sense impressions in relation to the states of pleasure and pain. Leaving aside Freud's distinction between inside and outside, Bion considers pleasure and pain to be as 'real' as sensory impressions. Lastly, he considers the capacity to understand to be an attribute of consciousness, to the extent that consciousness is 'a sense-organ for the perception of psychical qualities' (Freud, 1911). Consciousness had been reduced to a mental operation. Bion opened up the Freudian canon by bringing to it the major discoveries of the Kleinian tradition concerning the early stages of development: splitting, projective identification, the transition from the paranoid-schizoid to the depressive position, and the theory of symbol formation. Bion adds to this his own contribution on the development of verbal thought. It is accepted that the Oedipus complex remains a foundation of the new theory. What is new is that all these theories are thought of as factors capable of being combined into functions. Unlike the intentional indefinite-ness of the function, these theories of factors were to be used with as much rigour as possible.

THE ALPHA FUNCTION OF KNOWLEDGE

The alpha function is the cornerstone of the knowledge process. Alpha, the first letter of the Greek alphabet, signifies the presence of this function from the outset. With the alpha function Bion conceives a hypothetical mechanism capable of transforming sense data into dream thoughts and unconscious waking thinking. Within this perspective an emotional experience occurring in sleep is no different from an emotional experience occurring during waking life. In either case the perception of the emotional experience has to be worked upon by the alpha function before it can be used for dream thoughts: 'The alpha function operates on the sense impressions, whatever they are, and on the emotions, whatever they are, of which the patient is aware' (Bion, 1962b, p. 6). In so far as the operation is successful, alpha elements are produced which are suited to storage and the requirements of dream thoughts. Alpha elements resemble, and may even be identical to, the visual images with which we are familiar in dreams and which Freud regards 'as yielding their latent content when the analyst has interpreted them'. Bion does not reduce alpha elements to their visual characteristics alone, but also includes their auditory and olfactory components.

Whenever the alpha function is inoperative, sense impressions and emotions remain in their original state, which Bion described as beta elements. These are not amenable to use in dream thoughts, but are suited to use in projective identification and acting out. They can be evacuated or used in a type of concrete thinking. Alpha function protects the psyche from what is virtually a psychotic state. A patient whose alpha function fails cannot dream, and ultimately cannot go to sleep or wake up. Clinically, he seems to be in an acute confusional state.

For readers who are familiar with psychoanalytic literature, there is a further surprise. Bion uses Kantian concepts to differentiate between alpha and beta elements. He considers alpha elements as 'phenomena' and beta elements as 'things-in-themselves'. With a characteristic process of thought, Bion mirrors this philosophical abstraction with a concrete metaphor of digestive process. Beta elements are not so much memories as undigested facts, whereas alpha elements have been digested by the alpha function and are thus 'food for thought'.

There could be no learning from experience were it not for the way in which alpha function operates on consciousness of emotional experience. The child who learns to walk is able, with the alpha function, to store this experience. What had originally to be conscious becomes unconscious. The child can then use all the thinking needed for walking without being conscious of it. The alpha function relieves consciousness of the intellectual burden involved in all learning.

THE CONTACT BARRIER

Bion maintained that man must 'dream' an ongoing emotional experience as much during sleep as when he is awake. He reformulates this concept by suggesting that the 'dream' acts as a 'contact barrier' (the two terms are virtually interchangeable). Bion was reformulating the Freudian concept of a neurophysiological entity known as the synapse, the contact zone between two neurones. The alpha function transforms sense impressions related to emotional experience into alpha elements which cohere as they proliferate in order to form the contact barrier: 'This contact barrier, thus continuously in process of formation, marks the point of contact and separation between conscious and unconscious elements and originates the distinction between them' (Bion, 1962b, p. 17). There is a selective passage of elements between conscious and unconscious, and vice versa. Because dreams can give direct access to the study of the contact barrier, they retain the central position in psychoanalysis that Freud assigned to them. If the contact barrier is evident in clinical work, it takes a form something like that of dreams, protecting reality perception from being overwhelmed by emotions and phantasies emanating from within. Similarly, the contact barrier protects endopsychic phenomena from being invaded by 'realist' perceptions.

Adding to the concrete nature of his investigation, Bion cites some of the emotional experiences which led him to conceive of the alpha function. These occurred during the analysis of patients with thought disturbances. Bion had made 'orthodox transference interpretations' without any change being effected: the patients continued with their streams of disjointed associations. Bion noticed that the signs of confusion were linked to projective identification. It occurred to him that he was being used as the repository for the sane part of the patient's personality. As he was assumed to have the non-psychotic part, he was expected to be aware of all that was happening, unlike the patient. Bion sometimes visualized the situation thus: the patient was a foetus to whom the mother's emotions were communicated, but to whom the stimulus and source of these emotions were unknown.

At other times the patient seemed to be aware of what was happening, but could not have said how he knew. The problem then was to identify which part of the personality was at work. Using the theory of functions, Bion described the situation as one in which the patient was unable to dream owing to the absence of alpha elements: 'This would explain why I was a conscious that was incapable of the functions of consciousness and he an "unconscious" incapable of the functions of *unconsciousness*' (Bion, 1962a, p. 20). The two roles were interchangeable, and did not correspond to the theory of the contact barrier owing its existence to the proliferation of alpha elements and serving the function of a membrane, separating the phenomena into two groups: the functions of consciousness and the functions of unconsciousness.

In the psychotic situation, as Bion envisaged it, there was a functional division between analyst and patient, but one which offered no resistance to the passage of elements from one to the other. Whereas the distinction between conscious and unconscious derives its existence from the contact barrier composed of alpha elements, the lack of such a distinction brings to mind a contact barrier composed of beta elements. But if beta elements were incapable of forming links, how could it be possible to conceive of a 'composition' of such elements? In clinical terms the screen of beta elements resembles confusional states, and particularly the class of confusional states that resemble dreams. Comparison of the beta element screen with the confused states resembling dreams shows that the beta element screen is coherent and purposive. An analyst might be right in thinking that the patient pouring out a stream of material was aiming to destroy the analyst's power, or that the patient was more concerned to withhold information than to impart it. The beta screen has a quality which enables it to evoke the kind of response the patient desires. These conclusions are all the more surprising when one remembers that the beta screen is composed of elements that are not capable of linking up, or of making a functional division between conscious and unconscious.

With the beta screen the psychotic is more likely to produce the kind of material that aims to implicate the analyst's emotions rather than to receive an analytic interpretation. Bion's argument is that the theory of countertransference offers only a limited explanation of this phenomenon. It does account for the analyst's unconscious participation, but it leaves the patient's contribution unexamined.

I need examples here!

First, it was not developed to describe patients without articulate speech. This type of patient is incapable of grasping his own state of mind even when it is pointed out to him. His use of words is much closer to action 'intended to unburden the psyche of accretions of stimuli' than to speech. Secondly, the replacement of a (neurotic) contact barrier with a (psychotic) beta screen is a living process.

Bion questioned the Kleinian binarism of positions by adding an ambiguous resolution: the psyche can reach the border between psychosis and neurosis, causing the paranoid-schizoid and the depressive positions to coexist. Bion again employs his example of a 'reversible perspective' with the image that can be read either as a vase or as two profiles.

A contact barrier is formed when sense impressions are transformed into alpha elements liable to be used in dream thoughts or in waking unconscious thought. A reversal of the alpha function entails the dispersal of the contact barrier. The alpha elements of which it was composed are stripped of all that differentiates them from beta elements; this produces objects which resemble bizarre objects in that ego and super-ego traces are added to the beta elements. The contact barrier, as a function, is to be distinguished from the ego as a structure. The reversal of the alpha function also does violence to the ego, which is only one of the factors of the unknown function which transforms sense impressions into alpha elements. These distinctions became significant when Esther Bick put forward the notion of a 'psychic skin' derived from the notion of the psychic 'container' (unthinkable without the concept of the alpha function), and Didier Anzieu proposed the concept of the 'skin ego' derived from a different context.

THE THINKING APPARATUS

Wishing to give his abstractions a metaphorical model, Bion chose the oral phase of the alimentary process as the basis for constructing a sort of myth of the origins of thinking. He ultimately located the origins of the capacity for thinking within the apparatus geared to treating the sensory impressions emanating from the alimentary canal. The infant at the breast receives milk, and feelings of security, well-being and love. The mother gives milk with her mammary glands, the infant receives it with its alimentary canal. But what receives and deals with love? Emotional upsets may prevent the mother from providing her milk. The infant, too, may suffer digestive disturbances originating in an emotional upset. Thus Bion is led to suppose the existence in fact of a psychosomatic alimentary canal and breast. The infant needs this kind of breast in order to receive good internal objects with the milk. Bion deliberately avoided using the term 'wish' in place of 'need'. He did not attribute to the infant an awareness of this need, only an awareness of a need not satisfied. The infant is also attributed with a sense organ for the perception of psychic qualities through which frustration can be experienced.

An analyst treating an adult patient may be conscious of something of which the patient is not conscious. To an even greater extent, the mother can discern her infant's state of mind before the infant can be conscious of it. Bion imagined an infant showing signs of needing food even before becoming aware of its need. In this context the infant will be seeking not to receive a good breast but to evacuate a bad breast. What happens if the infant is fed? It may experience the taking in of milk, warmth and love as taking in the good breast: 'Under dominance of the, at first unopposed, bad breast, "taking in" food may be felt as indistinguishable from evacuating a bad breast' (Bion, 1962b, p. 34). (Bion transfers needs into the sphere of feelings, without explaining why.) Both good and bad breast are felt as possessing the same degree of concreteness and reality as milk. Sooner or later, the 'wanted' breast is experienced as the 'idea of a breast missing', not as a bad breast present (Bion does not indicate how the infant moves from the need for to the desire of the breast). Because it is wanted but absent, the bad breast is more likely to become recognized as an idea than the good breast, which is the existence of the milk the infant has in fact taken.

Bion again gives an example, another imaginary situation. He supposes an infant to have been fed, but to be feeling unloved. It is aware of a need for a good breast; and this 'need for a good breast' is a 'bad breast' that needs to be evacuated. The infant could be supposed to feel that the 'need for a good breast' (hence the bad breast) could be evacuated by passing a motion while taking milk. This physical act would then be associated with a result that we would call a change in state of mind from dissatisfaction to satisfaction. With this model Bion sought the origin of consciousness of psychic phenomena. The infant can be conscious of the psychic nature of its feeding only if it has transformed its emotional experience into alpha elements. The physical components – milk, the discomfort of satiation, or the opposite – are immediately apparent to the senses. This is why Bion accords chronological priority to beta elements over alpha elements.

The story is of the small child who learns to think with its mother. The infant contains a 'need for the breast' which is equated with a 'bad breast'. It must exchange the bad breast for a good breast. If it is able to tolerate frustration, the infant can have a sense of reality dominated by the reality principle. It works through the phantasies underlying projective identification with a certain realism, and begins to develop the capacity for thinking. It still needs the mother to receive and transform its projections in order to be able to reintroject them.

In other words, there can be neither learning from experience nor mental development unless there has been a maternal container at the outset. The mother's reverie develops simultaneously on two levels, the emotional and the intellectual (they are differentiated only for the purposes of analysis, as they are inextricably linked in reality). The mother modulates emotional experience. Her empathy enables her to know or guess feelings and emotions; she can tell whether they need to be mitigated or attenuated. When all goes well, an understanding mother adapts herself to her baby's needs. While responding in an adequate way, she helps it to discover its needs. What would happen if, overwhelmed with the fear of being a bad mother, she were to stuff her breast or bottle into the baby's mouth every time it expressed unease? If the baby needs to evacuate air from its digestive tract, its discomfort would increase, and this would be the beginning of a confusion between physical and emotional levels. The mother's response is right when she perceives a need; or, if there are several needs, when she is able to discover the most urgent need. In doing this the mother abstracts, so to speak, the most urgent need from a muddle of of distress. Eventually the child will internalize this process and become able to think for itself.

20   PSYCHOANALYTIC NOTATION

Bion was convinced that the only way to train psychoanalysts was through personal analysis. Being analysed offers an opportunity to have direct analytic experience. But having dedicated his life to this experience for some time, Bion had the feeling of being a member of an 'esoteric cult'. He felt that the only hope for wider relevance was to find a way of communicating psychoanalytic theories in a scientific way. The analytic session was the basic source of empirical knowledge. If it was to be made public, a way of recording it had to be found. Dissatisfied with the existing solutions, Bion wanted to create a system of scientific notation for this special kind of empirical testing. This system had to be of a sort that the analyst could still understand after a lapse of time, and communicate to other colleagues without serious loss of meaning. It would also allow the analyst to work on the problem that he had been able to record in this way. Ideally, psychoanalysis would become a discourse analogous to mathematics. Bion tried to reach this ideal by expressing his ideas in terms of the basic rules of mathematics.

THE PRINCIPLES OF NOTATION

Bion was careful to convey his thinking with the greatest precision by using mathematical notation. If psychoanalytic theory was rationally structured, it should be possible to signify the factors of the 'theory of functions' by universally applicable signs. A statement would then be replaced by 'a simple manipulation' of signs. The function of these special signs is to provide a form of denotation that is precise and clear while offering a means of abbreviation. The construction of a model can be the first step towards the abstract representation of a realization. But whereas an abstraction must be considered to be true, a model has simply to be 'good'. A model, in contrast to a theory, has a temporary existence and is set aside when it has been used or proved useless. If it repeatedly turns out to be useful, there is a point at which it may be transformed into a theory: 'The use of a model has a value in restoring a sense of the concrete to an investigation which may have lost contact with its background through abstraction and the theoretical deductive systems associated with it' (Bion, 1962b, p. 64). This process gives rise to the search for a new model, or the transformation of a model into a scientific system. Bion used the term 'model' to refer to a construction in which concrete images interconnect. The fact that these images are linked in a narrative implies that certain elements have a causal relation to others. The model gives greater weight to the real elements, the visual images, than to their forms of interconnecting links. Obversely, the elements of abstraction are linked not by narrative but by a process which aims to illustrate their relation to the emotional experience from which they emanate. These elements are less important in themselves. The model is constructed from elements culled from the individual's past, whereas abstraction is impregnated, so to speak, with preconceptions directed towards the individual's future.

Bion's developmental epistemology gives very little space to the father: the concept of the father is mentioned only twice in the examples cited in the text. His first – rather incidental – appearance is in relation to maternal reverie: this is beneficial only if it is 'associated with love for the child or its father' (Bion, 1962b, p. 36).

The second reference to the father is culled from his experiences with patients, with his children, and with other texts, and presented in the form of an imaginary story. Once upon a time there was a baby who was learning to say 'Daddy'. The baby had often repeated an emotional experience in which the following elements were constantly conjoined: the sight of a man, the sense of being loved by the man, a sense of wanting the man, an awareness of the mother's repetition of 'That's Daddy'. The child says 'Dad-da-da'. 'That's right; Daddy', says the mother. From its emotional experience the infant abstracts certain elements. These abstracted elements are given the name 'Daddy' in other situations in which the same elements appear to be conjoined. Bion considers that this story is a model, from which he develops the theory that 'Daddy' is the name of a hypothesis (or a conception). The hypothesis called 'Daddy' is a statement that certain elements are constantly conjoined. The infant may meet another child who also says 'Dad-da-da', but does so in circumstances which do not correspond with those with which 'Dad-da-da' is associated. There is a man, but he is the wrong one. However, elements of the new situation correspond to those of the initial hypothesis. The hypothesis has to be revised to represent both realizations. It may be abandoned for another, or it may become a concept. Using the model, the individual should be able to abstract from emotional experience elements that are constantly conjoined; and, among these, one element which is at one and the same time the name of the theory (or hypothesis, or concept) and the name of the realization that is believed to approximate to this theory.

THE ACT OF KNOWING

Before the elements of knowledge could be symbolized, the basic emotions underlying the alpha functions first had to be identified. It is clear that love and hate are fundamental to emotion. As for the rest, Bion was spoilt for choice: depression, anxiety, guilt, envy and gratitude, not to mention the sexual emotions. He thought that an emotional experience cannot be conceived of in isolation from a relationship, so he chose three emotional factors that constitute an intrinsic part of the link between two objects. The three corresponding signs express the part of the emotional experience which is invested in the link (here we recall Bion's concept of psychosis as an 'attack on linking'). Bion postulates that the three basic emotional relations are:

X loves Y; X hates Y; X knows Y.

Therefore he represents the basic emotional links by the signs L, H, K.

The LHK system can record only one part of the emotional experience of what has taken place in an analytic session. The selection of L, H and K is motivated not by the need to represent the totality of emotional facts of the session but by the need for a key which, like a musical key, can give the value of the other elements which combine to create a statement. It enables the analyst to establish the key of a session, as a statement in analysis derives its value and meaning only from its relation to other statements, thus giving a point of reference from which the analyst may derive the meaning of the other statements: 'L, H or K have to be decided in such a way that the analyst *feels* he has established a point of reference' (Bion, 1962b, p. 46).

Bion was well aware that the emotional relations of love and hate were to be found at the heart of Kleinian analysis.[29] He decided to dedicate himself to the study of the K link, which relates to learning from experience. L or H may relate to K, but neither is able, in itself, to lead to K. The knowledge activity represents a psychoanalytic relationship. This does not mean that X is in possession of a piece of knowledge, but that he is in the state of getting to know Y, and Y is on the point of getting to be known by X. In so far as X is concerned to know the truth about Y, the relationship can be said to be informed by a scientific outlook.

The process of abstraction is essential to the knowledge activity, since, by removing the concrete and particular, it effectively eliminates whatever might obscure the importance of the relationship between elements. Bion introduces a new criterion for evaluating abstraction: the success of abstraction can be measured by the amount of 'confidence' created, a feeling analogous to the feeling created by the fact of knowing that sense impressions are commensurate with other senses or shared with other people ('common sense'). Confidence is strengthened when the representation corresponds not only to the emotional experience from which it was abstracted, but also to other realizations not known at the point of abstraction.

According to Freud, it is motor action that has the capacity to create a distinction between internal and external. Insisting on the link between thought and action, Bion alters the definition of reality-testing. Recourse to action is no longer necessary, because reality-testing rests on the feeling of confidence that is the product of an adequate encounter with reality. Bion considered abstraction as a stage in publication – it facilitates the comparison between the representation that has been abstracted from the realization with other realizations, each different from the realization which initiated the abstraction. Concretization is a process which creates the inverse of abstraction, playing an essential role in isolating the relation characteristic of the K activity. It can be conceived as a form of publication which privileges correlation by common sense. A statement is concrete (sensory) if it facilitates experience by more than one sense or by the senses of more than one person.

PSYCHOANALYTIC ELEMENTS

Psychoanalytic theories seem to be inadequate in the same way as an ideographic script is inadequate as compared to an alphabetical one. The ideogram represents only one word, while a relatively small number of letters manage to combine to produce millions of words. Similarly, although they are not numerous, the abstractions sought would be able to be combined to represent all the theories necessary to psychoanalytic practice. The analyst would have access to the 'elements of psychoanalysis'. This term was not chosen at random – it has tremendous cultural and scientific resonance. But the explicit reference was to Euclid, the Greek mathematician whose *Elements* continued to be an authoritative text until well into this century. Bion also used this term because of its significance in chemistry: the elements of chemistry are the basic entities from which all others are composed.

To satisfy his hypothesis, Bion was looking for elements which could:

- represent the realization which they were originally held to describe;
- be capable of interconnection;
- combine to form a scientific deductive system capable of representing an unknown realization.

Bion had isolated three fundamental notions for which he had sought a form of representation analogous to mathematical notation. Eventually, he put forward these elements of psycho-analysis:

- the psychoanalytic links L, H and K;
- projective identification (female [♀] and male [♂] symbols);
- the interrelation between the PS↔D positions.

We have already seen that the signs L, H and K represent the links between psychoanalytic objects. They are culled from current realizations – love, hate and knowledge. The personality develops in so far as it is capable of establishing psychic links with real objects. The K link implies the existence of an apparatus capable of transforming the givens of experience and utilizing the products of this transformation.

The ♀ ♂ element represents the essential characteristic of projective identification. Bion refers to Klein's description of the mechanism used to transform infantile fears. The infant projects bad feelings, with a part of its psyche, into the good breast. These feelings are transformed by their reception in the good breast in such a way that the infantile psyche, having reintrojected them, manages to bear them. From this theory Bion constructs the model of container and contained. He defines the container as that which receives the projected object and the contained as the object being projected into the container. Container and contained are able to be joined and penetrated by emotion, in which case they can grow. If they are disjointed or stripped of emotion, they lose their vitality and become like inanimate objects. Pushing towards abstraction, Bion designates the container by the sign ♀ and the contained by the sign ♂ : 'These signs denote and represent simultaneously' (Bion, 1962b, p. 110).

Finally, the PS↔D element represents the interrelation between the paranoid-schizoid and depressive positions. It corresponds to Klein's theory which describes how, in certain contexts, elements that seem unrelated and associated with feelings of persecution interact and form an integrated whole associated with depressive feelings. This element designates the simplest mechanisms capable of transforming fragmentation into integration, and vice versa. PS↔D corresponds also to the reaction caused by the discovery of the 'selected fact'. The 'selected fact' is the name of an element which introduces order into the complexity of a psychoanalytic realization, precipitating a synthetic reaction which enables the analyst to make an interpretation.

Could these abstracted elements be readily identified? Bion's first criterion was that of observation; his perspective was that of a practising psychoanalyst. However, psychoanalytic reality is not observable through immediate sense data. Bion found a way of overcoming this difficulty by considering all the elements as functions. Abstractions or signs representing the elements are no more knowable than things-in-themselves. Conversely, the elements are manifested in observable phenomena of which the primary and secondary qualities may be known. For example, although the sign ♀ ♂ is by definition unknowable, it is indirectly known to the analyst and to the patient whenever there is a process of something being taken into the self or being put inside another, a question of containing or being contained, of 'container' and 'contained'.

Bion then passes on to a semantic game in which he takes the verb 'to see' in its literal and its figurative senses. The elements of psychoanalysis are chosen from all the functions of the personality which can be 'seen' in the course of an analysis. But which characteristics should be retained to declare some elements 'visible', since some analysts claim to see things whose existence is not even accepted by others? A similar disagreement can exist between patient and analyst even when they share an experience of 'seeing'. It can be only analogy, as others' experience of anxiety can only be deduced.

Bion reaches this paradox by attributing three dimensions to the elements obtained by extending the dimensions of sense, of myth, and of passion.

The extension in the sensory dimension signifies that the element must be an object of the senses. When an interpretation is given, it must be possible for analyst and patient to 'see' that it is about something audible, visible, palpable or olfactory.

The dimension of myth, which is more difficult to define, relates to personal elaborations without which the psychoanalyst could not construct models in his practice. It corresponds neither to statements about observable facts, nor to theoretical formulations aimed at representing a realization.

Passion is an emotion that is experienced with intensity, with warmth, and without the slightest trace of violence. It could be believed that the term introduces no more than the elements L, H and K described above, but this is not so. Bion considered that this element had many dimensions, of which passion would be just one. Passion is not manifested by the senses: 'For senses to be active only one mind is necessary: passion is evidence that two minds are linked' (Bion, 1963, p. 13).

THE GRID

Bion had postulated the existence of a mechanism which could transform the sense impressions of emotional experiences into 'thoughts', and invented an abstraction, the alpha function, to denote this mechanism. The emptiness of the term was to allow psychoanalytic research to have the space to hone its concepts by inflecting it with meaning. Bion then constructed another abstraction, as empty as the first, to represent the manipulation of these 'thoughts' in a thinking mechanism in the form of two axes combined as 'the grid'. It comprised a finite number of compartments which could contain the elements of psychoanalysis. The axes had been carefully selected – one to represent the uses of psychoanalysis, the other to classify functions genetically.

THE AXIS OF APPLICATION

Statements (mostly interpretations) can be differentiated according to their use, categorized according to the functions created in the psyche by the dominance of the reality principle. The horizontal axis includes the following categories:

1 The analyst gives the patient 'a definitory hypothesis'. He tells him, simply, about the constant conjunction of certain elements. For example, if the patient shows by his associations that he is depressed, the analyst can offer a definitory hypothesis: 'What you, the patient, are now experiencing is what I – and, in my opinion, most people – would call depression.' There can be no argument about it, because this category of statement requires only that statements should not be self-contradictory.

2 This category is the only one which is independent of Freud's 'two principles'. An interpretation can be used to deny that the situation is unknown and, consequently, dangerous. This state of affairs belongs to the countertransference, and thus to the analyst's own need for analysis. Analysts are not always fully analysed, and the statement, known to be false, can also be used as a barrier against other statements either unknown and liable to produce

The Grid

	1 Definitory hypotheses	2 ψ	3 Notation	4 Attention	5 Research	6 Action	... n.
A: β-elements	A1	A2				A6	
B: α-elements	B1	B2	B3	B4	B5	B6	..Bn
C: Dream thoughts, dreams, myths	C1	C2	C3	C4	C5	C6	..Cn
D: Pre-conception	D1	D2	D3	D4	D5	D6	..Dn
E: Conception	E1	E2	E3	E4	E5	E6	..En
F: Concept	F1	F2	F3	F4	F5	F6	..Fn
G: Scientific deductive system		G2					
H: Algebraic calculus							

anxiety, or else known and capable of producing a catastrophic change. Bion designates this column by the Greek letter psi (Ψ). He was probably referring to the 'proton pseudos' – the famous 'first lie' which Freud, in 1895, located at the heart of the psychopathology of hysteria.

3 Statements that are representations of past or present realizations. For example, the analyst gives the patient a brief summary, reminding him of what took place on a previous occasion. This corresponds to the function of notation aimed at providing a repository for the products of attention.

4 The next column denotes statements about attention which aim to go beyond sensory impressions and explore the environment. In

this way it has affinities with the preconception, and plays an essential part in discrimination (one of its functions is receptiveness to the 'selected fact').

5 In this column, interpretation is a theory used to explore the unknown. It aims to illuminate material to enable the patient to release still further material. The primary aim is to obtain material for the satisfaction of the impulses of enquiry in patient and analyst. The most obvious example of this is the Oedipus myth as Freud abstracted it to form psychoanalytic theory.

6 This category includes interpretations that are analogous to actions. This type of communication is aimed at enabling the patient to effect solutions of his problems of development (rather than problems *per se*). The transition of thought to a formulation from category 6 is most like the translation of thought into action.

Bion claimed that this list of categories in the horizontal axis is neither exhaustive nor exclusive. In the grid he represented the possibility of adding further categories by numbering them from 1 to n, with dots between 6 and n.

THE GENETIC ORDER

The axis of application excludes the temporal element. Bion decided to combine it with a classification of thoughts resting on the concept of time. He constructs a vertical axis allowing distinctions of degrees of evolution of the thoughts expressed. These degrees evolve from the top towards the bottom, from the most basic to the most evolved.

1 The A row comprises beta elements, the most primitive matrix within which thoughts can emerge. Beta elements may represent inanimate objects as well as psychic objects, without differentiating between them. In clinical terms, this is the concrete thinking of psychosis.

2 The B row corresponds to the work of the alpha function on sensory impressions. Alpha elements facilitate the formation and use of dream thoughts. These are not objects from external reality; they derive from the processing of the sensory data in relation to external reality.

3 The C row comprises dream thoughts, dreams and myths. The theory of dreams in classical psychoanalysis is sufficient for this level of thinking. With dreams one reaches a realm in which there is direct evidence of psychic phenomena.

4 The D row comprises preconception, a mental state of expectation, a mind adapted to receive a restricted range of phenomena. The prototype of this would be the infant's expectation of a breast after birth. Bion represented preconception taking his formulation from the psychoanalytic function Ψ (ξ), in which the factor corresponds to the non-saturated element (ξ). (The Greek letter ksi corresponds to our X, which is often used to represent the unknown in a mathematical problem or detective investigation.) When the preconception is mated with a realization, the non-saturated element is replaced by a constant.

5 The E row comprises conception. The theory of thinking has taught us that the mating of a preconception with a negative realization engenders a conception. Bion introduced a strange mobility in the grid, considering that conception could also be used as preconception. The mating also enlarges the preconception's capacity to become saturated.

6 The F row links concepts. Conceptions become concepts when a process of abstraction renders them 'free of those elements that would unfit it to be a tool in the elucidation or expression of truth' (Bion, 1963, p. 18).

7 With the G row we reach the scientific deductive system. By this Bion means a combination of concepts and hypotheses logically related to each other. The logical relation enhances the meaning of each concept and hypothesis thus linked, and expresses a meaning that the concepts, hypotheses and links do not possess individually.

8 The H row corresponds to algebraic calculus. With further work of abstraction, analysis could represent the scientific deductive system in mathematical terms.

Bion drew a line demarcating alpha and beta elements from the rest of the components of the grid – these elements were only theoretical hypotheses required for the explanation of observations of disturbances of thinking. Despite their names, alpha and beta elements cannot be classified as psychoanalytic elements, as they are not manifested in observable phenomena. Alongside this epistemological distinction we would emphasize the genetic division between the first row and the others. The A row is the only one to have no unsaturated (ξ, ksi or X) elements; consequently, it is unsuited for use as a preconception. On a developmental level, the evolution from the A row to the B row cannot be achieved without the mother.

Combining the Vertical and Horizontal Axes

An analytic session is unique in that the practitioner uses all the material for the sole aim of illuminating a relationship K. When he has a choice, or doubts, about what he might say, the analyst may refer to the grid. The horizontal axis shows him the functions that his statement might fulfil; it does not, however, account for the statement's degree of evolution.

For example – to take a statement which is at some remove from either extreme of the vertical axis – a patient says to his analyst: 'I think you hate me'. On the first level, this may be a simple convention. There can be no argument, because the patient is simply defining the feelings of his analyst. On the second level this statement, be it true or false, may be an attempt to avoid some unpleasant reality, such as a strong homosexual attraction. Thirdly, the patient may make a straightforward observation which will take its meaning from what follows. Fourthly, the statement indicates that the patient is giving his attention to this point, but will proceed further. Fifthly, the statement issues from a strong curiosity and a desire to know more about, for example, the reasons for this hatred. Finally, the statement heralds an eventual change in external reality, such as finding some protection against this hatred. It is fairly obvious that the patient's collaboration can become part of the interaction only with columns three, four and five.

The vertical axis enables the analyst to identify the type of intellectual process at work. The columns represent a number of developmental levels of the meaning of a statement such as 'I think you hate me'. Even though it is grammatically correct and semantically meaningful, this statement might in fact be the disguised expulsion of flatus, which, in popular phraseology, is tacitly understood in such terms as 'gasbag', 'long-winded', and other unconscious equations of speech with flatus. If this is the case, the analyst may classify the statement within the first level. The session may also indicate that the statement refers to a dream, or daydream, that the patient has had, which would classify it within levels B or C. In another context the statement appears to be a preconception and would therefore be classified in level D, where it is placed in a central position which is particularly favourable to mental growth. Lastly, the statement may have been articulated following an interpretation from the analyst. This statement would, as the result of mating a conception with a realization, be attributed to level G.

Let us suppose that the statement 'I think you hate me' turns out to be a preconception motivated by curiosity (D5). The analyst perceives that it is also a realization for the theory of splitting and projection. He will know that the patient is ready to receive an interpretation on the part of his personality that is full of hatred, which he has split off and projected. Instead of recognizing this hatred in himself, he is projectively attributing it to his analyst. Let us suppose that the patient then tells of a dream in which he experiences jealousy. Analysing the latent dream thoughts, it seems that the patient imagines that his analyst has a sexual relationship with a woman known to both men. The analyst then recognizes a realization of Freud's theory of the Oedipus complex. The analyst has identified the three elements of the psychoanalytic object: a dream made up of alpha elements, a mythic scenario and a scientific deductive system. The simultaneous presence in three levels indicates that he should be able to make a comprehensive interpretation.

Bion emphasized the importance of being able to have a freshness or naivety at each session. The analyst should not count on anything as having been won, since the way in which psychic contents are manifested in analysis does not depend on the length of the analysis. The analyst's attitude towards his patient should always have within it a non-saturated element (ξ).

From the outset of the epistemological period, Bion was wary of the defensive recourse to memory (which, later, would lead him to advocate analysis 'without memory or desire'). Consequently, he emphasized the capacity for anticipation. To recognize the grid classification in which material might belong would constitute a step towards anticipation.

Combining the eight degrees of evolution, according to the vertical axis, and the six uses, according to the horizontal axis, Bion constructed a grid. This enables identification of the elements which comprise a psychoanalytic object. Elements are the ideas and feelings that can be situated, through their context, in one of the categories of the grid. These elements interrelate to form psychoanalytic objects, in the same way as atoms combine to form molecules. In order to make them identifiable, Bion had endowed the psychoanalytic objects with a sensory dimension (alpha elements), a mythic dimension (dream thoughts) and passion. He presents the grid as a 'convention for constructing psychoanalytic phenomena'. To this effect he had transposed a system of Cartesian co-ordinates, in which a movement from above (beta elements) to below (scientific deductive system) implies growth. But does the development deduced from observations made in the consulting room resemble the rules of co-ordinating signs in the grid? It could be said that the movements within the grid represent the results of development or decline, but it cannot be claimed that the manoeuvring of signs represents development or decline them-selves.

THE USES OF THE GRID

The grid is a form of abstraction within a written convention. It can be used in many ways according to the analyst's state of mind, according to the preconception he can make of it. The grid is aimed at facilitating a form of thinking *outside* the psychoanalytic session. A session is far too valuable an occasion for observing analytic phenomena for the grid to be used within it. Bion considered two particular types of usage:

- a ' meditative review' in which the material of a session can be examined and controlled;
- a 'psychoanalytic game' through which intuition could be finely honed: 'in a kind of psychoanalytic make believe in which the experiential element is far less dominant' (Bion, 1963, p. 99).

The grid enables the analyst to scrutinize the contents of a session. He uses his memory to recall aspects of the work about which he is doubtful. Assuming that the preoccupation centres on some phrase of the patient's, the analyst manages to locate this phrase in a category by remembering the context in which it was made, and the intonation. It is a new way of registering what has taken place, starting from the elements of psychoanalysis, and of stamping the episode within memory. The grid enables the analyst to find a creative substitute for laborious and often meaningless note-taking. The grid also offers the analyst the opportunity to scrutinize his interpretations in the same way as he scrutinizes the patient's associations. The association and its actual or proposed interpretation are placed in the appropriate categories, and the ensuing *couple* association–interpretation is examined. But instead of focusing on the relation as known to classical psychoanalysis, the analyst can compare the category of association with the category of interpretation.

Besides mnemic registration, the grid offers the opportunity to engage with intellectual speculation: the analyst tries to locate the statement in various categories of the grid, and to see what would have happened. To do this the analyst must 'link' a number of elements and find the meaning of this hypothetical conjuncture. Instead of using the grid for real experiences, the analyst can play at 'make-believe'. Bion thinks of exercising the imagination in this way as an equivalent to the musician who practises scales and exercises rather than on any one piece of music. Just as the musician exercises with the elements of which every piece of music is composed, the analyst trains his intuition on the elements from which psychoanalytic objects are composed.

FROM PSYCHOTIC DREAM WORK TO THE ALPHA FUNCTION

In 1992 Francesca Bion published posthumously another of Bion's books. *Cogitations* gives us insight into the travail that leads from repetitive daily work to the glimmering of invention, and from the creative flight of imagination to conceptual rigour. One of the book's greatest surprises is discovering that the prose style which characterizes the epistemological period is the result of a constant practice of writing. Bion, like most of his Kleinian contemporaries, found writing a very important part of his practice. Even when it is expressed in a more straightforward style, however, his thinking generates many possible meanings. Ultimately, the *Cogitations* do not relieve the reader of ambiguity and uncertainty.

Despite the title of one of the chapters, the book is hardly ever about 'meta-theory'; it is almost always a psychoanalytic diary. The text is about clinical practice and theoretical reading. The reading in question is rarely psychoanalytic, since apart from some to the work of Freud and Klein, the references are for the most part to philosophy, science, the philosophy of science, and some poets.

Unlike most of the writing from the epistemological period, there are some references to clinical practice in *Cogitations*. An admiring reader can discover how theoretical thinking emerges from an event in the session. Bion's style of interpreting makes it evident that he had no desire to imitate either Freud or Klein, but wanted to be completely, recognizably and inimitably 'Bionian': 'More than one patient told me that my technique was not Kleinian. I think there is some truth in this' (Bion, 1992, p. 166).

Here we shall discuss only those parts of the book which concern Bion's attempt to build the cornerstone of his epistemology – the theory of the alpha function, derived from Freud's theory of dreams. Bion's writing allows us sufficient insight into his 'inner world' to enable us to see the steps that led to his epistemological leaps. It was by trial and error, by a cautious and tentative process, that Bion moved from understanding psychotic dreams and hallucinations in clinical practice to the formulation of a new concept which he used to construct a new, more comprehensive and more abstract system.[30]

Psychotic dreams are a means of expelling material absorbed during waking hours. A psychotic should be able to begin to dream if his analysis makes progress. What matters is not the content of the dream but the fact of dreaming. Through dream the psychotic can move from one position to another, to find the creativity necessary to discover the thing that would give depressive coherence to paranoid-schizoid chaos. A psychotic will avoid this emotional experience until he finds, or feels that he has found, sufficient support in a session. He needs this support because his greatest fear is is that the depressive synthesis will give rise to a 'terrifying' super-ego. Bion describes this as a 'murderous' super-ego because it has been rendered vindictive by being fragmented into tiny fragments, and because it behaved 'delinquently' before being fragmented through envy.

The intrapsychic reaching of the depressive position depends on the intersubjective relationship between patient and analyst (just as maternal reverie facilitates the baby's acquisition of the alpha function). Since his time working with groups Bion had thought of human beings as 'political animals' or, more specifically, group animals. He related the play of libidinal and destructive drives to the simultaneous play of narcissistic and socialist tendencies (those that move away from the group, and towards the group), since the group, despite being constituted of individuals, is indifferent to the individual's fate. Bion located 'common sense' at the intersection of these contradictory movements. This allowed him to formulate an understanding of patient's and analyst's shared experience of reality through perception, the elaboration of a characteristic common to all the patient's sensory modes. Reaching the depressive position allows the psychotic patient access to this common sense, which then allows him to dream and describe the dream.

Understanding dreams can progress if the dream can become an experience shared between the patient and his analyst, or at least a shared presence. Since the psychotic reaches the capacity to dream only with the depressive position, the analyst will be able to observe the phenomenon of a dream being experienced in waking reality. Consequently, Bion decided to extend the meaning of the word 'dream' so that it could 'cover the type of things that happen in the analysis of a schizophrenic'. Classical psychoanalysis, the analysis of the *Interpretation of Dreams*, takes into account only one part of dream work, although 'dreaming' is a continuous process which functions throughout waking life.

In one of the very few of his own dreams that Bion describes, we find an illustration of this reversible perspective (Bion, 1992, pp. 51–2). Before falling asleep on the night of 3–4 August 1959, he had been trying to understand a passage in a book by the American philosopher and logician Willard Quine. The theme of the passage was the 'negative'. He dreamed of a 'negro'. Bion uncovered the root 'neg', linking 'negative' and 'negro'. He then associated negative with native. Indigenous peoples reminded him of India, his mother, Hindus, people of colour thought of as inferior. He also thought of the dative in the sense of the gift and of dates, the exotic fruit he liked to eat (Bion does not consider the overdetermination of 'date' through its meaning of 'rendezvous':

with whom?). He adds 'ablative', with its connotation of removing, taking away. Unlike a Kleinian or a Freudian, Bion abandons this associative richness (and conflict) to consider the 'negro' – not as a real person but as an ideogram. He maintained that this ideogram enabled him to condense all these ideas presented (dative) to the reader.

What did Bion mean by proposing that the 'negro' was not a real person? Simply that it was a person from a dream. He differentiated between the status of a representation during sleep – where the 'negro' had appeared to be 'real', and had represented an 'undigested' fact – and the status of the 'negro' in the interpretation given to the reader. By making the 'negro' into an ideogram, Bion had partly 'digested' the fact. The visual image of the 'negro' evoked by the writing is part of the process of mental digestion. In other words, all 'dream thoughts' arise from an 'undigested' aspect of an event. If a person manages to dream about it, this means it has been 'digested'; this then allows them to learn from experience.

One essential difference between neurosis and psychosis is that the former tries to transform the frustration produced by the reality principle, whereas the latter manages to escape it. Although he may appear to have maintained contact with reality, the psychotic does not make use of such contact in order to learn from experience, because he does not have access to the 'dream work' to transform the events of internal and external reality. In this respect the dream seems to function, in mental life, in a way analogous to the process of digestion in physical life. Freud claimed that a 'dream' is the way in which the mind works during sleep; Bion added that the 'dream' is the way in which he worked during waking life.

Without formally stating his method, Bion worked by sliding across the meanings of words, which enabled him to move meaning onwards without completely fixing it. His use of inverted commas facilitated this sliding of meaning, which eventually resulted in a qualitative leap. To posit the existence of a waking 'dream work' was to make a significant theoretical innovation, the force of which Bion tried to attenuate by interjecting an intermediate concept of the 'alpha dream work'. Night dreams are no longer understood as seeking the fulfilment of a wish within an instinctual economy dominated by sexuality. Dreaming is part of the process of 'digesting' truth, which is as necessary to emotional development as food is to the body. Bion challenges Freud's view that a dream is analogous to a hallucinatory satisfaction of a wish, since hallucination is largely aimed at unburdening the psyche of what it cannot tolerate. Consequently, the dream work works in the opposite direction – towards containment, conservation and memorization.

Bion was tempted to contrast the unconscious thoughts of the previous day (the alpha function, which aims realistically to modify frustration, and produces dream thoughts) and night-time dreaming, which avoids the frustration that the dream thoughts would certainly have carried if they were being 'learned from experience' rather than dreamed. He settled for comparing the 'alpha dream work' with Freud's concept of the dream work. In each case he made a distinction between two opposed categories: on the one hand, the movement associated with the pleasure principle – that is, the way a feeling or an idea may be included in an ideogram in order to ablate it, to carry out a hallucinatory expulsion instead of a hallucinatory gratification; on the other, the work linked to the reality principle – that is, the transformation of stimuli received from internal and external reality in such a way that they are conserved, available and integrated.

Bion used the dream of the psychotic as a kind of scaffolding. Once his epistemological construction was built, he let it go. In clinical work he wanted to replace the dream by myth. A myth brings a social version of the phenomenon that an individual knows as a dream. In both cases an experience has been subjected to alpha function activity. Like the manifest content of the dream, the myth indicates that certain elements are linked as constants. It follows that each dream or myth can be understood by only one interpretation – that one and the same story may contain two different, but proximate, emotional experiences: one experienced through the dream, another through lived reality. Certain experiences cannot be understood unless they are interpreted in the light of the dream or myth.

When an individual tells a dream, his conscious communication is motivated largely by curiosity. He subjects a hypothesis to the test of common sense. The manifest content of a dream and a mathematical formula may fulfil the same function even though they are very different. They have the characteristics of the chosen fact and can bring coherence to facts which, although already known, would not seem to be related. Algebraic calculus provides us with a model for finding all the possible interpretative combinations, but this model runs the risk of leading psychoanalysis into an impasse of abstraction. Myth is likely to become, for the analyst, what mathematical calculations are to the scientist. The Oedipus myth brought Freud to more discoveries than any scientific process would have provided. Bion collected all the myths that might cast some light on the problem of learning, especially when learning is linked to a primary emotional experience. He referred particularly to four great myths: those of a Paradise Lost, Babel, Oedipus, and Narcissus. These all emphasize the fact of God's punishment of curiosity. Bion held a view somewhere between Lacan's concept of the 'big Other' [*grand Autre*], and Jung's concept of archetype: 'Berkeley says the stimulus may be God; so does Descartes. I shall maintain there is truth in that . . . ' (Bion, 1992, p. 189).

To summarize: Bion's method was rather different from the accepted view of psychoanalysis. Whereas the latter uses conscious material to interpret unconsciousness, Bion uses the unconscious to interpret a conscious state of mind, linked to the facts known by the analyst. The interpretation of the dream gives the analyst the meaning of the facts and feelings he has experienced.

21 GENETIC EPISTEMOLOGY

The concept of genetic epistemology brings to mind the work of Jean Piaget. Bion never referred to the Swiss psychologist, although he cannot have been unaware of Piaget's work, which was growing in popularity during the 1920s, so that by the 1960s it was very widely distributed, read and discussed. To outline the basic differences between their work, we can start with the fact that whereas Bion considered himself to be working in the context of 'active reasearch', since he thought psychoanalysis was first and foremost a form of treatment, Piaget's work remained at the level of pure science; he was a psychologist first and an epistemologist second. Secondly, Bion established close links between reason and emotion, intellectual development and the development of the whole personality; whereas Piaget studied the origins of intelligence in the socialization of action. Lastly, the psychoanalytic concept of object cannot be integrated into Piaget's epistemology, which explains development in terms of the transition from one structure to another.

The grid remains, above all, an original retheorization of psychoanalysis; it revealed a genetic epistemology.

DISTURBANCES OF KNOWLEDGE

Since theories of knowledge have changed since Freud's time, the psychotherapist, too, sees mental pathology from a different point of view. Bion finally proposed a theory of disturbances of knowledge: misunderstanding on one hand and reversible perspective on the other.

MISUNDERSTANDING $ENVY$

Some patients enter into a bitter struggle to prove themselves superior to the analyst by frustrating his attempts at interpretation. They misunderstand interpretations because they are convinced that an attitude of misunderstanding is superior to one of understanding. Bion proposed that the activity of knowing K is inverted into an activity minus K (-K). He suggests a model for this by infusing the relation between container and contained ($♀$ $♂$) with envy.

An infant may experience fear of dying, and react by splitting and projecting the feeling of fear. The breast, which would appear to protect its calmness, unleashes its envy, and the infant evacuates its envy along with its fear. In a good relationship the breast can attenuate the fear that has been projected into it and the infant can reintroject, in good time, the part of the personality that has been made tolerable. Mental development is thus stimulated. Envy, however, radically excludes this 'commensal relationship'. Instead of leading to K, it leads to -K. The infant feels as if the breast is trying forcefully to insert worthless refuse into it. A 'terror without a name' definitively replaces the infant's fear of dying.

Envy may give rise to an emotion so violent that it seems to lead to the evacuation of almost all the infant's personality. Envy continues its disastrous work by completely spoiling the part projected into the breast. Finally, there is practically no infant left at all to reintroject the terror without a name. The returning object remains envious. Bion, enigmatically, characterizes it as 'the fact of withoutness'. He adds: an internal object without an interior, a digestive tract without a body, a 'super-ego' claiming moral superiority without any morality. In short, this object is the result of an envious dissection and spoiling of all that is good within. This process continues until the negative of the container–contained is rendered invalid. Because of its resemblance to the super-ego, container–contained ($♀$ $♂$) continues to assert its superiority by finding more to pick holes in. It seems to hate any development in the personality, as if this would constitute a new rival.

With -K, alpha elements, however they were created, end up

being transformed into beta elements. In practice the patient feels that he is surrounded not by real objects (things-in-themselves) but by bizarre objects, residues of expelled thoughts and conceptions which have been stripped of their meaning. With the K link, the concretization and particularization of the general and the abstract is possible, whereas with the –K link, if there are abstractions they seem to become things-in-themselves, and particularizations become deprivations.

REVERSIBLE PERSPECTIVE

Bion shows how reversible perspective facilitates the avoidance of the mental pain that is essential to all growth. This conflict is not like neurotic conflict, in which one set of ideas is opposed to another, or one instinctual impulse is in conflict with another. Here the conflict is between the analyst's point of view and the patient's.

Bion returns to the image from Greek mythology. When Oedipus and Laius are opposed in neurotic conflict, reversible perspective pits Tiresias against Oedipus. Tiresias, having gone blind, had the reputation of interpreting the will of the gods better than anyone else. When Thebes was ravaged by pestilence, Oedipus sent for him and asked him whether he could discover the names of the guilty. To his dumbfounded indignation, the soothsayer refused to answer. But, provoked by Oedipus, Tiresias let fly with 'You yourself are the murderer you seek'. Oedipus rejected this interpretation. Inverting the perspective, he attributed this to the soothsayer's folly and expelled him from his presence.

In clinical work, analyst and patient seem to speak the same language, and to agree on many points. The analyst thinks that he is in his consulting room doing psychoanalysis. By going to the analyst's consulting room, in a kind of daydream, the patient imagines that he is also 'doing analysis'. In this fantasy of reality the patient feels filled with intuition and able to see where his problems lie without any help from the analyst. The analyst may feel amazed and delighted by his patient's brilliance and complaisance. Within this setting the patient will bring a dream. He may not believe in his dream experiences, but he succeeds in making his analyst believe in them. The dream, in fact, is an unpleasant experience being directly reported. The patient hopes that the analyst will interpret this reporting as if it were a dream. This would give some

Rubin's vase

Leavitt and Boring's 'young
beauty or old crone'

substance to his daydream reality, in which all this is nothing but a
dream. The patient mobilizes all his inner resources, including the
analyst's reality, to stave off all that might threaten his conviction.

This type of situation can readily be found in the treatment of
quite disturbed patients. The so-called 'dream' may become a
hallucination in the session, if the patient's capacity for daydream
is diminished. How is this possible? The patient seems to accept an
interpretation, while rejecting the premiss that he is consulting an
analyst in order to find a cure for his troubles. He strips the
interpretations of their impact by adopting another point of view.
The antagonism takes place in silence, set aside in a separate,
protected domain. If the patient were to emerge from his reverie,
he would eagerly acknowledge the fact that he is going to talk to
an analyst. The agreement between patient and analyst is analogous
to the representation of two people in diagrams illustrating
reversible perspective. Here Bion uses a more subtle version of the
diagram of the reversible cube which he used in the group period.
In diagram 1, Edgar Rubin's famous example, one person may see
a vase, whereas another may see two profiles. The meaning
attributed to a form depends on what is seen as 'figure' and what
is seen as 'ground'.

Moving from one point of view to another, the non-psychotic

personality acquires a sort of binocular perspective which facilitates psychic development. A psychotic patient uses the reversibility of perspective in order to maintain a single perspective; he 'sees' the interpretation as a function of his own hypothesis, and silently rejects that of his analyst. The reversal makes a dynamic situation into a static one, and prevents all psychic development. The patient may use fleeting hallucinations to shore up temporarily his capacity for reversing perspective. The inverted perspective enables the patient to avoid the discomfort of acknowledging the existence of the parental couple, and of being in overt conflict with his analyst; but the cost of this is that his perception becomes distorted and, in the long term, deluded.

MENTAL GROWTH

Somewhat arbitrarily, Bion offers us a definition of the psychoanalytic object: the notion of growth at the heart of the representation of the aims of psychoanalysis. At the beginning there is the constant Ψ with the unsaturated element (ξ) which determines the value of the variable when the latter is identified. When Bion was tracking the origin myth, he used the concept of the unknown variable to represent 'an innate preconception'. The model emerged of its own logic: the infant has an innate preconception of the existence of a breast that can satisfy its neonatal inadequacy. The unsaturated element and the unknown constant share a component represented by (M); this is an innate characteristic of the personality. The value of (M), like that of (ξ), is determined by the emotional experience created by a realization. In the example used above, it is the encounter with the breast which produces a conception. Bion adds a biological touch to his eclectic definition. A psychoanalytic object is inextricably linked to psychic growth. The latter is represented by $(\pm Y)$, the 'plus or minus' indicating, as it does in geometrical co-ordinates, that the growth may be positive or negative.

The final definition is represented by the formula

$$\{(\pm Y) \; \Psi \; (M) \; (\xi)\}$$

THE PROCESSES

Bion began by making a distinction between thoughts and the mechanism used for thinking them. He considered that thoughts pre-existed mechanism. This facilitated the epistemological approach, because thoughts could be studied without studying the mechanism of thinking, but he had to account for the origins of thoughts. Finally, he had to add a further distinction: between an elementary form of 'thinking' (for the emergence of thoughts) and the activity of thinking (for using thoughts).

The mechanism of projective identification (♀ ♂) and the interaction between the PS↔D positions contribute to development in the same way as they contribute to the use of thoughts. ♀ ♂ and PS↔D act together. Meanwhile, their differences lead us to differentiate between the ways in which each of these processes works. The PS↔D process has the power to unite elements with no apparent logical or factual links. PS↔D thus shows the relations and links between the thoughts already created by ♀ ♂. In other words, the transformation of beta elements into alpha elements depends on ♀ ♂, then the PS↔D process is engaged. Unfortunately, things do not always go to plan in the consulting room. Before ♀ ♂ can work, ♀ must be found. However, the discovery of ♀ (container) depends on the operation of PS↔D (selected fact). So it would seem that PS↔D is as much the cause of thoughts as ♀ ♂.

At the end of these formulations Bion concluded that the main problem was not whether PS↔D precedes ♀ ♂, or vice versa, as these are linked in a 'chicken and egg' sort of dialectic. He navigates the impasse by 'supposing that there is a mixed state in which the patient feels persecuted by feelings of depression and depressed by feelings of persecution'. He envisaged an original situation with dispersed beta elements. This state of dispersal can be understood either as a 'prototype aborted of container' as loosely structured as Jaques's reticulum, or as a 'prototype aborted of content' which compression has given the appearance of cohesion.[32] PS↔D and ♀ ♂ are not two separate activities but mechanisms which can assume each other's characteristics when necessary. Projective identification and the oscillation between the positions should be thought of as 'potentially primary'.

An object is not perceived and given the name 'dog' because from the object perceived a quality of 'dogginess' is abstracted: the term 'dog' is used when and because a set of phenomena is recognized as being interrelated yet unknown. It is used to prevent the scattering of phenomena: 'Having found the name and thereby bound the phenomena, the remainder of history, if so wished, can be devoted to determining what it means – what a dog *is*; the name is an invention to make it possible to think and talk about something before it is known what that something is' (Bion, 1963, pp. 87–8).

The hypothesis of the alpha element is an abstract way of understanding a spontaneous process which is inherent in the acquisition and use of language. The term 'dog' is a preconception which awaits a realization to produce a conception – in this example the presence of a real dog. Mathematical formulae are analogous to preconceptions, as is the grid. The term 'dog' at first signifies only certain elements that are constantly conjoined (a postulation derived from Hume); it is therefore a product of the PS↔D mechanism. Only after the term has served to signal and perpetuate the conjunction does the question of meaning arise. The term 'dog' takes on meaning when the ♀ ♂ mechanism begins to come into play.

Finally, Bion had clarified the relation between the two mechanisms of mental growth: 'On the PS↔D operation depends the delineation of the whole object: on the successful operation of ♀ ♂ depends the meaning of the whole object' (Bion, 1963, p. 90).

MYTHS

Myths offered Bion a privileged position from which to tackle the question of the contents of thoughts-in-themselves. The Oedipus myth may be considered as the tool which was usesd in the discovery of psychoanalysis. Freud abstracted a theory from the myth. When he was studying psychosis, Bion broached the myth from a 'naive' perspective and discovered that the sexual crime concealed an intellectual epic quest. The obstinate and arrogant way in which Oedipus pursues his quest results in blindness and exile. The riddle of the Sphinx expresses man's curiosity about himself. This self-consciousness prefigures psychoanalytic insight as it derives from the K link.

In other myths – not only the Oedipus myth but also the

narratives of the Garden of Eden and the Tower of Babel – Bion finds elements that signify the activity of knowing. Starting from this point of view, he discovers a primitive prototype of emotional growth. The elements he selects are those of the Sphinx, the Tree of Knowledge, and the Tower, respectively. In the Garden of Eden, the Father forbids eating from the fruit of the Tree of Knowledge. The serpent incites woman to transcend the prohibition. The knowledge of Good and Evil leads to the feeling of guilt and expulsion from earthly paradise. In the myth of Babel, men try to enter the kingdom of Yahweh and build an immense tower. Their curiosity is also punished by exile, and by the destruction of a common language. Confusion spreads over the world, so that co-operation becomes impossible.

From these myths Bion extracts components that are likely to 'pictorialize', within us, characteristics comparable to the elements of psychoanalysis:

- A God or fate blocking mankind in his search for knowledge. This superior force belongs to a moral system (it is described in terms akin to the envious super-ego of the psychotic which attacks the ego).
- Penetration or ingestion results in expulsion. Prohibition is especially directed against sexual knowledge and pleasure.
- In each of the situations described in the myth, there is stimulation of forbidden desires.

Bion considers that a private oedipal myth is an integral part of the human mind. It is this individual version of the myth that allows the young child to make real contact with his parents. In psychosis, the oedipal elements are scattered and the patient has no inner matrix through which to apprehend the parental relationship and adapt to reality. One of the difficulties in the analysis of psychotics is being able to recognize the oedipal fragments scattered in time, and to reveal their interconnections to the patient.

EMOTIONS

Psychoanalysis repeatedly proclaims: in the beginning was emotion. Bion's epistemological project would be incomplete without a theory of the emotions. He considered that the K link was an emotional link of the same kind as love and hate. The container is penetrated and the contained penetrates whenever one emotion replaces another. Container and contained should be held in a constant emotion which is open to being replaced by another. The recombining of mental systems requires a freedom which depends on the emotions that impregnate the psyche. These emotions materialize a connective tissue enclosing scientific systems as well as elements of the container.

Bion reminds us that an analysis is painful – not because pain has value in and of itself, but because the patient is moved to undertake an analysis by his suffering. Should suffering disappear once conflicts are resolved? Is the duty of the analyst, like that of the doctor, to relieve suffering in default of a cure? In contrast to these current ideas, Bion thought that the analytic experience should increase the patient's capacity for suffering, even if patient and analyst alike hope to reduce the patient's share of suffering. Bion draws an analogy with medicine: it would be disastrous to destroy the sensitivity to physical pain, unless that pain is accelerating the onset of death.

In order to avoid meaningless suffering, the analyst should be able to discover emotion in a premonitory state. Extending the model of the relation of a preconception to a conception in the realm of thought, Bion considers 'premonition' to be a precursor of emotion. He maintains the term's connotations of being a warning signal. The colloquial distinction between premonition and preconception enables us to reflect on analytic practice, but there is also a similarity between the objects thus differentiated. Therefore, the categories in the grid which enable psychic contents to be identified should also be useful for identifying the emotional content of experience. If the categories are as relevant to emotions as they are to ideas, there ought to be an emotional aspect to the beta elements.

We took as our example for explaining the grid the statement 'I think you hate me', and considered how each of the grid's categories could receive this idea. If the statement had taken the form 'I feel . . . ', the grid could also receive the emotion or premonition expressed in such a statement. In this case the transition from one level to another is still achieved by the ♀ ♂ mechanism. But the model is no longer based on that of the digestive system. Bion suggests that more appropriate metaphors are that of the respiratory system associated with olfactory processes, the auditory system and the visual system. Then the sense of touch can be used in opposition to the confusion created by ♀ ♂. Paradoxically, the proximity of relation that is required by the system of touch is less intimate than the distance in the relation characteristic of smell, hearing or sight. Tactile sensation is reassuring in that it gives the impression that there is a barrier between container and contained.

Bion considered feeling and emotion as virtual synonyms: he used these terms equally to describe acting out, a general tonality, a simple state and a complex arrangement.[33] Bion explores emotion mostly as one component of psychic experience, the other being ideas. It was perhaps through realizing the limitations of his theory of emotions that he then turned towards other directions, such as that of the transformations. The difficulty of covering and containing the richness and violence of emotions in mental life by use of a mathematical vertex led Bion to supplement it with aesthetic and religious vertices.

THE SOURCES OF THE EPISTEMOLOGY

Bion integrated many elements from philosophy and mathematics into his psychoanalytic theory. He gives their sources incidentally, even when the idea in question is employed as fundamental to his epistemology. These intellectual influences bear a family resemblance because they were selected for a shared sensibility and were then integrated into a common epistemology.

Bion turned first to the Vienna Circle, and thereafter to British analytic philosophy. Logical positivism was on a par with Hume (*A Treatise of Human Nature*, 1739). Another influence derived from two precursors of the Vienna Circle: Poincaré (*Science and Method*, 1908) and Frege (*Der Grundlagen der Arithmetik*, 1884) as he was seeking a system for logical abstraction. Bion finally turned to Kant (*Critique of Pure Reason*, 1781) for a theory of knowledge.

From the 1950s onwards there was an identifiably Kleinian school of psychoanalysis. Roger Money-Kyrle initiated this reintegration through his systematic collection of Klein's writings and his own clarifications of them. A scientific corpus that was so 'economically thought' should lend itself more readily to verification. In 1925, while Money-Kyrle was in Vienna being analysed by Freud, he obtained a doctorate in philosophy under the supervision of Professor Moritz Schlick. Schlick was part of the same movement as the eminent Austrian physicist and philosopher Ernst Mach.[34] The Kleinian school thus confirmed its filiation with Freud, each adhering to a philosophical conception of science. Meanwhile the future remained open as the Vienna Circle grouped itself around Moritz Schlick.

In his preface to *Man's Picture of his World* (1961), Money-Kyrle thanks Bion and Jaques for their useful suggestions on the content of his book. Reading the manuscript of this book was crucial for Bion, as it gave him an epistemological base for his own *Learning from Experience*. Bion includes Money-Kyrle's book in the very minimal bibliography of *Attention and Interpretation*, the last of the works from the epistemological period. With this psycho-philosophical model Bion felt that he had a 'scientific conception of the world', which was both empirical and positivist. This was the orientation of the logical empiricists of the Vienna Circle, grouped around Schlick, who in fact used the same phrase as the title of their book in 1929. Logical empiricism adhered strictly to the knowledge gained from direct experience of immediate givens; it also aimed to clarify the statements and problems of empirical science by logical analysis. It challenged the existence of any realm of thought over and above the realm of direct experience.

After the Anschluss, members of the Vienna Circle went into exile in Britain, where they had a strong influence on Anglo-Saxon philosophers and epistemologists. The indigenous tradition comprised a series of more or less parallel projects – from a shared base of presuppositions, albeit with very different objects. At the beginning of the twentieth century the idea of analysis was inseparable from formal analysis (in the sense of mathematical logic). The movement had reached a provisional classicism in Wittgenstein's *Tractatus Logico-Philosophicus*, published in 1921.

This movement opened itself to positivism at the beginning of the 1930s, and provided, through the work of Money-Kyrle, the foundation of Bion's epistemological period. The Neo-Positivists stated their attachment to empiricism (a philosophy which attributes the entire content of knowledge to experience). Philosophy becomes a positivist knowledge in so far as it adheres to the theory and practice of science rather than the transcendental objects of experience. The Neo-Positivists aim at a systematization of the language of knowledge, in the absence of a unified scientific practice. Bion was a Neo-Positivist in that he linked a formalism of language to Mach's scientific empiricism (Ernst Mach, the great Austrian physicist, studied the role of supersonic speeds in aerodynamics, his name becoming used to designate units of speed reached by supersonic aircraft. He later became a philosopher and his critique of Newtonian mechanics was a significant influence on Einstein's work.) This was useful to Bion because he returned consistently to Freud's 'Two principles of mental functioning' (1911). The French historian P.L. Assoun (Assoun, 1981) suggests that Freud based some of his scientific 'capital' on principles discovered by Mach, at times employing his ideas literally.

Mach claimed that a theorist must respect the 'principle of the economy of thought': the task of science is is to reveal facts in such a way that it uses only those representations that are strictly necessary for its experience. While thinking should be turned towards facts, it should also be internally coherent. (Bion proved himself to be a firm believer in the economy of thought; he always maintained that the value of the analyst lies in his ability to encompass every experimental outcome with the minimal number of theories.) Mach thought that each specific science should set out the different forms of interrelation among its elements. There is a continuity between physical and psychic reason because the relations between their respective elements can be unified in one world. In his theory Mach does away with notions of substance, causality, and so on. He denies the duality between psychic and physical realities. 'Empirico-criticism', which he created with the German philosopher Averianius, was both empiricist and idealist. This 'subjective idealism' attracted Freud, Money-Kyrle and finally Bion.

Whereas Bion discovered Mach's theses through secondary texts, he read the work of Henri Poincaré with great care. At the beginning of the century both Mach and Poincaré produced a 'philosophy of knowledge' which had an international impact that is still felt in the intellectual heritage of contemporary thought. Bion was very much struck by Poincaré's creativity. Well past his 'mid-life crisis', he aspired to the creativity of these young geniuses whose dazzling achievements assured them a place among the great mathematicians. A further affinity emerged when Bion introduced the aesthetic dimension to his epistemology. Poincaré was one of thos thinkers who maintained that the main element in mathematical creativity derives more from aesthetics than from logic. This was to be a decisive turning point, verging on Platonism.

Choosing Poincaré was also a question of logic. Bion aspired to create a science which would deal only with the fundamental elements of psychoanalysis. By turning towards the mathematical method he hoped to find these elements, since mathematics is the discipline that makes least reference to sensory data. Located on the borders between logic and physics, mathematics is equidistant from the two founding instances of knowledge: the mind and the senses. Logic and physics were considered to constitute the boundaries of scientific knowledge. However, psychoanalysis could not be said to be a science in the same way, as it is defined by its practice within a reality which is known through the senses. Bionian epistemology, Janus-like, looks both ways: to experience and to pure mind.

In the wake of Poincaré, Bion chose to locate himself upstream of the late-nineteenth-century crisis generated by Cantor's theory of sets. We have seen that he sought to formulate the elements of psychoanalysis in the same way as Euclid sought to formulate the elements of geometry, and that his grid was overtly inspired by Cartesian geometry. We will also see that he derived his inspiration for his system of notation from Frege.

When he was writing *Learning from Experience*, Bion had in mind Frege's *The Fundamental Laws of Arithmetic* – the first book in which a writer attempts an ideographic exposition of a thesis. The parts of the book in ordinary language are simply commentaries on the deduction itself. In seeking a unified science, the Vienna Circle adhered to the principle of rendering concepts and deductive processes with greater precision through the use of symbolic representation, conceived according to a mathematical model. Analytic philosophy later turned away from this logical formalism in order to focus on the analysis of ordinary language.

The evolution of Bion's work moved in the opposite direction. He sought to give psychoanalysis what Frege had sought for mathematics: a 'perfectly scientific' method. Frege, judging ordinary language to be inadequate for this, following Leibniz, developed an ideal language. He considered that exact sciences need a mode of expression which simultaneously prevents errors in interpretation and avoids false reasoning. Such faults were understood to be caused by imperfections in language. Frege judged that an ideographic representation (*Begriffsschrift*, or language by formulae of pure ideation) would be the most appropriate tool for correcting these faults of imprecision and distortion. He sought to augment this language with mathematical formulae, or signs for new logical relations. Ideography borrowed from and restored to mathematics the dual distinction between constants and variables, functions and arguments. Frege presents an analogy between concept and function. Both can be represented by signs comprising two dissimilar parts where the unsaturated sign is complemented by the other. This need for completeness may be represented by empty parentheses or by letters (ξ). We have seen that Bion makes significant use of the concept of Ψ (ξ). He clearly takes his notational system from Frege's ideographic notation, using part of Frege's notational system of the Greek and Latin alphabets, in both upper and lower case. Bion recognized one of the difficulties inherent in the ideographic principle: how could a science progress through the use of ideographic notation when the latter presupposes the former? Similarly, language seems to make rational development (and scientific knowledge) possible, but how could humans have invented language without first developing reason? Rather than perfecting his system of notation, Bion preferred to go back in history. Kant is generally recognized as the originator of something of a 'Copernican revolution', addressing all the major questions of the eighteenth century and giving them new meaning. Seeking 'pure reason' for his theory of knowledge, Bion did not so much 'return' to Kant as select from his *oeuvre*.

Neo-Kantianism (or post-critical philosophy) was often thought of as a theory of scientific knowledge. Great thinkers such as Poincaré decided to base their philosophy on this epistemology. The Vienna Circle had been set up in reaction to the idealism of the post-Kantian schools of thought. Philosophy needed to be revised in the light of the revolutionary early-twentieth-century developments in physics.

While he adheres to logical empiricism, through the work of Money-Kyrle, Bion bases his epistemology on Kant's *Critique of Pure Reason*, and employs the concept of the 'thing-in-itself'. Kant articulated his system in a series of dualities: sensation and understanding, understanding and reason, phenomenon and noumenon. Bion retains the last of these dualities. As a neo-Kantian, he wondered what status to give the thing-in-itself, and decided that it constitutes the limit of our perceptions and cogitations. Materialist principles led him to reject the dualism of sensation and understanding, and he replaced this with a duality between the sensory impressions which constitute perceptions and the logic of relational discourse which makes sense of the perceived objects. Rational activity is thus aimed at elucidating the nature of beta elements. In the end Bion composes a bricolage of intellectual sources, using the 'associative penumbra' of the borrowed concepts to provide unity, while his associative montage generates unexpected links between them.

PART 4b:

THE EPISTEMOLOGICAL PERIOD: THE QUEST FOR ULTIMATE TRUTH

Bion introduces his third book, *Transformations*, with the regret that it cannot be read independently of the two previous works. He finally gave up the hope of writing an independent text, as this would have required an 'intolerable degree of repetition'. In fact, to realize this hope he would have been obliged to rework the first steps of his epistemological system in order to unite a mathematical quest with a mystical hope.

In his sixth book, *Attention and Interpretation*, Bion completed his epistemological project. He wanted to explore the difficulties inherent in representing an experience which does not derive from sensory impression within the framework of a scientific system. By dint of reformulating and communicating this experience, the analyst must necessarily use a vocabulary and syntax which make use of analogy. This language necessarily conceals as much as it explains the search for, and communication of, an ultimate truth. Returning again to Melanie Klein's theories, Bion attempts to build an analogy between theologies, contemporary mathematics and certain psychoanalytic concepts.

22 A Mathematical and/or Mystical Psychoanalysis

On first reading, *Transformations* appears to extend the project set out in the early texts of Bion's epistemological period, but its innovatory use of language speaks of another project at work, one which is initially presented as incidental and complementary to the epistemological project. Little by little Bion introduces us to the hallucinatory world of psychosis, by means of a text which moves between tedium and illumination, bewilderment and genius. How can we learn about origins from anti-thinking? Bion was in no doubt that much could be learned from psychotics and their psychic creations. Is it possible to trace the reality of a patient's hallucinatory experience of an analytic session from the analyst's transformation of that session into a form of representation which will enable it to be communicated to others? Using the mathematician's method and reflecting the psychotic's experience, Bion thought it was possible to develop a theory with which to resolve this problem, and to think about the situation at one remove.

There follows a description of three successive, and interpenetrating, methods. The artist transforming a landscape into a painting enables Bion to re-create the links with the Neo-Positivism of *Learning from Experience* and *Elements of Psychoanalysis*. The concept of the thing-in-itself breaks the links that connect Bion's method to post-Kantian scientific method. A vertiginous return to Plato, fleetingly glimpsed beneath the concept of the thing-in-itself, accords great significance to geometry, but a geometry that is very much more sophisticated than Euclid's or Descartes's. Bion makes illuminating and illustrative use of the abstract structures of modern mathematics. In the final analysis he passes from the negation of

INVariants

language to a negative theology. This disconcerting train of thought readily combines mystical vision and scientific method. Despite its occasional reprising of clinical analytic material, the book applies aesthetic understanding to the concept of deity.

THE THEORY OF TRANSFORMATIONS

Deliberately choosing a concept that derives simultaneously from physics, chemistry, biology and mathematics, Bion proposes to call the immutable elements of transformation 'invariants'. He borrowed the concepts of invariants and transformation from projective geometry in order to apply them to painting. The concept of invariants was fairly widely used at this time – the painter and critic André Lhôte, working in the 1940s, aimed to integrate his concept of modern art with stable aesthetic principles called 'plastic invariants'.

Geometric figures can be subjected to all sorts of transformations, including translation, rotation or projection. The mathematician finds whatever is common to the figure before and after its transformation. Just as the projection of a geometric figure on to a plane alters certain properties while it leaves others unchanged, analysis alters some properties of the session while it leaves some unchanged. Without an epistemology the analyst must discover those invariants that are proper to the discipline, and the relationships between these invariants.

The difficulty here remains the difficulty expressed in *Learning from Experience*: how to develop the conceptual tools required in order to represent psychoanalytic knowledge and the psychotherapeutic process? Whereas Kant, somewhat less ambitiously, enabled thought to move from pure reason to practical reason, Bion works something of an intellectual conjuring trick as he erases the difference between science and art by reducing painting to the representation of the external world. He chooses to ignore the fundamental challenge made to the tradition of pictorial realism by the invention of photography, and the conceptual upheaval generated by abstract and non-figurative art. This act of identifying himself with the historical antecedents of his contemporaries in science and philosophy enables him to adhere to the perspectives derived from Euclidean geometry; but in this field, too, he ignores other geometries that had been in circulation and in use for over a century. From the first chapters one senses that Bion will not find it easy to carry his aesthetic solution through to the end of the project.

Next, Bion turns to the early years of psychoanalysis – to Dora's case of hysteria. With Freud's text he establishes his first link between psychoanalysis and art. Freud gave us a literary account of his patient. Although it is not a painting, isn't this text analogous to a painting? Freud represented his analysis verbally, just as a painter represents a landscape pictorially. He was able to find psychoanalytic invariables in his description. The result of psychoanalytic work should, then, be evaluated as a work of art. Bion suggests that a significant component of the success of Freud's work is its literary quality (for which he was awarded the Goethe Prize). By fusing psychotherapy with its written representation, Bion intended to locate it predominantly within the realm of art. With the theory of transformations, he integrates psychological elements within the genre of aesthetics. However, he does not abandon his previous project to claim psychoanalysis as a science. The rest of the book constitutes his search for a solution to the problem of squaring this circle.

With progressive shifts in meaning, Bion reaches a point at which he can state the fundamental thesis of his second epistemological cycle: it is useful to consider psychoanalysis as part of a set of transformations. Analogous to art and mathematics, the work of an analyst is the transformation of a realization (the analytic experience) into an interpretation or a series of interpretations. The painter works at transforming a realization (for instance, the experience of a landscape) into a representation (a painting). If he succeeds, it is because invariants make his representation comprehensible. Invariants vary according to style and technique, so that an Impressionist painting has characteristics that differ from a Realist painting. Similarly, different psychoanalytic theories and techniques create as many different transformations. It goes without saying that for Bion a Kleinian transformation will not be the same as a classical Freudian transformation. There will also be differences between interpretations of two Kleinians, although they 'belong' to the same school of thought.

Bion finds the sense of his theory of transformations in every situation in which analysis entails a controlled form of breakdown.

Its sense would be more difficult to establish in situations where breakdown has already taken place, or cannot be prevented. Bion cites the example of a patient A, a 'borderline psychotic'. The analysis seems to proceed slowly. Changes in A take place, and his friends and family can no longer deny his illness. The patient behaves strangely, sitting morosely in a chair for hours on end. He seems to be hearing voices and seeing things. In analysis he is hostile and confused. There is a sudden deterioration, and his family become overtly alarmed. They communicate their alarm to the family doctor and to the analyst; the latter has good reason to be alarmed. The analytic experience, which is normally confined to the couple in the consulting room, is now the concern of a number of people.

The psychotherapist should take his own anxieties into consideration, as well as those of family and friends whenever these are made available to him. But above all, the analyst should consider the analytic sessions themselves. If the patient breaks down, the analytic experience undergoes a catastrophic change. It is then that the concepts of invariance and transformations may help. Before the catastrophe, the analysis is not emotional, and is devoid of any marked outward change. Hypochondriacal symptoms are prominent. Violence is confined to phenomena experienced by psychoanalytic insight: it is a 'theoretical violence'. After the catastrophe violence becomes patent, but the ideational content appears to be lacking. Violence invades the analytic experience, whereas hypochondriacal symptoms are less evident.

Bion categorized catastrophic change into three elements: subversion of the system, violence and invariance. The analyst must search the material for the invariants of the pre- and post-catastrophic stages. Bion compares the change to an explosion: the patient's violent emotional state creates emotional reactions in the analyst and in others. They too tend to be dominated by their overstimulated internal objects, thus producing a massive externalization of internal objects. The theory of transformations can usefully be applied to the catastrophic event described.[35] Bion uses the word transformation to refer to three different processes:

- a total operation T, which includes the act of transforming and the end product;
- the process of transformation: $T\alpha$;
- the final product: $T\beta$.

As a psychoanalyst, Bion was interested in a 'function of the personality' in this process of representation, but he did not want to imply that a function of the personality has a 'form', as the word transformation might lead one to suppose. He uses the grid to 'escape' from the implications of form. (Etymologically, the term 'transformation' derives from the Latin verb denoting 'to form beyond'. The concept of transformation also carries connotations of the Platonic theory of form.) The grid's symbols refer to abstract categories which can represent Tα and Tβ. Similarly, Bion introduces another sign to designate 'realization', something which is not a mental phenomenon and can never be known. We can share something of the analysis of Dora by reading Freud's text, even though we have not personally analysed the patient.

Bion illustrates this with a brief clinical example. The patient enters and, according to the convention of that analysis, shakes hands. It is this external fact that Bion calls a 'realization'. In Kantian terms it is a thing-in-itself, and unknowable. Bion designates it by the symbol O.[36] The phenomenon corresponding to the external act, as it exists in the patient's mind, is represented by the sign T (patient) α. This sign, in turn, can be replaced by one of the categories of the grid, the selection of which is determined by the analyst's judgement of the symbolic meaning of the phenomenon.

Bion hoped that in a range of different analytic experiences he would find different types of transformation, which could then be categorized into a system of classification. In fact, he limits his classification to the distinction between psychotic and neurotic types of transformation. He begins by exploring the transformation in which the transference tends to repeat the repressed as an experience, lived in the present, which always contains elements of infantile sexuality, of the Oedipus complex and its ramifications. This entails a faithful reproduction of the original situation. The feelings and ideas appropriate to the infantile sexuality and the Oedipus complex are transferred, almost without distortion, on to the relationship with the analyst. Bion therefore proposes to describe this set of transformations as 'rigid motions'.

He opposes rigid motion to projection. In geometry, transformations by rigid motion – such as inversion, translation or rotation – retain invariants such as size and the fixed angles of a form. Transformations by projection, on the other hand, do not retain these invariants, and are thus more complicated. In psychoanalysis, projective transformations are most often found in borderline patients. They stimulate and frustrate, intellectually. Analysis is so transformed that the intention that it should be healing and rewarding is frustrated by actions intended to wound. Material representing O is brought in a destructive way. Bion compares these patients to landscape gardeners who work to transform the landscape rather than painters who transform the landscape into a painting. Often it is the analyst himself that the patient is trying to transform: the patient considers events far removed from any relationship to the analyst as aspects of the analyst's personality. In this state, the patient is indifferent to the limitations of time and space.

So Bion employs the symbol O to designate reality – in other words, the sense impressions that an individual subjects to the process of transformation. He likens this to Kant's concept of the thing-in-itself, an essentially unknowable entity. By Tpβ or Taβ Bion designates the representation of the process of transformation made by patient or analyst. When the analyst makes an interpretation that is felt by both to be true, the processes of representation, and thus the symbols, can be linked by 'and'. Tpα and Taβ thus denote a representation akin to what Kant describes as a secondary quality. Bion likens it to 'common sense'. In rigid transformations it is the invariants that establish the relation to O. In projective transformations the differences between Op and Oa do not permit of a process of arguing back from Tpβ and Taβ to Op and Oa. The stimulus for projective transformation is apparently Op. Psychic reality has the same capacity for initiating a train of mental events as is possessed by an event in external reality.

At this point Bion refines the analogy between analyst and artist. He differentiates the work of a 'great' artist from that of others. The 'great' artist does not simply make a technical transposition of the elements in the landscape into the elements on canvas – he manages to communicate an emotional experience in a universal and durable way. The analyst helps the patient to transform the part of his emotional experience of which he is unconscious into an emotional experience of which he is conscious. If he does this, he helps the patient to achieve private knowledge. But the analyst has further to transform his private experience into a public experience, to communicate his discovery to other workers, since it is through shared knowledge that scientific work progresses.

Bion uses the artistic process as a model because the analyst's writing must stimulate in the reader the emotional experience that the author intends; its power must be durable, and the emotional experience stimulated must be an accurate representation of the psychoanalytic experience.

Why should truth have been taken as a criterion, and how can it be recognized? Because 'healthy psychic development' seems to need truth, much as the growth of the body depends on food. If truth is lacking, the personality begins to deteriorate. Bion holds this as axiomatic. He justifies his work by saying that he resolves more difficulties than he creates. In opposition to the psychotic period, he classes this axiom in the realm of aesthetics, as it cannot be scientifically verified. Following this, he returns once more to the grid. The grid, however, does not take account of aesthetic reality. Such reality is not part of a high level of abstraction and elaboration: perhaps it shares the categories at the base of the grid with passion and the scientific deductive system?

Bion maintained that the principles of research should be the same whether they are applied to art, mathematics or psychoanalysis. At one end of the process he located the concrete elements that initiate the transformation; at the other he located the equally concrete result. He gives the following example of transformation:

On a calm, bright day a man looks at a lake. The trees on the bank of the opposite shore are reflected in the water. Suppose the man can see only the reflections. He is nevertheless able to deduce, from what he can see, the nature of O. It would be relatively easy for him to recognize the reflection as trees, more difficult for him to identify the species of trees, and impossible for him to deduce the nature of the microscopic structure of their leaves. If changes in the atmospheric conditions of observation distort the reflection, the observer's deductive abilities will be impaired to a greater or lesser extent.

Bion transposes this model of observation on to analytic observation, replacing the atmospheric conditions with the L, H and K links. In this model the trees on the lakeside are deemed to be O. What is the counterpart of O in analysis? He postulates that O is a fact known to both patient and analyst, available equally to both analyst and patient for transformation. Any O that is not available to both cannot be the object of analytic investigation (the perturbation that might be produced by the analyst's personality is minimized by the fact that the latter has, ideally, been sufficiently analysed).

The opportunities for an analyst to observe the relation between different psychotic phenomena is unlimited. No phenomenon located within the field of observation can be ignored because of the general interdependence of phenomena. The mere fact of employing terminology such as invariants, variables and parameters limits the universe of discourse. Analytic interpretations possess certain types of relation which may be applied to the universe of discourse; but they are not identical to the phenomena they represent, because such relations are those of an infinite universe.

Freud had taken a similar path when he defined a universe of discourse in which conscious behaviour is studied by postulating the existence of an unconscious. Bion, on the other hand, did not seek to differentiate between conscious and unconscious, but between finite and infinite. He could only represent the relational forms at the heart of an infinite universe by means of relational forms operating within a finite discourse. Whereas Freud remained focused on the past, essentially living his reconstruction, Bion emphasized the prospective dimension inherent in the Kleinian theory of object relations.

THE GEOMETRY OF HALLUCINATION

In his epistemological period Bion reduced the interaction between the PS↔D positions to its operational aspect, leaving aside the entire emotional and moral aspect of reparation. This – as it were repressed – aspect of 'emotion' was now to make its return. Bion, however, was not the kind of man to allow it to return without transforming it in line with his project. This is the best way of understanding the mysterious emergence of the aesthetic: 'His thought processes were extremely disturbed, many of his utterances being incomprehensible even after prolonged analysis. When I thought I grasped his meaning it was often by virtue of an aesthetic rather than a scientific experience' (Bion, 1965, p. 52). 'Aesthetic' should be taken in its philosophical sense. Bion seems to refer to the division between a transcendental aesthetics and a transcendental analysis, as outlined in Kant's *Critique of Pure*

Reason. Kantian aesthetics studies the *a priori* conditions of perception. If one removes from the object of perception all qualities of sensation, everything that endows it with particularity, the remaining forms are those that are *a priori* to sensation: space and time.

The analysis of psychotics is made difficult by the fact that such patients have little or no capacity for using intellectual or symbolic functions in the presence of a real object. They seem, at times, to be waiting for something to happen in external reality in order to be able to 'think' about it. Similarly, they seem unable to imagine a situation instead of enacting it. They do not seem capable of producing a Tpβ with which to work in the absence of O – in other words, they do not manage to transform O into T.

While the neurotic can know only the primary and secondary qualities, not the thing-in-itself, the psychotic can never know anything but the thing-in-itself. From the time when a psychotic can express himself in words and sentences, it would seem reasonable to attribute to him the capacity for thinking, but it would be more accurate to describe such a patient as 'speaking as if he could transform O into T'. Many Bionian approaches could be used to answer the question: 'Why then, to revert to the point and the line, do these visual images lead in one case to the efflorescence of mathematics and in the other to mental sterility?' (Bion, 1965, p. 57). The term 'mental sterility' does not altogether express Bion's thoughts. Previously he had emphasized the destructive effect of psychosis on the human mind. Now he began to think that the psychotic has something to teach us, as if hallucination and delirium, at least in the context of mental activity in the course of an analysis, are signs of creative power. The psychotic began to become the shadow of those people whose genius is expressed in art, mathematics and mysticism.

In order to forsake the specific explanatory power of science for the study of transformations of the universal, Bion turned to the concept of causality. The psychotic uses a personal theory of causality which merits consideration. But how to consider it without opposing it to the analyst's theory? Klein's study of the intolerance of depression is useful here. The psychotic is persecuted by feelings of depression. His intolerance of depression hinders the interchangeability of the positions: 'The proposed chain of causation can then be seen as a rationalization of the sense of persecution' (Bion, 1965, p. 57). The chain of causation re-emerges in the argument, just as the analyst's presentation of phenomena also rests on a theory of causality.

Psychotics find it easier to resolve their problems if they locate them on a moral plane. Their feelings of omnipotence can be expressed by sheer force of control (instead of feeling that they are impotent in the face of a totally external reality). Every one of us is liable to collude with such a solution, as is evident in the dominance of morality in all human groups. The atmosphere of a basic assumption group is fundamentally hostile to individual thought.

Bion returns to the example of the hammer which 'forces' in a nail; he considers the relationship between two people when one feels that the other is forcing him. The beta elements and the bizarre objects are constituents of morality. For this reason the link between two of these types of object, or between this type of object and the personality, will be imbued with feelings of responsibility and guilt. The theory of causality, in its scientific sense, is used to move an idea from the moral plane to an inappropriate domain. Nevertheless, Bion uses the notion of causality in relation to clinical material: 'The patient entertains a transformation (it might be of a loved object) because of the hatred he feels for the person O of the analyst' (Bion, 1965, p. 68). But he claims to use the notion only for convenience, to make himself more easily understood.

Although the content of the material is very important for analytic practice, the theory of transformation touches only tangentially on the question of content. Bion aims to focus on the form of the communication. His thinking weaves an intellectual slalom through the fundamental figures of geometry, illuminated with elementary representations of psychoanalysis:

- the point or dot: the breast;
- the line: the penis;
- the circle: inside–outside.

Bion conducts what is dangerously close to an exercise in style when he considers that every end result of the transformations is capable of being represented by points, lines and circles. This exercise is intended to prepare the analyst to 'see beyond the superficial', to enter into contact with 'the central experience'.

It all starts with the infinite varieties of the presence and absence of the object to which we relate from the beginning of life. Some patients use the point and the line – or equivalent signs in painting, music or everyday speech – as if they were things. Moreover, they are convinced that other people do so too. When they hear someone say the word, or when they see the sign in print, these patients behave 'as if the point marks the place where the breast or penis was' (Bion, 1965, p. 76). This is the basic statement from which Bion builds erudite logical variations. The patient seems to endow 'this place' with the characteristics that a less disturbed person might attribute to a ghost.

The point (.) and the word 'point' are understood as manifestations of the 'no-breast'. The observer begins to realize that words or signs are being used to indicate the presence of an absent breast. The place where the breast was takes on the characteristics of a hostile breast (since its disappearance is cause enough to make the patient operate a negative transformation of it). Instead of representing a breast, the word 'breast' is thought of as the external manifestation of a 'no-breast'. This new perspective makes it impossible to use the point as a mathematician would, to construct a geometric system. This same perspective is also opposed to the elaboration of artistic, anatomical and physiological systems from the starting point of the abstraction of the breast. When (.) and (–) correspond to preconceptions, the latter represent the place where (.) and (–) used to be. These signs could be used for thinking about objects in their absence. They can be combined to form a geometric figure, a drawing, or alphabetical letters.

Bion thought that the narrative form given to the Oedipus myth could be misleading. The story links the narrative events by introducing a causal relationship, aiding memory by registering a constant conjunction. The notion of causality is appropriate to the story, but not to the corresponding realization in which the elements are simply linked. The realization derives from a transformation. No transformation can take place without an emotional experience, the model of which is the violent scene that takes place at the crossroads to Thebes. The existence of psychosis means that all the terms used in *Learning from Experience*, *Elements of Psychoanalysis* and *Transformations* can have two values: one as sign of a constant conjunction, the other as the position occupied by the object. Bion gives the conventional notation of minus (–) for the 'position it does not occupy'.

A change is brought about when a fragmenting attack against the present is carried out, reducing time to a continuous 'now'. The minus point (–.) and the minus line (– –) retain meaning, as no-things, because a trace of the object remains even when the object no longer occupies the position it once occupied. But when time is reduced to a moment without future or past, all meaning vanishes. This state is not static; a destructive force continues to operate even when everything has been annihilated. The problem of this process (represented by ← ↑) may be stated by analogy with existing objects – it is violent, greedy, envious, ruthless, murderous and predatory, without respect for truth, persons or things. Bion suggests that it is what Pirandello might have called 'a character in search of an author'. But in so far as it finds an 'author', it appears to be a completely immoral conscience: 'This force is dominated by an envious determination to possess everything that objects that exist possess, including existence itself' (Bion, 1965, p. 102).

Since the object no longer exists after its total annihilation, the characteristics we have attributed to the force that destroys it should also cease to exist. This would seem to be true – except in the mind of the patient, who appears to entertain the phantasy of a self-contradictory object, and to identify with such an object; so that the contradiction then lies in his existing sufficiently to 'feel that he does not exist'. The rule that a thing cannot both be and not be is inadequate; in its place we find the rule: 'A thing can never be unless it both is and is not'. To put it another way: 'A thing cannot exist in the mind alone, nor can it exist unless at the same time there is a corresponding no-thing'. The rules that apply to the thing do not apply to the no-thing. By analogy, if Shakespeare's character Falstaff is a no-thing, Falstaff also exists; and if he has more 'reality' than people who really exist, then this is because an actual Falstaff exists![37] In psychoanalysis the invariant is the quantitative ratio of no-thing to thing.

The patient wants the analyst to make interpretations in order to deny the complete absence of meaning. The breast plays an important part in learning by supplying the infant with meanings. Ultimately the fear of the total destruction of the breast implies not only the fear of the annihilation of the infant (who cannot materially survive without the breast) but also the fear of the disappearance of meaning itself (as if meaning had a material existence). The fact that the analyst gives interpretations masks this fear, as they seem to offer proof of the existence of meaning. The patient, for his part, lets out a flood of words, in order to provoke a reply confirming the existence of meaning. It is impossible to find the meaning of a given conjunction unless it is acknowledged that the phenomena in the conjunction may not have any meaning. The inability to tolerate the absence of meaning prevents curiosity from emerging; the same holds true for feelings of love and hate. The patient also manipulates the analyst's countertransference in order to prove that love and hate exist. He reassures himself by using his energy to deny a nonexistence; but he also deprives the interpretations of all effectivity.

Due to its extreme envy and greed, the nonexistent 'object' goes as far as annihilating space and time. In turn it fears either being the victim of this annihilated 'space', or becoming its slave and having to satisfy its insatiable desire for destruction. The psyche seems unable to coexist with this 'space'. These kinds of fears may be found in the analysis of claustrophobic or psychotic patients. The Mad Hatter's tea party in *Alice in Wonderland* gives us some idea of what happens in this type of world.

An accumulation of conceptual slippage led Bion to a boundary: on the one side the sphere of scientific mathematics, on the other the sphere of mathematicians, artists and mystics. A little later he makes explicit reference to 'Dodgsonian mathematics'. He intermittently defines his wish to find a system of notation, both supple and precise, which would simplify the psychoanalytic task. His efforts to do so succeeded only in uncovering problems of still greater complexity, and in adding philosophical enigmas to scientific problems. Meltzer describes it thus: 'In the present work no such hope sustains us in the face of the proliferation of mathematics-like notations, pseudo-equations, followed by arrows, dots, lines, arrows over (or should it be under?) words, and not just Greek letters but Greek words. How are we to bear such an assault on our mentality?' (Meltzer, 1978, p. 71). In his text Bion reproduces the difficulty which is experienced in encounters with psychotic patients. It comes as no surprise when he writes: 'If I re-read one of my own notes, knowing it embodies what to me was knowledge when I wrote it, it can seem tautological or to express a meaning so inadequately that if an interval of time separates me from the state of mind in which I wrote it it fails to communicate its message even to myself' (Bion, 1965, p. 109).

The first problems encountered concern the link which unites two people. The breast can be thought of either as an inanimate object or as an object endowed with personality. Furthermore, it can happen that no distinction is made between animate and inanimate. Depending on the problem in treatment, one or other solution is taken. The efficacy of the solution is judged by the extent to which it is or is not a source of growth for the patient. Certain patients change their attitude towards an object by changing their point of view. This strategy implies a split in time and space; the result depends on the intention that motivates such a change of perspective. A perverse perspective does not permit a solution to be found, as existing 'binocular vision' has been destroyed. On the other hand, it might be that a scientific method approaches a solution by providing a substitute for the 'binocular vision'. The split helps to establish a correlation, as all the split-off fragments have then to be reassembled. Correlation, which implies a creative reunion or reassemblage, is impossible when the splitting is the result of aggressive drives; creativity may stimulate aggression.

In *Transformations* Bion presents for the first time a clear explanation of his concept of vertex. The use of the term 'vertex' indicates that a sophisticated mathematical term is being used (category H1) and that it is being used as a model (category C1). In the period of transformations the fundamental method of knowledge consists of a binocular psychic vision and a multiplicity of interchangeable vertices.

The analytic situation was first conceived as providing the patient with a base on which to carry out his transformations (a 'frame' in Bleger's sense?). Even though this base may not always be ideal, Bion considered that it was stable. It allows the patient to transfer his images on to the person of the analyst, but this description of analysis does not adequately include the mechanism of projective identification. To recognize the elements of projective identification as and when they appear in the analytic situation is not of much use – the analyst must be able to identify the signs of projective identification in a (so to speak) multidimensional field. The mathematical concept of vectorial space is useful for conceptualizing these multidimensional objects. This conceptualization allows Bion to discern the relation of the paranoid-schizoid position to vectorial space, which he describes as being analogous to the two points of view in a reversible perspective. The analytic space requires a breadth and depth greater than can be found in a model drawn from Euclidean space.

PSYCHOANALYTIC GNOSIS

Rules are by nature arbitrary. Bion turned his attention to the speech of patients that can be seen as emanating from category A6 of the grid, when the mind functions as if it were a muscle. The psychotic patient fails to differentiate between things and thoughts, so that the real meanings of words, such as would be understood in a rigid transformation, seem to be expelled from the mind much as the lungs expel air. From the moment when a communication is part of a projective transformation, it can rightly be assumed that the patient is expelling 'something'. The patient uses his eyes and the mental equivalent of sight to effect an expulsion. Bion had discovered a 'transformation in hallucination' corresponding to what he had considered to be a 'catastrophic change' maintaining the 'transformation into O'.

The psychotic patient considers hallucination to be a means of mastering independence. He creates material using the organs of perception as a means of expulsion. This gives him the feeling of having entirely created the world which surrounds him, and if that world is not perfect, it is because malevolent forces have intervened. Pleasure, like pain, becomes a means of scoring points in a mental confrontation. In treatment the patient finds means of affirming the superiority of rivalry, envy and hatred over compassion, co-operation and generosity. (Note that gratitude is still excluded from the Bionian vocabulary.)

A patient who hallucinates presents the analyst with a dual problem: the problem of his real trouble is overlaid by the problem of his self-generated solution to his trouble. This takes the form of a conflict between the patient's method and the analyst's method. As long as this duality has not been illuminated, no progress is possible. The illumination of the problem does not make it disappear – it persists, but this time within the patient. The more the problem emanates from an innate disposition, the more the patient deems hallucinatory transformation to be a superior solution, and the greater is his need to be the 'victor'. The problem is that such patients are convinced that their feeling of well-being and their vitality emanate from the very characteristics that cause their trouble. They are intensely afraid of losing parts of their personality, as even if they are 'bad' in the eyes of their analyst, they appear to themselves to be the source of all mental 'health'.

A person hallucinates when they saturate a predetermination with an evacuation of the personality, and are convinced that they have entirely created the product of the evacuation. What is this predetermination that has taken the place of the preconception? To reply to this question, Bion 'borrows' more philosophical material which he considers likely to facilitate his task. He begins with borrowing from Plato's theory of Form (it is worth noting that most commentators prefer to use the concept of Idea rather than the concept of Form). Ideas or essences are perceived only by intelligence, which is not dependent on sensory experience. Our senses hamper us by being bound to material reality. The allegory of the cave locates the sensory world in the cave lit up by the fire, and the intelligible world outside illuminated by daylight. The soul connects man to the sacred sphere of Ideas. Desiring Goodness or Beauty would be impossible if we did not already have some idea of these things. We seek Truth only because we have already known it, and must have encountered Ideas in a previous existence. The goal of philosophical work is to make us remember what once existed. This theory of reminiscence is based on faith, and the belief in the reincarnation of the soul in successive lives. Plato, it seems, shared this faith with the Pythagoreans. Although this area is not one in which the influence of oriental philosophy has been detected, it is nevertheless present, as it is in other aspects of Bion's work.

Throughout *Transformations*, philosophy provides Bion with the project of a totalizing theory which then prefigures a new epistemology, and a new approach to the theory of knowledge. Philosophical intuition becomes a mediating point at which Bion reorders his ideas in relation to facts. Like Freud before him, Bion felt the need to find epistemological legitimation of his ideas in the writings of philosophical genius. Thus Plato becomes a precursor of Klein's theory of internal objects.

Klein considered that envy had a basis in biological constitution; she also thought that the infant had an innate and unconscious knowledge of the mother's existence. But she insisted that an internal object cannot be formed unless there is a perceptual encounter between internal and external realities, and that this encounter transcends the limitations of representation. In *Transformations* Bion sought to formulate a general theory of the internal object, drawing on the Platonic aspect of the Kantian philosophy he had already used in his developmental epistemology. Any psychoanalytic practice inevitably deals with Kantian phenomena. The interpretation of such phenomena, however, stems from transformations such as a representation of the individual's experience of O: 'but the significance of O derives from, and inheres in the Platonic Form' (Bion, 1965, p. 138). In Plato the discourses of philosophy and religion are fused, as it is the soul that connects man with the sacred sphere of Ideas or Forms. Next Bion makes a lateral move by replacing the philosophical description of the internal object (Plato) with the representation of the internal object in the discourses of mysticism.

Within Christian mysticism Bion deliberately chose the work of Meister Eckhart, a fourteenth-century German Dominican monk whose work became the basis of late-nineteenth-century Renan mysticism. Unification with God becomes destiny, and is also the basis for the discovery of material reality. God can be described only within the limitations of our forms of thinking, although He transcends all the terms that we may use to describe Him. Because of the limitations of thinking about that which has no beginning and no end, Eckhart used the term God [*Gott*] to designate the God of the Trinity and of Creation, and Godhead [*Gottheit*] to designate the divine power and origin of the Trinity. God and Godhead are as different from one another as earth and heaven. (Bion conceived of birth as an incarnation of the psyche, and stressed the importance of the caesura of birth.) God operates, whereas Godhead is irreducible to activity. God and Godhead differ, just as activity and inactivity differ, and Bion sees this difference as related to the opposition between K as a form of knowledge which implies action in the world, and O as a form of knowledge which emanates from being. Eckhart's representation of the nature of Godhead or divine essence is built up through repeated negations; in some ways he was the originator of a growing movement in philosophy which uses negation to define hypotheses. The Word was made flesh, and became Christ, so that mankind, justified by grace, could return to God through him and by him. Here we can see Bion's intellectual affinity with a doctrine for which the redemptive aspect of divine incarnation is relatively unimportant, or at least secondary; this is very much like his own view that gratitude and reparation have a relatively secondary role within Kleinian psychoanalysis.

Renan mysticism is often criticized for seeking to translate something which transcends reason into rational terms. Eckhart, too, made an effort to explain everything in logical terms, even at the cost of losing whatever surpasses discursive thought. Frustrated by the expressive impotence of words, he was led further and further to try and communicate the unspeakable. These same observations could be made of a large part of the work of *Transformations*. Eckhart's prose leaves as little space for emotions as it does for visions.

Anxious at the prospect of sacrificing mystical genius to burgeoning scholasticism, Bion makes a characteristically surprising about turn. He explores the work of St John of the Cross, a Christian mystic whose lyrical poetry retraces a mystical journey and whose work expresses intimacy with God in terms which are very evocative of the emotions of human love. Bion's intuition completes the circle, as St John of the Cross was certainly very much influenced by Pseudo-Dionysius, a disciple of Proclus, one of the most systematic and classical of the Neo-Platonists. St John also influenced the mysticism of Renan.

Bion was very much taken by the 'extraordinary agreement' which unites all the disparate mystics who describe an experience of encountering ultimate reality (although, as we have noted, he actually limits his selection of mystics to the Neo-Platonists). He thought that St John's text *The Ascent of Mount Carmel* was the best description of his inexpressible experience, and that the soul seeking to be united with God provides an accurate analogy of the suffering of the psyche growing through psychoanalysis.

Through the terrible Ascent, the goal is reached. One meaning of O is simply the original experience of which the patient speaks – or, in other words, the experience which includes the facts and events that form the basis of his reactions. Above O there is ultimate Reality, absolute Truth and aspects of the Primary Cause. Bion adds to Plato's concept of Idea (or Form) and to Eckhart's concept of the Godhead, respectively, the philosophical and mystical descriptions of the problem, his own concept of hyperbole. All scientific research involves a certain amount of distortion, because some elements have to be amplified in order to become significant. Exaggeration can help to clarify a problem.

Primitive emotions need a container to 'detoxify' (Bion, 1963, p. 67) them. Emotion must be exaggerated in order to obtain the help of a container, but it may be that the container cannot tolerate the emotion. The emotion then becomes amplified through neglect and in a desperate effort to obtain attention; this may, unfortunately, result in its being evacuated ever more violently. This gives rise to hyperbole, a constant conjunction of an emotion and an increasingly powerful process of evacuation. Using the term in a psychoanalytic sense, Bion emphasizes the factor of exaggeration and the sense of distancing, of projecting outwards. Hyperbole refers to the realizations that psychoanalytic theory describes as projective identification. A transformation in which envy and evacuation are at work can be recognized through manifestations of hyperbole.

At the end of *Transformations* Bion asks how it is possible to bring about a transformation from knowing about a real self to being a real self, through the use of psychoanalytic interpretation.[38] While Klein conceives of growth simply as a process of integrating the split-off parts of the self in order to strengthen the ego, Bion explores the process of this alienation and the trajectory of the split-off elements of the self. He focuses on the abyss which separates the personality from reality, and on the inaccessibility of O. Rather than conceiving of O as the starting point of a transformation, O is made into the representation of ultimate reality, of good and evil. Mystics alone believe that ultimate reality is not inaccessible, and in the end Bion's sympathies are with the mystics.

The personality must – in the words of Milton's *Paradise Lost* – be 'won from the void and formless infinite'. Before we can begin to make the unconscious conscious, we must engage in a process of linking through K, which contrasts with the process by which O is brought into being. K enables us to differentiate between feelings of inside and outside, between internal and external objects, between container and contained. How are we meant to understand the transition from Eckhart's dark and formless Godhead to the Holy Trinity of the Scriptures? Bion suggests that the transition between unknowable and knowable is brought about by the number three: 'The Godhead becomes, or is made,

space between opposites
tension of opposites
ouroburos

mathematical' (Bion, 1965, p. 70). The configuration which seems to coexist in all developmental processes – be they religious, aesthetic, scientific or psychoanalytic – is a progression from a 'void and formless infinite' to a saturated formulation which is finite and is associated with a number. For a long time Bion had been of the opinion that a discipline cannot be considered scientific if it is not mathematical. With tremendous regret, and with wry humour, he realizes at the end of *Transformations* that all his efforts have led him only to create a mathematics worthy of Lewis Carroll.

23 Psychoanalysis without Memory or Desire

Following from *Transformations*, Bion began to revise his system of notation of psychoanalytic experience. His 'second thoughts' (later to be used as the title of his annotated work from the psychotic period) enabled him to begin a radical change in his conception of the thinking processes of the practising analyst at work. He subsequently wrote and published *Attention and Interpretation*. There he discovers a psychoanalytic practice defined negatively, the analyst's frame of mind of being without memory or desire, and ultimately without comprehension. Achieving this frame of mind requires much time and effort, and is essentially a spiritual approach to the self.

Bion's clinical concerns move from the psychotic's misunderstanding of reality to the 'perversion' of knowledge by lying. A liar's inventions are evidence of a certain creativity. A lie, like a notation, is not the product of an individual but requires the existence of an interlocutor or group. The relationship of a group to the exceptional individual such as the mystic is based on the relationship between container and contained. The final thoughts of the epistemological period deal with the transition from catastrophic change to the language of achievement. True thought manifests itself as a prelude to, or substitute for, action.

REVISION OF THE SYSTEM OF NOTATION

After *Transformations* Bion collected together his articles on psychosis and published them in their original form. He satisfied a public demand for access to what was seeming, in retrospect, to be a unified corpus of work. But a man like Bion, who was so driven by the need to be creative, could not be content to rest on his laurels. He took the opportunity afforded by collecting his articles to add a commentary, and the collected essays were published as *Second Thoughts*. The commentary is not so much a revision of the perspective gained in the psychotic period (a vertex which he always recognized as of value) but, rather, a series of thoughts on the notation and recording of analytic practice.

The juxtaposition of the original articles and the new commentary shows how much psychoanalysis had changed over the fifteen years that separated them. This temporal gap which separates the texts gives rise to a dual perspective that is greater than the sum of the two parts of the early and later perspectives. Memories of experiences in clinical practice over the preceding decade linked Bion with his earlier self, but by 1967 he felt alienated from his earlier notation and rendering of that practice.

The mature analyst reread the works of his analytic youth and felt uneasy. He thought his good intentions had proved to be the worm in the apple of truth. Nothing is more fundamentally commendable than the concern to protect the anonymity of the patient, the basic rule of confidentiality. But this type of falsification inevitably fails through a sort of 'basic lie'. Bion was aware of distortion in his writing, as he knew it was impossible to write a true version of what really happens in analysis. The analyst has a technique which allows him to acknowledge his involuntary distortions of memory. But even despite this, in writing he works with memory as a historian or a scientist rather than a psychoanalyst. Memory, the product or residue of sensory experience, best serves experiences of this kind. Notations based on sensory perception also record only what is foreign to psychoanalysis.

The analyst's reaction to his patient will be all the more subtle for being less bound to sensory data. The greater his wish for a precise interpretation, the greater his difficulty in describing a state of mind in terms of sensory impressions: 'The patient's associations and the analyst's interpretations are an ineffable and essential experience' (Bion, 1967a, p. 122). The psychotic's reaction to an interpretation is usually orientated more towards the ineffable aspect of the communication than towards its verbal meaning. In the course of an analysis this difficulty of communication is minimized by the shared nature of the experience. The difficulty becomes amplified when the analyst tries to communicate this experience in writing. Bion took the opportunity offered by the second publication of his essays to explore the complexity of this difficulty, since it presented him with the problem of the communication between the analyst who had written the essays and the analyst who was rereading the work of his 'former self'. However, conditions for perfect communication were still not present. In his early years Bion had developed the habit of taking detailed notes on sessions. He was aware, even then, that in the short time between writing the notes and reading them later he became less able to follow their meaning. In fact, he now speculated, he probably understood them no better at the time of writing them than he did rereading them some ten years later. They seemed to him like notes made in a half-waking state of mind in order to record an important dream; in the morning the scribbling is still there, but the latent content of the dream has disappeared.

This kind of preoccupation led Bion to experiment with different ways of taking notes and, years after publishing his article, to decide to stop taking notes altogether. One reason for this was his feeling that although notes have meaning, they do not refer to a past event but are formulations of a sensory image which is evocative of the future. The visual images relating to the past and the future belong to the grid categories C3 and C4 respectively. Although on the page these categories appear adjacent, they are in fact separated by a great mental 'distance'. When notes record the past, they aim to evoke so-called unconscious memories (either forgotten or repressed). If they aim to describe the future, they must be conjecture or prophecy on what has not yet happened.

A related problem is the evaluation of the 'speed' of thought. Again, this is not simply a matter of intellectual debate but is grounded in clinical practice, where it is of significance. It may happen that a patient perceives the meaning of an interpretation very quickly. The analyst, however, realizes, a few moments later, that the patient has not understood anything of what he has apparently heard. The speed of thought has enabled him to foreclose the statement he heard before he has had time to understand it. The formulations of 'time' and 'space' should be transformed in such a way as to make a new formulation that is not so abstract as to become a form of wordplay, nor so burdened with meaning that it prevents growth. The capacity for anticipation is one of the main things an analyst should develop. An analyst should be able to have the widest possible range of thoughts and emotions. He should be able to think about the patient's potential suicide as part of becoming a psychoanalyst.

FROM MEDICINE TO PSYCHOANALYSIS

In *Attention and Interpretation* the reader is made aware of a sense of closure. The elaborate logico-mathematical and linguistic apparatus of the preceding books becomes little more than an infrastructure to be referred to when appropriate. It is used as an accessory, and the main object of study is the state of mind of the analyst and his analysand. Bion now uses the term analysand rather than patient, as medicine is no longer an appropriate model. An unbridgeable chasm separates the doctor treating sensory experience and the psychoanalyst who deals with an experience which is not derived from sensory data. Bion repeatedly states that anxiety has no form, no colour, no smell nor sound. He proposes to use the term 'intuit' to designate the work of the analyst in contrast to the sensory action of the doctor.[39]

This new state of mind, without memory or desire, is necessary not only for treating psychosis – it becomes necessary for all analytic practice, as hallucination exists alongside thought – as a kind of anti-thinking. The fundamental tension is between patient A, who is incapable of tolerating frustration or pain, and patient B, who is capable of becoming or being a psychoanalyst, and capable of such toleration. Some patients have very great difficulty in accepting reality, especially if this reality happens to be their state of mind. They are so incapable of tolerating pain that they feel pain without being able to suffer it; they cannot be said to 'discover' it. What is it that they are unable to tolerate or to discover? The answer to this can be inferred from the experience of patients, like the analyst, who allow themselves to suffer. The problem is that the patient who does not want to suffer pain is not able to 'suffer' or endure pleasure. Where B can understand that a word represents a constant conjunction, and can thus explore its meaning, A feels something which is not there; he is incapable of distinguishing between the thing which is not there and what is there, or hallucination.

As the concept of hallucination has a long and loaded history of meaning, Bion prefers to use the term 'beta element'. This enables him to relate the 'hallucination' encountered in clinical practice to the 'thing-in-itself' of philosophical speculation. These parallel concepts are grounded in the basic axes of space and time. For a long time Bion had been fascinated by the discoveries made in geometry about the nature of space. He realized that in order to be able to use its abstract concepts – such as point, line and space – in psychoanalysis, he should be able to identify them in relation to their psychic origins. This is not so much the perception of the three-dimensional nature of space as the realization of the emotional life of the psyche. The concept of geometric space is a product of an experience of the perception of 'a place where something once was'. This, in turn, must become part of a discourse in which it is meaningful to say that a 'feeling of depression' is 'the place where there was once the breast or any other lost object', and that space is 'where depression or any other emotion used to be'. The realization of three-dimensional space is present to our minds as visual mental images, which therefore have limitations that disappear into mental space as soon as any attempt is made to represent them in terms of verbal thought. In the imagination an infinite number of lines can pass through a single point, whereas the representation of such an image on paper would limit the number of lines that could be depicted. Bion hypothesized a 'mental space as a thing-in-itself, which is unknowable but which can be represented in thought' (Bion, 1963, p. 22).

All thinking is a form of realization about objects which can be represented in three-dimensional space. Patient A cannot tolerate this because it implies the frustration inherent in all realization, which necessarily occurs within the reality principle. Patient A lacks the alpha function: he has no access to spatial mental images. He lacks the apparatus which would enable him to represent mental space. What happens to him when he has an experience in which patient B might have recourse to projective identification?

Bion conceived of a kind of antithesis of the mechanism of projective identification. A cannot project parts of his personality because the very limited nature of his reality has prevented him from recognizing objects. He has no concept of a container into which projection might take place. Nevertheless, A needs to evacuate undesirable parts of himself, and he expels them into what the analyst understands as the realization of mental space – that is, a mental space which lacks the visual images that might fulfil the functions of a co-ordinating system (which has O as the point of intersection). As a result, the patient feels a sense of such a vast immensity that even the astronomical concepts of space cannot provide representational metaphors for it. The analyst, however, must be able to contain this explosive experience within the limits of the human body.

Bion describes this process using the analogy of surgical shock: 'In this the dilatation of the capillaries throughout the body so increases the space in which blood can circulate that the patient may bleed to death in his own tissues'. Compared to any realization of three-dimensional space, mental space is so vast that the patient's capacity for emotion is felt to be lost, because emotion itself is felt to drain away and become lost in the immensity. What emerges as images, thoughts and verbalizations must now be considered as the debris of dialogue, or as emotions floating in a space so vast that its limits, either spatial or temporal, cannot be defined. In this mental space all events are synchronous, and time can be thought of as a distance.

PSYCHOANALYTIC ASCETICISM

'The analyst must focus his attention on O, the unknown and unknowable' (Bion, 1970, p. 27).[40] The success of psychoanalysis depends on maintaining this point of view in which O signifies the psychoanalytic vertex, ultimate Reality, absolute Truth, the Godhead, and the thing-in-itself. O may be an evolution or a development, but it can never be known. The analyst can identify himself with the vertex represented by O; he must 'be' it. In so far as he can become O, he is capable of knowing the events that are the evolutions of O. This absolute occurs only incidentally in the sphere of knowledge, when it has evolved to the point of being known from experience and formulated in terms of the sensory world. In other words, everything that is part of the sphere of knowledge comes to us from the elaboration of O.

Translated into the the terms of analytic practice, this means that the analyst uses his senses to know about what the analysand says or does, but he cannot know the O of which words and behaviour are a transformation. He must wait for O to be manifested in the K of actual events. At times clinical manifestations may seem to him like obstacles in his aim to become O; at times they may seem like actual events that put him on the path of O. The encounter between analyst and analysand cannot occur except through the senses, but the psychoanalyst is concerned only with psychic qualities which the senses cannot apprehend. The more he focuses on actual events, the more his activity depends on thinking, which derives from a background of sense data. Inversely, the more the analyst is real, the more he manages to engage with the analysand's reality. He then has the opportunity to make an interpretation which facilitates the transition between knowing reality and becoming reality. The same holds true for the reader: he should disregard what Bion writes until the experience of reading has evolved to a point at which the actual events of reading give rise to an interpretation of experience.[41]

This is why Bion advises a radical change in the analyst's attitude when he is working in sessions: a state of mind in which memory and desire have been set aside. This is one of the aspects of Bion's work that the psychoanalytic institution found most intolerable. He locates the origins of memory in the process of projective identification, which he identifies as the mental mechanism which performs certain tasks before thinking is able to take responsibility for them. Projective identification creates an exchange between a container and a contained: at first a breast and a mouth, then an introjected breast and mouth. Under the pressure of the pleasure principle, the contained is evacuated in order to become transformed into something pleasant, or something considered to be pleasant; or, more simply, it is evacuated in order to find the pleasure of being contained. The container absorbs evacuations for complementary reasons. It has the option of rejecting in turn, or of receiving. Thus it is a prototype of memory which forgets or retains. This faculty of memory retains the limitations of its sensory origin. The more memory accumulates, the more it is full of saturated elements. Furthermore, the impulse to rid oneself of painful stimuli means that memory retains only objects of pleasure and expels objects of unpleasure. As a container for the evacuations of projective identification, memory cannot be of much use to the psychoanalyst who seeks O, or absolute Truth.

Memory works with desire. If one could live without memory, desire would also disappear, and vice versa. Even while he differentiates between memory and desire, Bion notes the characteristics they have in common. They are both derived from sensory experiences, and from feelings of pleasure and pain. They both exist in experiences of pleasure and pain. To allow oneself to be totally immersed in memories or desires entails total saturation. Preconception is excluded as desire and memory occupy a space which should remain unsaturated. An analyst may find an illusory feeling of security in becoming totally immersed in memory and desire, for these provide instantaneous saturation, but he then loses all possibility of being unified with O. Bion uses the 'opacity of desire and memory' as the foundation of a general theory of resistance (a concept which Kleinian analysis overlooks). The psychotic has no recourse to the defence of resistance; he obtains a similar effect by multiplying the resistances of his analyst. Using this mechanism the psychotic will activate the desire and memories of his analyst, and lead him to choose understanding over intuition.

'The analyst has to *become infinite* by the suspension of memory, desire and understanding.' He will inevitably feel dread, like 'one on a lonesome road . . . who knows that a frightful fiend doth close behind him tread'. The suspension of memory, desire and understanding would seem not only to be in direct opposition to the established psychoanalytic technique and practice, but also to duplicate what in fact occurs in severely regressed patients. Bion himself warns us that 'there are real dangers associated with it' (Bion, 1970, p. 47). This process is recommended only for those practising analysts whose own analysis has brought them to some recognition of the Kleinian paranoid-schizoid and depressive positions. The mysteries of *Attention and Interpretation* are revealed only after a long apprenticeship. And yet, however prolonged or thorough his training analysis may be, the practising analyst who tries this 'disciplinary procedure' will find it disturbing. The more he manages to exclude memory, desire and understanding from his mental activity, the more he is likely, at least at first, to feel painful emotions that are usually excluded, or concealed by social conventions.

He must be able to believe in the existence of an absolute Truth: otherwise the ultimate reality of O cannot evolve to the point at which the mental functions, linked to the senses, can recognize it. As soon as memory and thought intervene, faith (F) is no longer needed. The act of faith is based on an acceptance of the unknown, since nobody knows what will happen. The hypothesis that it is possible to be at one only with absolute Truth is as essential to science as it is to religion, even if it is the mystics who are closer to the experience of it. From Bion's point of view, the act of faith derives from a scientific state of mind, and should be freed from its usual religious connotations.

Bion recommends that some essential notes should be made about the patient's age, members of the family, past illnesses, life circumstances, address, telephone number, and times of sessions. These facts can then be forgotten, because the sensory background of which they are a part can be given notational form. The mind then has greater freedom to recognize inherently psychoanalytic phenomena. 'By rendering oneself "artificially blind" through the exclusion of memory and desire, one achieves F' (Bion, 1970, p. 57). F brings us to the psychoanalytic vertex. It frees us from the peculiarities that make us creatures of circumstance, leaving us with those features which are invariant, with the 'irreducible ultimate man' (who can become at one with ultimate reality).

Bion returns to this theme in the Brazilian Lectures, citing the scientific discoveries in radio astronomy of the 1950s. An idea that was once thought perverse and stupid – listening to the interference noise on radio rather than to the broadcast programmes – led to the discovery of the 'noise' of stars. Radio astronomers discovered 'black holes' in the spatial equivalent of the astronomical field. The black hole is a part of space in which the gravitational pull is so intense that no light can escape from it. A large star can become so condensed that it becomes a black hole, a point of immense energy. This analogy may help us to recognize the nature of the psychoanalytic asceticism Bion describes. Just as radio astronomy was discovered by setting aside the field of vision, so a psychoanalysis of ultimate reality is reached through leaving aside sensory data; as Freud describes to Lou Andréas-Salomé in a letter: 'I have to blind myself artificially to focus all the light on one dark spot'. This statement becomes a leitmotiv of Bion's work; he links

Zen

it with Milton's blindness, through which Milton was able to find access to God, the Light of all.

Since desire and memory rest on sense data, the analyst must try to suppress them. The closer he is to achieving this, the more likely he is to slip into a sleep akin to stupor, a state which resembles some acute psychotic states, characterized by the amplification of residual sensory perception, particularly hearing.[42]

The exclusion of sensory experience decentralizes the pleasure principle from its prevalence and reintegrates the reality principle. One can easily conceive of the extraordinary discomfort thus produced. Two types of reaction aim to avoid this discomfort: one consists in accumulating knowledge by isolating it from the process of growth; the other is to attribute events to the 'supernatural', and thus prematurely to saturate the process of experiencing.

Bion realized fully that to exclude memory, desire and understanding is to some extent to sever one's connection to external reality. To avoid misunderstanding, he explains how this analytic technique differs from a pathological breaking of links with reality – that is, the way in which his technique differs from psychotic thinking. First, Bion's method implies a partial and temporary exclusion of reality, followed by a conscious, disciplined and deliberate process of transformation of intuition into speech. Secondly, this technique is not aimed at forming a psychotic defence: whereas the psychotic aims to break links, the analyst is aiming to establish and strengthen them. Bion aims to diminish the contact made through the senses in order to allow psychic reality to be apprehended in its own dimension. He concludes this explanation with some thoughts on symbolism.

The psychotic does not always behave as if he were incapable of forming symbols – in fact, some psychotics seem to find symbolic meaning where none is apparent to the analyst. These actions, symbols or events seem to them to have the meaning of a message that is personally addressed to them. The 'symbol' of the psychotic is less a symbolic equivalent of something than a message to the patient that he is intimately connected to a deity or a demon. It represents a conjunction between the patient and a divinity which the patient regards as a constant. A symbol usually represents a conjunction which a group or society regards as a constant.

what about Numinous? Zen?

THE INVENTION OF THE LIE

As he encountered more cases that could be classified as being on the borderline between neurosis and psychosis, Bion became fascinated by the extraordinary ease with which some patients boldly assert statements which are obviously untrue. Liars present the analyst with a difficulty which could, on reflection, lead him to explore the philosophical problem of truth. Both psychotic patients and liars attack the foundations of psychoanalysis by destroying free association. Whereas the psychotic will unconsciously prevent any association from being formed, the liar deliberately falsifies the play of associations.

Bion had often heard Klein say that 'liars are impossible to treat' (Bion, 1977c, p. 215). Like her, he considered the tendency to lie to be a symptom of severe personality disorder, but he did not think it impossible to treat liars psychoanalytically. If it was possible to treat schizophrenics, despite their disintegrating attacks on the associative chain, so it ought to be possible to analyse patients who punctuate the associative chain with pure invention, or even present entire fabrications. At one point Bion thought that every schizophrenic capable of maintaining treatment must have a neurotic part to his personality. Similarly, he anticipated discovering in liars in treatment a coexistence of false and mendacious statements. The false are simply the result of humans' inability to accept the truth, whereas the mendacious are the falsification of those who have perceived the truth.

Bion thought that liars tend to create a veritable 'counterculture'. With his characteristic flair for irony and droll humour, he tells a mythical narrative of the 'universal liar' who attempts to establish the superiority of the lie over science (taken in the inclusive sense of a universal search for truth). Liars throughout history and across the world have known how to maintain a protective illusion for those who might be shocked by scientific truth. For its lack of sincerity, humanity should be mourned and remembered at the tomb of the Unknown Liar.[43]

Lying, unlike psychosis, need not hinder social existence – and it may even confer highly prized competence in some spheres, such as espionage, national security, and some religious sects. Bion thought that the psychoanalytic sphere should be expanded to deal with those mental states which are usually the 'hunting ground' of professionals such as thieves, burglars, sexual perverts, murderers and blackmailers.

The liar's speech can be as plausible and convincing as the speech of a scientist. Are all words equally valid, then? No, because reality puts words to the test when they become enacted. A man who throws himself off a cliff because he believes in his ability to fly will probably find himself in hospital, or end up in the cemetery, because of his belief. An intellectual approach to the same experience leads us back to the concepts of O and the vertex. The Bionian system does not countenance a split between the O of belief and the vertex of survival, nor between the O of survival and the vertex of belief. Every belief can find a vertex that will utterly validate it. The problem may remain purely epistemological, as everything becomes a matter of 'precedence' or priority.

Bion tended to categorize lying as a form of human creativity, and to attribute to it the 'pleasure of creation'. He places it somewhere between a *folie à deux* and artistic collaboration, but refers also to the sadomasochistic collusion between a poisoner and a victim (a metaphor connoting physiological intoxication as well as moral corruption). Unfortunately, his use of paradox does not allow this interesting hypothesis to be fully explored. The reader experiences a conflict (followed by lassitude and boredom) when Bion continues to oscillate between the lie as pathology and the lie as the art of survival. He finally reaches the conclusion that true thoughts have a different status from lies.

Exploring another dimension of the problem, Bion supposes that the liar needs an audience in order to be satisfied. He needs a public to value his inventions. In the analytic situation, the patient can lie successfully if he manages to get the analyst to accept his statements as being true. Bion maintains that the PS↔D reaction, which makes a coherent unity from disparate and scattered elements, cannot be the same in falsity as it is in authenticity. The scientist discovers a unity which seems to belong to a pre-existent reality, while the liar needs to pre-exist the pseudo-discovery. Just as, epistemologically, thoughts precede thinkers, the liar, epistemologically, precedes the lie.

With these epistemological reflections Bion provides a way of separating the wheat from the chaff in psychoanalytic practice. The truth does not necessarily need a thinker, whereas the lie cannot be separated from the liar who thinks and formulates it: in other words, the thinker is logically necessary to the lie. A true interpretation may be recognized by the fact that it is not derived from the knowledge, character or experience of the analyst who speaks it.

THE RELATIONSHIP BETWEEN THE MYSTIC AND THE GROUP IN TERMS OF THE MODEL OF CONTAINER – CONTAINED

Bion returns to explore a familiar idea: since extremes resemble one another, genius must be close to madness. However, his original thinking turns this familiar adage into an interesting observation: 'Psychotic mechanisms require a genius to manipulate them in a manner adequate to promote growth or life' (Bion, 1970, p. 63). Such an exceptional individual may be considered to be a genius, a messiah or a mystic. Bion prefers to think of such exceptional individuals as 'mystics'.

The mystic and the group are mutually dependent, but the relationship between them is necessarily one of conflict. The group needs to maintain its coherence and identity. This need works against the need for growth, and the group needs an exceptional individual in order to achieve growth. Similarly, the mystic cannot develop his gifts and reach his aims without the group. He must conform to the laws of the group, and help the group to achieve its destiny, but at the same time he could not be a genius without casting doubt on, or even destroying, the rules of the group; this, in turn, threatens its coherence. In other words, all (institution-alized) groups have difficulty in containing the mystic.

Some patients present similar problems, for they cannot, or will not, explore their conflicts or predicaments within the analytic setting. Theories of 'acting out' may be of some use in such contexts. However, the patient who 'acts out' can be contained within existing theoretical formulations. The process of acting out also has its analogy in the psychic sphere: it can generally be contained within analytic theories. The mystic is an exception; he contains the idea that is likely to bring about catastrophic change, and because of this the Establishment has difficulty in containing the mystic.[44] At this point Bion turns to the example of the groups that run psychoanalytic societies and institutions. One of their most controversial activities is the formulation of rules and regulations for the group so that those without any aptitude for being psychoanalysts can at least have an experience of psychoanalysis. At the same time, however, the rules must help rather than hinder the affiliation of exceptional individuals, since they are indispensable to the existence and vitality of the analytic group.

Bion challenged the difference that is sometimes made between the nihilistic mystic who provokes the destruction of his community and the creative nihilist who refuses violence against his own group. He asserts the necessarily 'disruptive quality of the mystic' (no doubt because the hagiographical tradition idealizes creative qualities), and reinterprets the main features of the Jesus legend and Christianity within a psychoanalytic framework. He finds in this legend a striking illustration of a society's attempts to contain and control collectively a particularly explosive idea and individual. At the same time, the group dynamic was nothing more than the particular forms created by this society's attempts to contain. After Christ and Eckhart, Bion discusses Isaac Luria, one of many Jewish mystics, known as the proponent of the new cabalism which grew among exiles in Spain in the sixteenth century, and sought to transmit its culture throughout the Jewish community, to prepare it for the coming of the Messiah.

It would be wrong to attribute to Bion social, political or religious objectives. He chose to address himself specifically to a psychoanalytic vertex, leaving others the opportunity to bring complementary configurations to the same subject. Bion claimed to have identified a configuration which is repeated across different historical eras and has taken many different forms. This kind of mythological narrative is constructed by the group in order to give imagistic form to people's inner worlds. Imagistic language is opposed to the metapsychology approved of by classical psychoanalysis. For instance, in the second topography, where the psyche is described in terms of ego, super-ego and id, there is both an abstract formulation (Category F) and verbally formulated imagery (Category C), which is a direct product of the senses.

Bion conceives of the relationship between the messianic idea and the mystic, and between the mystic and the group, in terms of a container and a contained. The relationship between a container and a contained can be one or more of three types: commensal, symbiotic or parasitic. Bion gives several definitions, varying according to whether it is a question of the relationship between thought and thinker, or of mystic and group. The mystic can, in fact, contain the idea as much as be contained by the group. In the commensal relationship each term exists in its own right, and the two coexist peacefully. In symbiosis, the two partners influence each other mutually and productively. Parasitism, by contrast, creates general destructiveness. Bion thought he had found a universal structure for the representation of the relationship between two part-objects, such as the mouth and the breast; two whole objects, such as the patient and the analyst; or an individual and the group, such as the therapist and the group, or Freud and the analytic community.

FROM CATASTROPHIC CHANGE TO THE LANGUAGE OF ACHIEVEMENT

A good analyst must practise at the risk of insanity, just as a good officer commands at the risk of losing his life. In the analysis of psychosis, all change is inevitably represented as catastrophic. Generally, a successful treatment must include the treatment of the psychotic part of the personality. The mark of the experienced practitioner is not that he avoids crisis, but that he can successfully control it. Conversely, a novice risks leaving his patient with the 'terror without a name'. Such a patient may well break down, and the violent emotions within him will then be directed outwards against his environment and the community. What should have remained a question of thoughts will be no more than a series of actions and reactions.

Bion thought that catastrophic change and the human mind were inevitably linked. In 1966 he wrote an article specifically about this, and he takes up its themes again in the final section of *Attention and Interpretation*. The relationship between the messianic idea and the mystic, between the mystic and the group, steers a course between the Scylla of phobic avoidance (stultifying conformity, empty petrification) and the Charybdis of explosive acting out. The path towards emotional growth is scarcely wider than the biblical eye of the needle. The group fears that the messianic idea or the mystic might provoke a schism, a splitting, or even an explosion within its centre. The group usually finds it difficult not to fall back on drastic defence measures: to compromise or spoil the messianic idea; to destroy, bureaucratize or drive out the mystic. Whenever ordinary people must follow an exceptionally gifted individual, there will inevitably be a crisis. Bion often uses the metaphor of a nuclear explosion to indicate the scale of the subjectively felt danger. (Did Bion here replace Klein's concepts of persecutory anxiety and depressive anxiety with his own concept of catastrophic anxiety?)

Psychoanalytic thought must lead to action, or to some equivalent. Bion's solution to the conflicting needs of thought and action was formulated in his concept of the 'language of achievement'. His concept of this is very much influenced by a letter Keats wrote to his brothers in 1817, in which he describes his admiration for great writers, particularly Shakespeare, in terms of their 'negative capability; that is when a man is capable of being in uncertainties, mysteries, doubts, without any irritable reaching after fact and reason' (quoted in Bion, 1970, p. 125). Leaving aside Klein's concept of the depressive position, Bion takes on, almost to the letter, Keats's definition of the 'state of patience' which is as indispensable to cultural creativity as it is to interpretation.

An idea, nurtured by love, develops from a basic matrix and functions only if it is translated into the language of achievement. The counterpart of this 'celestial' destiny is psychotic hell. Envy can make the idea undergo repeated splitting. Ideation (the production of ideas) increases, but on inspection all ideas turn out to be the same one. This pathological process is based not on the splitting of the object but on the splitting of envy. Each 'bit' grows independently of every other 'bit'. Rather than using the concept of the negative therapeutic reaction, Bion proposes the more accurate definition of a 'proliferation of fragmented envy' (Bion, 1970, p. 128).

PART 5:

THE FINAL PERIOD

The stages in Bion's work can be grouped into temporal phases with some degree of accuracy, especially since each period has a major unifying theme; we have identified these as groups and their structure, the subjective structures of psychosis, and the problems of a general theory and epistemology of psychoanalysis. Towards the last stages of his life we cannot apply this model of a unified theme; instead, we find a new tendency to review and conserve the past, while speculating on the future of the discoveries made and charted. All the earlier themes are juxtaposed, synthesized and partially renewed. We have chosen, therefore, to characterize this phase in terms of the new forms of expression that Bion develops here. These include:

- accounts of discussions and conferences;
- a literature of fantasy (The Trilogy);
- the autobiography.

Before discussing each of these in more detail, we will sketch a general outline of this group of texts, which are mostly based on spoken material or on self-referential writing. During his years in California Bion felt, in a confused way, that he was creating for the last time – he felt that his 'abilities were not what they had once been'. He adapted to this partly by expanding and renewing his forms of creative expression, partly by compromising and finding an equivalent to his abundant, rapid and definitive creativity as it was before this mid-life crisis. The first stage of this comprises the conferences and seminars. Since he no longer wanted to write – or, perhaps, no longer felt able to write – Bion began to speak. He introduced turbulent sentences, he improvised; within this nascent discourse, some of the formulations were already familiar; some of the anecdotes had already been told, and were repeated as a kind of discursive ritual.

Then this revered psychoanalyst wanted to show that not only did he appreciate poetry, but he was also a poet. He was able to listen to the voices of his reverie, and to find words for them in a literary trilogy of fantasy. The author comprises a multitude of often illustrious people; he choreographs their appearances and exits, and orchestrates their interactions. The author is completely incarnated in his writing – sometimes as an omniscient and timeless being making universal syntheses, sometimes as an obscure and fragmented individual making a specific and subjective comment. In the flow of writing Bion tries to find an alternative to becoming petrified in the caesura of death. No longer seeking ultimate reality – a reality beyond language – he transforms language into a form of intoxication. Why did Bion set about writing his life story? It is difficult to write an autobiography that is not an apology, or a justification, or a personal search for understanding. Bion refuses to lie in his autobiography – not only to not write untruth, but above all not to inflate himself or his actions. Always wary of being mistaken for someone else, with his typically ironic black humour he emphasizes that his autobiographical efforts run the risk of reinforcing the very connotations he detested.

Deliberately avoiding the anecdotal, Bion's self-referential writing oscillates between the trivial and the significant, so that the meaning of these diffracted texts is not always immediately apparent. All the projected characters are alike because they appear on the screen of a waking dream. Much remains on the surface, even towards the end of a long life, so that the power of memory must reanimate significant events to rescue them from disappearing into the depths of oblivion. It is the form in which Bion chooses to transmit the secrets of his life that gives power and significance to what might otherwise be a rather narcissistic literature.

24 THE CALIFORNIA YEARS

Towards the end of the 1960s, some analysts in Los Angeles became interested in the work of Melanie Klein. They invited some of the better-known Kleinians from London to speak to them. Bion was their third guest, and his hosts were so impressed with him that they asked him to stay on indefinitely in Los Angeles. Bion agreed. Close friends knew that his decision to leave London was based on his reluctance to take on the mantle of the leadership of the Kleinian group after the death of the founder herself.

The Bions left for the USA on 25 January 1968, and settled at 225 Homewood Road, Los Angeles. In his letters to his children, Bion shares his sense of wonder. He could hardly believe it was winter – the sun shone all day in an azure sky. It was a joy to discover the 'real rain' of his childhood in the Punjab. Moving to the west coast of America was not an easy business. The couple had left behind a peaceful, rather traditional world, and entered an environment that was quite foreign to them, as well as being itself in rapid transition. These social changes were to be as challenging as they were stimulating. This move took place when Bion was over seventy years old. He realized that an Englishman in California would not be entirely welcome; and with his characteristic dark humour, he added that if an analyst is ever welcome, he is failing in his work . . .

The invitation to California came after much considerable and long-term work. Bion's professional reputation as an outstanding analyst was beginning to spread beyond the shores of England. He was very pleased to be invited to participate in a conference in South America. In the same year as he moved to Los Angeles, he went to Argentina, where he was shown around by Leon Grinberg, an eminent Kleinian. His hosts here also proved to be very impressed with their guest – in 1972 they wrote and published the first book on his ideas, which was subsequently translated into many languages.

It was the vast scale of the continent of America that reactivated some of Bion's memories of his childhood in India. Flying over the Amazon, he remembered the Ganges he had admired in Delhi. But this trip was also a time to reflect on the situation in California. Compared to the 'very enthusiastic reception' in Argentina, Bion found the atmosphere of Los Angeles 'astringent'. He made a great impression on the few analysts who were interested in the Kleinian School – the memorial anthology which Grotstein edited for Bion's eightieth birthday testifies to this. But Bion was almost unknown outside this narrow circle. The Los Angeles Psychoanalytic Society even stipulated that there should be a limit to the number of their training analysts with an object-relations orientation.

The rate of population growth in California was one of the highest in the world, so that the population of Los Angeles consisted of people who had moved from all over the USA. This accounts for the fact that part of the population was very receptive to radical counterculture, and to exotic religions. Bion arrived in California at the height of the Vietnam War, the race riots and student protest demonstrations. He was not prepared for such cultural competition.

Bion developed an enthusiastic following among some groups, but he rapidly began to feel pessimistic about this success, and found that 'Envy, rivalry and hatred are the spiritual nourishment from which we must live' (Bion, 1985). Psychoanalysis had serious rivals in other forms of therapy: family therapy, behaviourism, non-verbal Gestalt groups, biogenetics, to name but a few. Moreover, there was a tremendous vogue for all sorts of esoteric practices of oriental inspiration.

Bion's own 'return' to India was through the great literature of Indian culture and history. He had wondered why the *Mahabharata* seemed familiar to him as he read it.[45] He discovered that the narratives of these Sanskrit texts must have been told to him as stories by his Indian *ayah*. It seems that the journey to California allowed him the opportunity to reintegrate his earliest thoughts.

After 1973 Bion was accompanied by his wife on all the major journeys and conferences. She had already been of tremendous help to him in his writing and publishing, not least because she had some secretarial training. She now became a true collaborator. That year the Bions went to São Paulo for two weeks of seminars and lectures (at the invitation of Frank Philips, who had once been Bion's analysand after being analysed by Klein). His reception in Brazil was even more enthusiastic than it had been in Argentina. He was such a success in 1974 that he was invited to return to São Paulo and Rio de Janeiro to give more lectures and supervision. In 1975 he went to Brasilia and then, in 1978, to São Paulo for one last time. The proceedings of the seminars and conferences he gave there were rapidly published to enable wider dissemination of his work and ideas.

Bion had gradually become known as an author who refused to market himself. Only once, in 1977, did he allow a New York publisher to reprint the four books of the epistemological period. Over the years he had had to settle for publication through small or unknown publishers. Both volumes of the autobiography were published posthumously, and his literary trilogy *A Memoir of the Future,* which proved the most controversial and least understood of his works, was published at his own expense. The book that sold the most copies was the small book on groups, the collection of his first writings.

Family life, however, was a source of great happiness and satisfaction to Bion. Parthenope married an Italian musician, Talamo, and moved to Turin to work as a psychoanalyst. Julian had read medicine at university, and was working as a GP. Nicola trained as a linguist.

In his spare time Bion often visited the good bookshops in Beverly Hills. He could be recognized by his idiosyncratic walk: 'a military parade-ground gait'. He surprised people with his distinguished accent, which evoked an 'aristocrat from another time and another place . . . and paradoxically a great commoner, albeit a most uncommon one' (Grotstein, 1981, p. 4). In 1978 the Philipses invited the Bions to spend the summer with them in their house in the Dordogne in France. This inspired Bion to buy a very old farmhouse nearby, and he spent many happy summers rebuilding it. Bion had always loved France, and found great happiness there.

25 TRADITIONAL OUTPUT

For the last time, Bion returned once again to the grid. With its double function, the grid could now be seen to offer mutual protection to the mystic and to the 'Establishment'. He then turned to a new subject: the 'caesura' which separates intrauterine life from the years of early childhood. Returning, metaphorically, to the embryonic mind which can lead either to psychosis or to genius, Bion wrote a final article in which he speculates whether it is possible to work analytically with this caesura and its emotional turbulence.

Bion signified the important changes that had taken place for him by giving the name *Seven Servants* to the new edition of his collected works on epistemology, published by the New York publishers Aronson. The metaphor is Kipling's, and his six 'honest serving men' are named What, Why, When, How, Where and Who. The seventh pillar of wisdom is one, Bion suggests, that we, as individuals, each bring for ourselves. This title signified the passage from knowledge and apprenticeship to wisdom.

FINAL THOUGHTS ON THE GRID

The grid had not been altered since its original formulation, but the new state of mind which now informed psychoanalysis meant that it could be reviewed in a different light, and Bion explores this in *Two Papers: The Grid and the Caesura* (1977c). Whereas at first the use of the grid had been illustrated with the Oedipus myth, Bion now turned to the illustration of the excavation of the royal cemetery of Ur, the city of ancient Sumeria. Burial and pillage now became the two images which represent the typical domain of the analytic activity. Around 3500 BC, in Sumeria, the kings were buried in a special place, the 'rubbish dump'. Buried alongside the royal corpse were the bodies of a sacrificial group of royal courtiers. Eventually the sacred burial ground was used to inter less illustrious people, and gradually it lost its significance. Some five hundred years later the riches buried along with the bodies attracted pillagers, and most of the treasures of Sumerian funerary culture were stolen.

Bion deconstructs the images of the burial and the pillaging as if he is analysing a dream, thereby freeing the constitutive elements from the narrative thread which connects them. From the new disorder of the elements, a new structure emerges. What kind of emotional power could lead a small elite group to kill themselves? Could it be claimed that they acted unknowingly, as in the accidental death of a young child? Ignorance, or not-knowing, is simply not an adequate solution, so something else, such as the power of religion, must be taken into account. Bion reflects on the pillaging of our Western pantheon of science. Could it be that scientists, archaeologists and – especially – psychoanalysts are motivated by greed? Bion took some time to explore these questions, and his explanations were characteristically frank. While the title of this book indicates that it is primarily about the grid, Bion's thoughts range across a number of ideas, from a clinical vignette to analysis of myth, searching for a final expression of an essential, absolute and ultimate Truth. He ends, inconclusively, on the antinomy between omnipotence and distress. Unable to provide theories of these, psychoanalysis nevertheless makes fundamental use of them to understand psychosis and phenomena such as basic assumptions in groups. Bion finds a potent metaphor in the myth of the death of Palinarus.[46] A young child overcome with envy and greed feels his distress as an injustice inflicted on him by the 'gods', just as Palinarus rages against the unjust sacrifice ordained by Venus.

From this narrative fragment of the *Aeneid* Bion constructs a model to which an analyst can may refer in formulating a construction from a patient's material. Differentiating between interpretation and construction, he considers the former as formulated in contact with the patient and the latter as worked

through and evolved at some distance from the material, especially
through the use of the grid. The grid functions as a buffer,
protecting psychoanalysis as a nascent science, still in its infancy,
from the upheaval that genius may create, and offering the ordinary
analyst a method of bringing his own intuition closer to the
intuition of genius.

ALL IS NOTHING BUT CAESURA

Throughout Bion's later works we come across the metaphor of
psychic birth, which he found so significant at this time. Like Freud,
Bion emphasizes the objective fact of the newborn infant's
helplessness. Without the capacity for effective co-ordination, the
newborn infant is completely dependent on its environment,
especially the mother. Helplessness at birth and during infancy
gives rise to a state of emotional distress – *Hilflosigkeit*, as Freud
terms it. The psyche is entirely dependent on the relationship to
another for its development and its growth. Bionian theory suggests
that the helpless infant soon develops fantasies of omnipotence,
which protect it from the realization of the mother's real power.
The baby is able to achieve some emotional control through this
illusion of megalomania, if the maternal care offered allows it to be
retained and used.

Through desire to overcome and master these humble origins,
the infant develops superior forms of knowledge. Mental growth
takes place in sudden and abrupt stages which release anxiety
about change. Every significant stage brings with it a paroxysm of
anxiety as the psyche is threatened with disintegration and
collapse. This anxiety also accompanies every act of emotional
creativity. Bion's original contribution was to identify the origins
of this ongoing process in the irrevocable separation of birth. Freud
conceived infantile distress as the prototype of every traumatic
situation which creates anxiety. Bion returns to this concept,
integrating it into his theories of omnipotence and mysticism.

In 1926 Freud made a major revision of his theory of psychic
conflict in the neuroses, to provide an explanation of anxiety which
did not depend on the binary opposition between the two basic
instincts. Klein did not follow Freud; she proposed instead that the
unconscious includes the death instinct from birth, and that from

the earliest days of life the ego is subject to anxiety emanating from the conflict between the two basic instincts. Bion had gradually removed instinctual conflict from his epistemology; although it returns with some force at the end of *Attention and Interpretation* as a major component of envy.

Somewhat later Bion takes up Freud's comment that 'inter-uterine life and early infancy are much more continuous than would be imagined from the striking fact of the caesura of the process of birth' (Bion, 1977c, p. 243). Out of context this comment becomes ambiguous, as the caesura can be interpreted in a number of ways. Freud meant that the mother's early 'psychological' care is an equivalent of the biological environment before birth. Bion reverses this point of view, and interprets Freud as meaning that something of the spiritual or mental life must exist before birth, in intrauterine life. This long journey of the soul or psyche accounts for the fact that humans find it so difficult to achieve spiritual growth.

Bion then sought a guiding principle – like Freud, who was trying to make a metaphorical equivalent of Haeckel's speculations on embryology. Haeckel had discovered vestiges of earlier evolutionary forms of physical organs within the organic forms of the embryonic human body. Freud wondered whether there might be, in the adult human mind, vestigial traces of foetal sensory and cognitive activities. If Freud was right about the caesura of birth, there ought to be a continuity between emotions and thoughts, before and after birth: 'Or exaggerating the question in order to simplify it, should we consider that the foetus thinks, sees, senses and hears? And if so, to what extent are these thoughts, feelings and ideas primitive?' (Bion, 1977c, p. 44).

In the consulting room we sometimes come across events that evoke intense and inchoate feelings, which may be so basic or so powerful that they may be experienced as physiological or anatomical. Bion spoke of 'sub-thalamic' or 'para-sympathetic' feelings.[47] He notes that when pressure is applied to the eye sockets, images are formed which cannot be a response of the optical system. It may be that we re-experience the way in which the optical cavities responded to pressure before birth.[48] This may be one of the intuitions that a practising psychoanalyst has; however, he cannot use it as the basis for an interpretation unless he connects intuition with its corresponding concept. The 'thalamic feelings' imagined by Bion are based on transitional thoughts, between intuition and concept (analogous to the models used at the outset of the epistemological period).

There are some symptoms which cannot be understood if they are only seen as having developed after birth. 'Sub-thalamic' fear should also be taken into account, and those emotions which have not been able to become conscious, thought or verbalized. The analyst should be able to recognize the vestiges of an archaic state of mind. Hallucinations, for instance, may be the vestiges of a capacity to see or hear things that were once real. Bion was interested in prematurity, whatever comes into the world before being mentally ready to be born. He was also interested in autism, where some sensory capacities, analogous to the animalistic, exist (and in this respect we have all experienced what it is to be emotionally premature to some degree). The sudden and unexpected 'breakdown' of a child who has been too good, or of a 'too brilliant' scholar, will remain incomprehensible unless we think about the possibility of the resurgence of psychosomatic primacy.

How can we overcome the obstacle constituted by the caesura of birth? Bion proposes that there is a continuity of experience in both directions: between the pre-mental experience of gestation and conscious postnatal thought. His image of the dual process was also an anatomical one: men penetrate women in two directions – once from the inside to the outside during birth, and then from the outside to the inside during sexual intercourse. We are wrong if we think it is possible to 'return' to childhood, even if this is a legitimate use of the verb 'return'. We must find a formulation which allows us to overcome the obstacle – of the caesura of birth – in the present.

Analysis has a temporal rhythm, partly determined by social conventions, and we might therefore be led to think that the situation described by the patient is also organized temporally. It is a mistake to think that analytic material has a past – in fact, a constantly changing personality speaks to a personality in constant transformation. But the personality does not expand and stretch like a piece of elastic: 'It is as if it were something which developed many different skins as an onion does' (Bion, 1977c, pp. 48–9). This model can help us to understand the situations in which the patient feels forced to change from one state of mind to another. A positive temperament manages to cross the layer separating the two states of mind when there is opportunity to do so, or to make the best of an apparently disastrous situation.

A true interpretation can be made only by not offering the other possible interpretations. Since the human personality exists as a complex unity, choice may require the mind to be split into several possible ideas or interpretations. Bion calls this a 'non-pathological splitting'.[49] This process takes place more rapidly during speech; action takes place more rapidly than speech. The analyst can wait until an order of priority among ideas has been set up. Even if analyst and analysand speak the same language as a means of communication, there is a good chance that they will be speaking from different vertices. The analyst must employ a non-pathological form of splitting because the situation in its entirety is beyond his capacity to understand it, just as the small child's capacity to grasp the world as adults understand it must also be outgrown. It is natural for the young child to see only one part of reality, from a point of view which is not false, but inadequate. The splitting which the adult analyst chooses to make enables him to perceive things which the young child or analysand may perceive quite easily.

It is surprising to find Bion comparing the caesura of birth to the caesura of marriage, as if marriage were analogous to the severance of the biological connection with the mother. The analyst and the analysand, like the lover and the beloved, have a decision to take: to make a demand and to accept a demand. Just as the first years of life have much in common with what happened inside the womb, so marriage and its emotional life are experienced very much in terms of what happens before the marriage: 'The events at the heart of time end up by becoming part of the conscious life of the person concerned who then must act in a situation which has become real' (Bion, 1977c, p. 50).

Bion had concluded his introduction to *Attention and Interpretation* with precisely these analogical links. We should not confuse the things we use with what these things represent or symbolize. Symbolically, a gun can resemble a penis. The truth can be found only in the relation between these objects – in the analogy which connects them rather than in the objects themselves. The concluding pages of the paper on the caesura urge us to discover the links which connect phenomena that would appear to exist on opposite sides of the rupture. It was Bion's contention that there is greater continuity between the conscious and the unconscious, the transference and the countertransference, sanity and madness, the analyst and the analysand, than the impressive caesura of classical theory would have us believe.

THE EMOTIONAL TURBULENCE OF GROWTH

Invited to give a paper on the borderline personality, Bion focused on 'emotional turbulence'. He thought that the concept of the borderline personality was sufficiently new to sustain a *tabula rasa* approach. It seemed to him that the concept of 'latency' was in some way implied in the structure of the borderline personality. As the concept of latency was too familiar to convey fresh meaning, he went back to question what it is that is latent in borderline personality. In borderline cases, he suggests, what is latent is emotional turbulence. Turbulence is what is manifested when an apparently co-operative, quiet, docile and admirable child becomes noisy, difficult and rebellious. If a psychiatrist is consulted, he may find symptoms of schizophrenia or manic-depressive psychosis.

Adolescence is a stage at which this turbulence is normal and to be expected. The caesura of birth may be so striking that it prevents us from thinking about a foetal 'proto-mind', but Bion emphasizes the continuity between different states of mind. The caesura of birth, like that of death, may grip the imagination because it seems to happen suddenly. However, repression is a kind of death, and repression, as Freud taught us, does not happen suddenly or all at once. If emotional difficulty sets in, we may find it difficult to distinguish between repression and death. Growth seems to necessitate repression; progress requires a withdrawal back to the previous mental stage. Mental troubles may be dramatized around the significant changes of life: birth, adolescence, the onset of old age, and death. Analysis can be carried out only within specific constraints.

Like Socrates, Bion hoped to awaken minds by using humour and dialectic, provoking his interlocutors to come out with their own conceptions and to think for themselves. His own solution was not to be taken as law, but simply as opening up a new universe of questions.

People seek to mask their ignorance. Mankind, like Nature, seems to abhor a vacuum, and tries to fill up every space that ignorance leaves empty. All theories, including psychoanalysis, might be considered as elaborations that exist to fill a space. Freud demonstrated that sometimes the inability to answer questions is not a deliberate attempt at avoidance. He understood some erroneous memories as attempts to fill the space created by an amnesia. An analyst should think about whether he is giving a true response or simply filling up space, as paramnesia does.

Human beings have always managed to survive by preserving the capacity for growth, which depends on a gifted person's ability to slip away and communicate his intuition to less intuitively gifted people through visual images. Leonardo da Vinci's drawings of swirling waters and long hair in disarray are one such example of an intuitive grasp and illustration of the meaning of emotional turbulence. When an analyst 'demonstrates' (a term that Bion uses particularly in relation to groups) the presence of the disturbing emotional turbulence of growth, the response will often be one of trivializing the recognition of its existence. This response of 'I know' erects a barrier against the emergence of the unknown, and against recognition of the cause of the not-knowing.

Bion uses the image of the spiral as a metaphor for growth. Two years earlier he had compared his talks to a helix: 'We repeatedly return to the same point, but on different levels of the spiral' (Bion, 1979b, p. 85). He also considered the psychic development of the human species in terms of a helical movement. He thought that our scientific culture should enable some people to return to earlier levels of the spiral and draw resources from archaic episodes of turbulence. Turbulent emotions would give some dynamism to the spiral of knowledge. According to Bion's 'scientific fiction' we will never know what a foetus might be thinking, but this should not prevent us from supposing that a foetus does feel. Bion imagines a living being who, despite being immersed in amniotic fluid, is extremely sensitive. Our date of birth is not the date given by the obstetrician in medical records, but the date at which the personality is born.

An analysand in treatment once told Bion: 'I can remember my parents at the top of a Y-shaped staircase and me at the bottom . . . and . . .' That was all. The analyst waited for the rest, and had ample time to free-associate. Such a succinct statement offers many unspoken associations to an analyst. Bion imagined a Y-shape which, if pushed towards the point of intersection of the three lines, forms a cone or funnel. If the shape is further extended from the point of intersection, another geometry reveals the shape of a breast. Bion did not know how to communicate the kind of image the statement had brought to his mind. He suggested that over and above what the analysand had already said, the statement was a sort of 'visual pun'.

In his obituary of Charcot, Freud notes his idea of concentrating on an unknown situation until the point at which a pattern emerges and can be interpreted. Charcot's frame of reference was medicine, particularly neurology and surgery. Psychoanalysis works differently, but following Charcot's advice, Freud was able to temper his speculative impulse and leave things in abeyance until they speak for themselves. Bion, in turn, acknowledges that the object of psychoanalysis is not a sensory object, even though initial contact with the analysand is established through the senses. He advises analysts to set aside memory and desire because these are linked, respectively, to the past and the future.

The need to attain an almost empty state of mind is all the more necessary because every individual begins with the caesura of birth. Do we ever forget anything? Psychoanalysis would seem to indicate that nothing really disappears. Memory is complicated by the fantasy of omnipotence, which makes us split off and disregard whatever we do not like. Nothing seems to change, and what remains is the belief that something has been eliminated. It could be supposed that nothing is ever forgotten, and that the 'something' still exists in rudimentary form in the unconscious mind.

A psychoanalyst can only use words, sometimes well-worn words, to work with this state of mind. He must learn to speak to this foetus that is almost ready to be born, since part of the adult analysand is, or is derived from, this foetus. To put it another way: the question is one of how emotional reality and feeling can be introduced into a conscious and rational discourse – perhaps by plunging into fantasy, the 'infancy of our thinking'. Bion imagines a foetus towards the end of the term of pregnancy, who senses unpleasant movement in the amniotic fluid of its environment. Might the trouble be due to parental discord?

The same foetus might also hear loud noises coming from the father and the mother, or noises from the mother's intestinal tract. Bion supposes that a foetus that is relatively developed already has the basis of its future personality, that it directs its omnipotent hostility towards these rudimentary ideas and feelings, and is capable of splitting off and evacuating this hostility. A more developed foetus might get rid of its personality, and intelligently acquire words and language. This baby would eventually learn to differentiate between what is correct and what is mistaken, but this knowledge would not affect one level at which it did not know the difference, while still maintaining a sense of guilt. This model of development could explain certain resounding failures arising after a lengthy and well-hidden latency. 'It may be the case that we are here dealing with things that are so slight as to be virtually imperceptible, but so real that they can destroy us without our being aware of them' (Bion, 1987).

THE WISDOM OF ANALYSIS

'Making the best of a bad job', the title of Bion's last paper, reflects this state of mind. He was obviously referring to psychoanalytic practice. An 'emotional thunderstorm' is inevitably created whenever two people meet. Psychoanalysis can take place only if one of the two is prepared to cut his losses. Moreover, the analyst has to be sincere. He runs the risk of playing a role if the analysand manages to evoke such powerful feelings in him that he is unable to think. Bion employs a military metaphor: the enemy tries to terrify so as to stop one from thinking clearly; his object is to prevent one from gaining a true perception of 'reality'.

We may feel impelled to escape from an unpleasant world either through the body or through thought. Escape is a fundamental response in human beings. An infant already wishes not to know about its distress: it denies or idealizes it. Distress gives rise to a phantasy of omnipotence which tends to be projected on to the person of a parent or deity. The psychoanalyst uses his mind to rectify false solutions to the problems of distress. Existence is not enough; our existence must also have a certain quality of aliveness.

Bion continued to maintain his adherence to the philosophical principle of monism: the tenet that mind and body are one. Like

Milton, an analyst should 'see and tell of things unvisible to mortal sight' (Bion, 1987, p. 257) – in other words, the analyst should be able to hear 'not only the words but also the music'. Acknowledging that these ideas might be considered self-evident, Bion emphasizes the difference between knowing and knowing about. Idealization must give way to a realization through which one can perceive the shortcomings of the idealized image.

Bion continued to maintain that ego development and physical development are parallel, but he considered this development in terms of the adrenal gland. He reprises, in so many words, Selye's concept of the 'adaptation syndrome', which posits that adrenalin is more productive of initiative than attack or escape. The embryo does not anticipate (does not think), neither attacks nor escapes, but its body develops in 'anticipation' of having to produce organs which form the apparatus for thinking, attacking or escaping. This bodily development is the prototype of mental mechanisms. Comparing the transition from waking to sleep with the transition from amniotic fluid to a gaseous environment, Bion does not privilege one over the other. Sleeping is as valid as waking, but which state should we choose to interpret? Our culture does not yet accept 'rhapsodic response', the direct translation of drive into action.

26 DISCUSSIONS AND LECTURES

It seems that Bion did not have very much more to say in his discussions and lectures – nothing that he would have taken the trouble to publish in written form. We should read the texts for meaning, above and beyond their declared intentions. A psychoanalyst of renown accumulates a mythic capital which eventually elicits a process of reification and conservation. From the moment when Bion found success, his entourage and his followers decided that everything about him was worth preserving and publishing. The first domain of conservation was sought in his teaching seminars.

Bion gave lectures where certain members of the audience elected themselves interviewers. He had constructed an intellectual self-image through his writings. His lectures enabled him to play a mirror game with this chosen self-image in which his audience voluntarily accepted the role of reflecting it back to him. He was endlessly obliged to remodel and re-create it. The public's desire was expressed in two opposite directions simultaneously. On one hand, the questions asked aimed to elicit repetitions of statements he had already written and published, and avoided areas which were not part of his success. Rather than being party to work in progress, the audience came to see and admire the throned and crowned king. Yet on the other hand, some questions sought to make him talk about things he had not yet written about, or to push him towards anticipated revelations.

In the course of his peripatetic teaching, Bion often elicited a group dynamic. He was aware that colleagues treated him as though they were his patients. Their training led them to believe that they were entitled to learn something from an analyst reputed to know more than others. His public came to him to find answers, whereas Bion wanted primarily to be the analyst. André Green accurately describes this misunderstanding: 'which arose from the fact the audience believed themselves to be in the presence of the author of the books they had read, whilst not realizing that they could, in fact, only meet the author of the books he was currently writing, and who, in many ways, was no longer the same person' (Green, 1992).

Eventually Bion dedicated himself increasingly to teaching psychoanalysis. As his success grew he gave more lectures, seminars and discussions. He returned to a fundamental epistemological problem: the written communication of lived experience, and the teachers whose learning was disseminated entirely in spoken form – Jesus Christ, Luria, Socrates. Just as we can only speculatively reconstruct the thoughts of a young child and even, perhaps, the foetus, so we can only speculate on the meaning of ephemeral speech.

27 THE FANTASY TRILOGY

Bion was very fond of the three-volume literary work that he published under the title *A Memoir of the Future.* Through his method – which he modestly called 'science fiction' – he constructed a speculative account of the future of psychoanalysis. Bion placed himself as the prophet of psychoanalysis for the year 2000, and each volume represents a different way of bridging the gap between prophetic vision and writing.

SPOKEN DREAMING

The first book could be described as perfectly circular, if it had a beginning and an end. Is the preface the beginning? The author divides himself into a dyad of A (author) and Q (questioner), and launches into a close dialogue about the work. He alternately takes the point of view of writer and reader. From the start the reader is somewhat jostled around. The dialogue is about a new form of psychoanalysis, a strange business which requires considerable sacrifices of time and money without any preliminary questions being asked. This may not be the best way of drumming up custom, but the artist will not be reduced to commerce. In the text's structure the preface is symmetrically matched with an afterword. A and Q turn to each other to discuss the outcome of the book. Bion pre-empts the reader who might want to know the ending without having read the book, offering him a structure which begins with alpha and ends with omega and berating him, ironically, for his laziness, reminding him that the volume is the end result of an entire lifetime of intellectual work.

Is the beginning in a 'pro-logue' that precedes dialogue? Bion dons his psychoanalyst's hat to offer some first-person-singular explanatory sentences. He tells the reader that he is tired of nights that are as full as his days, and as disordered as his days are well planned. To the drowning reader he throws a first life belt, the concept of reversible perspective. One has only to use two different and separate vertices. Bion considers the alimentary tract transformed into a telescope. The reader should use his imagination to observe the mouth from the perspective of the 'arse hole', just as he can see how his arse hole looks from the point of view of his mouth. Bion recalls *Transformations*, in which he suggests that there may be two separate but coincident vertices: it is as if one of these points of view was rushing to meet the other.

Bion declares: 'This is a fictional account of a psychoanalysis with an artificially produced dream' (Bion, 1977a, p. 8). The fiction is to be taken as seriously as analytic practice. *The Dream* rests on a paradox: fictional characters do not actually exist, yet they none the less live within us. The book is an almost zoological collection of these fictional species which are indispensable to human survival.

Does it start with chapter one? There is no first chapter. The number eleven is printed at the head of page eleven. Each 'chapter' is indexed according to the number of the page on which it begins. The first 'chapter' begins with Alice waking up, rubbing her eyes and saying that she had been dreaming that she was empress of India. Although this Alice is explicitly a reference to the protagonist of the Lewis Carroll books, she also, like the other characters in the text, is occasionally liable to cross the threshold of dreams (rather than the looking-glass) in order to make contact with the author, and thus with the reader.

The basic scenario is an exchange between the partners of two couples. One couple comprises Alice and Roland, who are the 'masters'; this is paralleled by the servant couple, Rosemary and Tom. The drama starts out as a farce:

On waking up, Alice feels strongly ambivalent towards her servant, Rosemary. She decides to seduce her rival, who has already seduced Alice's husband, Roland. Rosemary's husband,

Tom, a robust but rather dimwitted agricultural worker, does not know how to resist Alice and has almost raped her. Despite her own beauty Alice is overwhelmed with envy of her young servant, who has just been fired. Conjugal love fills Alice with murderous hatred and weighs on her like an unwanted obligation.

The entire household awaits the arrival of mysterious enemies. Having missed the last train, Rosemary returns to the house. She manages to give some physical pleasure to her mistress who, for some time, has been deprived of passion and sexual gratification. The author suggests that this might be a hallucination. The sexual and narrative climax is interrupted by the arrival of two enemies who steal all Alice and Roland's belongings. The enemies think that Alice and Roland are dead. The protagonists endure a situation which has a finality of which they are unaware.

Following this administrative death, the situation disintegrates still further. Rosemary sleeps with Roland while Alice proudly goes upstairs to sleep in the servant's bed. Rosemary is triumphant: she has used her sexual power to take possession of the desirability and class of her employer. She secretly encourages Tom, who has returned mysteriously, to go to Alice's bed. Fascinated and anxious, the couple listen to the battles that rage at night. At dawn the two men and two women are taken away to be interrogated. England has been occupied by an enemy power.

Roland manages to dupe the enemy and begins to walk towards Munden. Thinking only of saving himself, he abandons Alice to her fate, telling himself that he never loved this woman, although she is still very pretty. Not being a mother has given her a hard appearance – perhaps Tom had even impregnated her with a 'deformed' baby.[50] Meanwhile Alice and Rosemary are kept as prisoners, Alice suffering most from the experience of humiliation and promiscuity because up until now she has mixed with and known only 'gentry'. The women become unable to distinguish between the world of reality (facts) and the world of dreams (the unconscious).

Roland, for his part, has come across a friend of his, Robin, who does not accept 'pacification'.[51] He joins up with his friend, but then the two of them have an unexpected encounter with an armed soldier. This encounter turns Roland into a murderer and the two friends into fugitives, on the run from the police. They are soon tracked down but manage to escape. They are being pursued once again.

The reader is at a loss to know who is who, and who is doing what to whom. The thinking has become disorganized; each individual character in turn begins a long, rambling monologue. Up to this point the story has taken the form of a banal novel. From page fifty-nine everything changes, and the narrative then claims to be 'science fiction'.

Still in pursuit of the eternal, Bion pursues the real throughout his fiction. He underscores the initial paradox by giving an artificial language to his fictional characters. His literature is a composite of polylogues. All the characters chatter on endlessly; they can do nothing else. Their voices interweave in one night of thought. At times the reader may identify with the character of 'Paranoid-Schizoid': 'It's like being bombarded with bad puns, fragments of Shakespeare, imitations of James Joyce, vulgarizations of Ezra Pound, false mathematics, religion and mysticism, visions of adolescence, second childhood and old age.' Sometimes, with the 'Depressive Position', he may think: 'What are the counterparts of disturbances, perturbations, turbulences that are violent, invisible, insensible? Analogous to the models made visible by Leonardo's drawings of hair, water? And occasionally by schizophrenic or other formulations?' (Bion, 1975, p. 61).

The voices address one another in apparent chaos, mastery over which is kept by Bion alone. The author accumulates the effects of surprise by introducing characters who become increasingly bizarre. Even the narrator is divided into 'Bion P.A.' (psychoanalyst) and 'Myself'. Literary characters sometimes lead the dance: Sherlock Holmes, Mycroft, Watson, Big Brother. Mythical, literary-historical characters are assembled from time to time for some speaking parts. Some of them remain anonymous: Nurse, A Neighbour, Supporter, Captain; others are scarcely individualized at all: Voice, Memory and Man. The author uses every conceivable linguistic register and sphere: jargon, swearing, literary and philosophical discourse; from onomatopoeia to formal logic, from intellectual dialogue to street talk.

This deliberate chaos serves to prepare the reader for an illumination: if the reader is capable of tolerating the chaos and solitude of the monologues, he can discover the pattern which underlies fundamental reality. The author lets loose a myriad of philosophical, literary, religious and psychoanalytic tropes and syntheses. He pays homage to his personal pantheon of great authors: Shakespeare, Milton, Kant, Plato and Freud. He introduces some newer ones more recently added to the canon, such as the writer of the *Baghavad-Gita*.

Mathematics are no longer an adequate model for representing the unconscious. Real people must learn to coexist with imaginary creations, since the latter are to play a role much like the part played by the negative numbers which broke with the tyranny of real numbers. The characters of a novel or in the theatre can be 'thoughts without a thinker'. While they seem to be real, they are the product of something like hallucination. The character 'Bion' is identified with a hallucinating patient as the author demonstrates that he is simply a construction of the text. All the characters of *The Dream* attempt to work through the catastrophic changes experienced by the author, as he considers that his life and experience are relevant to humanity in general. The author tries to give form to the future by working through the emotional turbulence of the past.

The book ends, on page two hundred and twenty-nine, as arbitrarily as it began. In a dialogue with the two personages of the author ('Myself' and 'Bion'), Alice tells him that they seem to have ended up where they began. The circularity of the statement derives from the impossibility of escaping from the word, whereas real life is as much a matter of muscular, sensory, affective and active processes. Even psychoanalytic language is not adequate to describe the process of dialogue. But this first volume has, perhaps, allowed something new to be glimpsed: the fact that there might be some psychoanalytic principle, like the Heisenberg Principle in physics, which allows the recognition that observation alters the object of observation. As this is only an analogy, it should be possible to resort to the 'as if' metaphor. The individual can be thought of as a group, and represented by a dramatization between his ego, his internal objects and his thoughts without a thinker.

THE PAST PRESENTED

The second volume is as arbitrary as the first. Each chapter is named simply after the number of the page on which it starts, but in this volume the chapters are considerably longer. This makes the overall structure much more homogeneous, even more monotonous. The narrative voice of the author has disappeared, and all the words constitute part of 'dialogues' between a number of characters.

Chapter five, the beginning of volume two, starts by setting limits to the sense of chaos created in the first volume, as it locates the action in space and in time. The trio of Roland, Alice and Rosemary are still in the London area.

Roland begins by asking what day it is. Alice replies that she has no idea, and can't see why it should be of any importance. Roland reprimands her and tells her to wake up – to external reality. In fact Alice is not as unaware as he imagines and she specifies the year and the day: the action takes place in the 1970s (the years in which the book was being written). While talking to the others, Alice pursues her reverie. She has refound her social position and her husband, and the country is no longer at war. She hopes that Roland remembers their wedding anniversary. Time passes. She finds it difficult to accept her reflection in the mirror: her beauty and her husband's love are not what they used to be.

Alice and Roland, a cultured and sophisticated couple, entertain many guests. Some are invited, others arrive as unexpectedly as characters in a dream. Many of them are already known to us from volume one. But they now make a 'demonstration of their existence' instead of theorizing. To do this they speak to each other without stopping. This group exists only in a game of verbal associations.

The reader's experience of this narrative resembles a parabola, as the simple plot is conveyed in a more sophisticated and evolved prose style which aims to facilitate the discovery of insight, just as the circle and the line facilitated the evolution of geometry. But just as these material representations can also constrain and impede the evolution of abstract thought, so the physical basis of speech can also constrain the 'requirements of the mind'.

The character of Harlequin maintains a discourse which unfolds at length through the text but is nevertheless constrained and interrupted. It puts together a number of very short extracts taken from the books of the last two periods. The Psycho-Analyst is seeking a language which could be universally understood. From time to time the reader begins to tire of the interminable dialogues which start up incessantly. All the themes explored in the articles, discussions and lectures of the last period are rediscovered, from a slightly different angle, in the second volume of the trilogy. The diverse characters appear as interlocutors, allowing the Psycho-Analyst to restate and recapitulate his views on the search for absolute Truth. When he is told that psychoanalysis forever returns to the same point, he remarks that one can never return to the same geophysical space, as time moves on perpetually.

The characters evolve in an analytic context, their interconnected associations allowing something of the unconscious to emerge into the foreground. Bion pushes himself to represent extraordinary experience, and in order to do this he includes dreams within thought. The privileged interlocutor of P.A. is as much the astronomer, the doctor, the mathematician, as the priest. Whether it be 'Paul' or 'Priest', Bion often follows and takes their part. Treatment should enable the patient no longer to be terrorized by his divine attributes, while he continues to have faith in his divine qualities. The Psycho-Analyst tries to show the patient that one of the roots of the idea of God is the memory of the real father, but memory does not necessarily exclude other sources for the origins of this idea.

From chapter fifty-one onwards the atmosphere begins to become unsettled. Roland is confronted by DU, and Roland's past – the author's past – returns forcefully.[52] Roland nervously questions this extraordinary being, and manages to identify him only through negations: he is not a devil, nor a nightmare, nor a ghost. DU explains: 'I am the future of the Past, the shape of things to come . . . I am only one of your thoughts' (Bion, 1977a, pp. 51–3). This being represents the deepest level of the unconscious, which Roland will one day call God – A 'mother idea' which will be accessible only if he remains in communication with the foetal part of himself. Roland argues strenuously, as he cannot believe that a mere metaphor could behave as if it were a fact. DU demands that it/he not be expelled, as it/he has the right to exist without being forever dependent on a thinker. Roland, for his part, wants to be able to choose whether to become sane or mad, and conflict arises.

The author's representation of this surreal theme pays homage to Lewis Carroll's literary style of punning. Roland fuses the idea of a primary obligation 'ought' with the idea of autism, and creates the neologism 'oughtism'. DU advises Roland to be wise rather than use his intelligence; DU might be considered 'oughto-nomic' in the sense that it emanates from the primordial level of the psyche. It is time for Roland to listen to this archaic ego, despite his attempt to silence it with the conceptual rubbish he uses to fill up his mind. When DU puts him into contact with his past as an officer, Roland has to listen. DU disappears with the reminiscence of the ending of the war, and Roland finds himself talking to the Psycho-Analyst. He wonders, aloud, why people are so resistant to any truth which seems to threaten them. The Psycho-Analyst replies that to reach the truth that exists beyond the specific context within which we live is too frightening, too terrible, so that we live, instead, within the matrix of our own ignorance.

When he began the trilogy Bion already had some great literary antecedents – people such as Virgil, Dante and Milton. But the structure of the three volumes is especially evocative of the Divine Comedy: the paranoid-schizoid hell of the first volume is followed by the purgatory of the second, which oscillates between these two Kleinian positions. The characters purge the author's conscience of the suffering of guilt at being a survivor. Reversible perspective again emerges, and the 'servants' take the place of the 'masters'.

From this point on, the conversations take place in the kitchen. Rosemary becomes the new lady of the household. She now has absolute power because she is no longer bound to oafish Tom, but has replaced him with a new partner: Man, a representative of the occupying army. The occupation has overturned the hierarchy, and Man proposes marriage to Rosemary.

The situation stabilizes as Rosemary's dominating sadism is mirrored by Alice's masochism; a fact which P.A. acknowledges publicly. While all around him the world revolves round sex, through Rosemary's seductions and her immorality, P.A. pursues his Byzantine discussions with other intellectuals in quest of truth. Our specialist wishes he could make something in the material world, like a mirror, which would enable everyone to see himself as he is in his soul. But every glimmer of insight that psychoanalysis reveals becomes distorted by jargon. The specialist can find refuge only in fiction, where truth, thus predictably distorted, can emerge again.

Rosemary becomes increasingly intolerant of Roland's peremptory demands. Man calmly suggests that he should annihilate Roland the irremediable individual. Rosemary does not say no,

*but remains undecided. Man again proposes marriage, which she
finds rather flattering. Rosemary becomes more angry with Alice.
She threatens to fire her, which would place Alice in great
difficulty given the problem of finding another job. Man loves
neither Alice, nor Roland, whom he thinks of as dangerous; he
urges Rosemary to fire Alice and to let him eliminate Roland.
When Robin and Roland get together to rail against Rosemary,
'Roland drops down dead' (Bion, 1977a, p. 133). Man has just
shot him with a revolver.*

Rosemary and Man dominate the others because they are violent
and are prepared to behave ruthlessly. For all that, they are far from
stupid brutes. Rosemary offers some pertinent arguments when she
discusses psychoanalysis with P.A. Man turns out to be a lucid and
well-informed administrator who wishes to adapt the Priest and the
Psycho-Analyst to the new order. He reproaches the Priest for
wasting time on the past. The Priest is no longer important,
although his remains are in evidence and influence the present. He
urges Man not to live only by repeating the past. Finally, Man asks
the Psycho-Analyst to become director of a 'Department of Truth'.
The Psycho-Analyst does not know what to say, so lost is he within
an infinity of vertices. Man does not want to know about what is,
essentially, a subjective truth. Like most of the characters facing a
catastrophic change, P.A. reacts by embarking on a soliloquy which
cuts him off from external reality. He thus manages to disorientate
even the most attentive of readers.

*Man only soliloquizes and proclaims on the state of his soul. He
tells Rosemary that he is going to marry her before long. By
assassinating his protagonist, Roland, in cold blood, the author
can take the fiction wherever he chooses. He summons together
all his entire psychic family, which is both ancient and
innumerable. One of the characters notes 'What a crowd!'. The
pretext for this final party seems to be Rosemary's marriage to
Man. An orchestra adds singers' voices to the festivities and we
even read of a celestial choir. Roland is inexplicably resuscitated
and takes his place in the word game. Several characters wonder
who the party is being given in honour of. Is it Alice? Rosemary?
P.A.? Each of them disclaims: 'No, it's Time Past's Party'.*

All this sound and fury screens out knowledge of the inevitability of death. First Betty's death, as P.A. comments: 'Women have greater reason to fear death than men as they know that they may die in childbirth' (Bion, 1977a, p. 166). Then the many, many young men who died between 1914 and 1918. The verbal party ends with a final exchange between P.A. and the ghost of Auser.[53] Auser's ghost asks Bion, survivor and war hero of the First World War, a final question: 'I wanted to ask you: Did we win?' (ibid., p. 179). The only reply he can give is a long – very long – silence.

We also find the death of the eighty-year-old author himself. Immediately before meeting Auser's ghost, P.A. sees his own. He has difficulty recognizing him, as they are so completely different from each other. Whereas one wants to warm his old bones by clothing them with flesh and blood, the other wishes only to be completely disembodied, to be only a 'figment of the imagination'. Although he gives only two brief replies, the ghost of P.A. throws light on the meaning of the title of the second volume. *The Past Presented* is that of a man who is psychically dead: 'I died at the English Farm and since I have worked in purgatory' (Bion, 1977a, p. 177). This encounter had been set up by P.A. since the second chapter: 'I will not go back to the road between Amiens and Roye, for fear of meeting my ghost – I died there' (ibid., p. 35). Bion again confirms this in his autobiography: 'Oh yes, I died – on August 8th 1918' (Bion, 1982, p. 265).

THE PAST FORGOTTEN[54]

The author still seeks a 'communication of pure nonsense' – that is, a form of communication which has not been distorted by the constraints of sense. He apologizes for still resorting to the 'language of experience and reason', as the entire book will be nothing but one immense conversation. The first two volumes plunge us straight into a space that is somewhere between science and fiction, presenting memory as something that originates in a nebulous dream. The third volume, *The Dawn of Oblivion*, achieves the aim expressed in the title of the work: a reconstruction which opens up on to the future. Night has finally dissolved into dawn to give birth to a new day; just as in *Paradise Lost*, light prevails over the shadows following Adam and Eve's repentance; just as the *Divine Comedy* ends with a dazzling vision of the sight of God.

If the trilogy structure is inspired by Milton or Dante, the final volume reads as theatre. The author could well have structured it in acts and scenes rather than chapters. P.A.'s admiration of Shakespeare is very much in evidence: he is 'the greatest man who ever lived . . . ' (Bion, 1979a, p. 3). Bion follows his illustrious predecessor, and declares in his turn that life is but a tale told by an idiot, signifying nothing. The author uses characters to dramatize his efforts to discipline his thoughts and emotions into literary form; in this sense the past evoked by the characters structures potentially catastrophic changes. Verbal exchanges, dialogues and soliloquies offer aesthetic containment to archaic impulses. The author decides to return to the primordial change which obliges us to live outside the maternal matrix; but thoughts pre-exist the thinker, and the history of his thoughts began before physical birth.

Bion reactivates the circularity set up in the first volume. Once again he negates the concept of a beginning and an end by framing the text within a Pre-prologue and a Post-epilogue. Q questions A about the new *Memoir*. His interlocutor does not try to reassure him – quite the reverse. It is taken as understood that the reader was unable to enjoy the previous volume, and will therefore be even less appreciative of the last one. The relationship between Q and A is rather like the relationship between Rosemary and Alice – the more A tries to rebuff and reject Q, the more Q declares himself satisfied and clings on. Of course, A expects Q to turn immediately to the end of the book. Although A addresses him with irony, Q refuses to be put out and begins to interview A: Did he enjoy his visit to America? (The last volume was published by a British publisher in 1979, the year that Bion returned to Britain.) A declares that he was delighted – it was far better than his journey in the Belgian Ardennes in 1916. Q would like to know more, but he has not got much time if he wants to be present at his meeting with Destiny. A says goodbye to him, and wishes him a happy holocaust!

The book's first surprise is that it starts with chapter one. The next surprise is that the pre-, neo- and postnatal beings have been replaced by conventional flesh-and-blood characters: the only exception is P.A. The range of characters is infinite, as they are identified only by their ages. Things are relatively straightforward when they are named in relation to being twenty months, twenty-four or thirty years old, and so on, but we also find a dialogue initiated by a mysterious Em-mature – not an immature or premature being but a 'symbolic embryo' (Fourtina, 1987, p. 577) who is evidently destined to become a renowned psychoanalyst. He takes on an organizing role in relation to other beings, analogous to the role of P.A. Em (mature) is destined to disappear as soon as he reaches the stage of birth.

While he aims to lead the reader to Paradise, the author begins by plunging him into the 'Darkness of Origins'. Em declares that the book is a psycho-embryonic attempt to write a proto-scientific narrative of the journey that leads us from birth to death. Em would like to tell his story at first hand, starting with the spermatozoa meeting the ovum, but he has to acknowledge that he has been able to complete his memory only with the help of the narratives of science that he came across much later. Similarly, it is only in hindsight that he is able to understand his earliest experiences as being those of a 'self'; and only in retrospect that he is able to relate changes in hydraulic pressure to a pleasure ego or a pain ego.

Into this sort of surrealist animation the author brings more illustrious people: Leonardo da Vinci, Milton and Krishna . . . By this he means to signify that prenatal experience can be communicated if it takes on an 'artistic form' (Fourtina, 1987, p. 579). To avoid employing a language that is already formed, and thus liable to saturate this primitive experience and communication, Bion makes full use of non-sense and pseudo-stupidity. Em imagines that he might be able to use a small suitcase or box as a temporary exoskeleton. Term protests strenuously that Em will never emerge if he satisfies himself with borrowing; by swallowing his incorporation he incorporates it into his ego, thereby strengthening his endoskeleton.[55] This is his means of advancing on the path of progress.

Officially the trilogy ends with the *Dawn of Oblivion*; however, Bion returns to the solitary mental journey which leads us from birth to death. The final volume soon re-creates the situation of guerrilla warfare set up at the beginning of the trilogy, locating this situation in terms of the constraints that Nature imposes on Mind and Body. Mind and Body will never be able to get on together, and generate Psyche-Soma or Soma-Psyche. There will sometimes be open warfare from Birth onwards. Another struggle soon emerges into the war zone: the struggle against sex and the war between the sexes. There is nothing peaceful about the coexistence of brother and sister. Girl and Boy find it yet more difficult to make the transition from latency to adolescence, for they hate apprenticeship and growth.

Confusion and hatred are accurately expressed when the children chase a cat to trap it under a flowerpot, then make it take abrupt flight from the terror and noise of captivity. The cat gives us a soliloquy, noting that the children are unable to differentiate between a flowerpot and a container of gestation. (Fourtina suggests that the children caricature the act of birth which, they feel, has robbed them of their foetal omnipotence.) Everything is nothing but a terrible repetition. Having had barely enough time to grow up, Boy sees armed soldiers. Now there really is war.

A Memoir of the Future may be seen as the author's attempt to re-establish contact with a lost part of himself, and so with reality itself.[56] The veteran of the First World War had experienced the negative of a religious experience as he had felt his soul, rather than his body, die after the battles of Ypres and Amiens: 'For although the soul may die, the body lives on forever' (Bion, 1985, p. 35). At least it lives on to about the age at which Bion was writing the trilogy, when he was sensing the caesura of death, as close to him as it was difficult to traverse.

Rather than compulsively repeating the past, we must find a way to traverse the caesura. The psychoanalyst must facilitate emotional growth, as all knowledge – somatic and somitic – contributes to futurist knowledge. It should be a 'transitive theory', a theory on the path to knowledge, not knowledge itself. This credo, which was first strenuously affirmed in *Transformations* and *Attention and Interpretation*, is further explored as the author brings in the personae of Bunyan and Schreber.[57] Like the genius Shakespeare, both these men wrote about their self-questioning on the nature of existence. But these 'old companions' did not really experience what they wrote about; rather, like a woman, they settled for being containers of the seed of knowledge. Alice, who has experienced pregnancy, is the only one who can really understand a psychosomatic complaining of stomachache.

P.A. suggests that disparate elements could be brought together so that what appears to be false can generate a growth of knowledge from generation to generation. The innumerable discussions that men have among themselves, and between themselves and their scientific entities, prevent the ideogram fulfilling its function of communicating to a fellow human being. An exemplary writer is Ezra Pound, who found a way to transpose poetry across continents and across centuries.[58] Picasso, painting on glass, showing us both sides of the screen, is another example used by Bion. We should, he thinks, protest at the way in which people of genius become entombed in culture. P.A. considers James Joyce to be the contemporary mind most able to achieve the innovations in articulation necessary to shatter the 'mental ossification' of our times. The author willingly brings back the body after each intellectual flight. Alice does not avoid telling P.A. bluntly: 'My clitoris is passed unnoticed by your mouth, "blinded", "glutted" by your penitential penis' (Bion, 1979a, p. 36). Phallic arrogance makes us forget that the mouth takes pleasure and is nourished, as well as speaking.

The characters of the trilogy exist only in so far as they speak, the fundamental quality that allows us to explore the problems of verbal communication. The apparent precision of scientific and social discourse disguises its inherent ambiguity. We should learn to hear and value the 'rhapsodic' quality of what can be sensed. Rosemary's discourse is punctuated with sexual insults such as 'bloody cunt', which are used to connote her sadomasochistic sexuality. Is it a fantasy when she tells us that her mother was beaten almost to death by a 'gentleman' with a leather strap? Swearing and blasphemy are used to convey the fundamental baseness of our existence which begins in amniotic fluid full of meconium.

The final chapters recapitulate the fundamental questions of the trilogy. Talking to a resolute Priest, P.A. states that psychoanalysis is not just another religion – it simply helps the human being to grow, and so helps him better to choose and worship his God. On the question of original sin, P.A. answers that some observations might be better explained by the concept of 'original guilt'. This fundamental language, linked to archaic existence, is correlated to fundamental guilt, which shares some of the attributes with which Freud characterizes the id. Although he does not believe in life after death, P.A. believes that there is such a thing as prenatal mental life. Therefore, psychoanalysis runs the greatest risk when 'pre- and postnatal personalities are reunited'. The meeting of two individuals, two groups or two nations can be equally dangerous.

P.A. offers a 'hypotheory' which is capable of explaining the unease of gifted young people, such as Bion, when they leave school or home. The gifted person has always tried to be without feelings and without emotions, even before birth. If it is impossible to take flight from inherited characteristics, it may be possible to try to escape from acquired characteristics, since these are only 'phenomena'. Bion thought that the quality of love between the parents, and the mother's state of mind in responding to the world, could affect the foetus. The gifted child soon learns an innate language, and appears to be socially well adjusted. In the grip of a violent emotion, however, he may be susceptible to 'war neurosis' or being 'brainwashed', depending on historical circumstances. There is a more or less conflicting coexistence of the premature and post-mature personalities inhabiting the same body. At times the two personalities cannot coexist; in their place is a relationship between complementary pairs which may be of such intensity that it can result in a *folie à deux*.

The author writes page upon page in an attempt to avoid falsifying this idea. A ray of hope illuminates the conclusion. P.A. is now used to his words being found incomprehensible, then declared to be common sense, and finally plagiarized. He finds that Melanie Klein's fate was not very different, and that it is difficult for him to understand what she writes, despite – or perhaps because of – the fact that he was analysed by her. He begins to find that there was some truth in her interpretations, and that she had literally been able to shed light on him: 'It was as if night had been replaced by dawn' (Bion, 1979a, pp. 121–2). This is what enables him to understand Milton's invocation of light in the third volume of *Paradise Lost*.

Although he was reaching dawn, the future remained uncertain. The author saw the approach of a final catastrophic change, and his readers were not to be spared his knowledge. Human beings must face a decision: either they choose wisdom and a capacity for choice, or there is oblivion and physical destruction such as nuclear war. From circle to circle Bion seems to have been drawn towards the truth – that is, towards death. A sympathetic reader sees an art which reaches the height of freedom because it is no longer bound to proving anything; a critical reader sees the unhappy restlessness of a man who, having lost the freshness and energy of his youth, is striving compulsively. Anxiously confusing the pleasure of creation with that of writing, Bion interposes his image of the leading athlete of the mind. To become a great psychoanalyst is to make people love everything one produces. People become dependent on one's ego as if it were necessary and desirable nutrition.

28 THE NAKED TRUTH, OR THE AUTOBIOGRAPHY

For a substantial part of his life, Bion lived alone. His immense pride made him erect a wall of silence between himself and others, while he felt the need to make his exemplary destiny a public matter. But it was only the anxious tension of old age that made him decide to share his nostalgia for childhood, his suffering as a schoolboy and his ordeal as a soldier. He entrusted the manuscript to Francesca, who published it posthumously in 1982. This autobiography, which covers the years from his birth to the First World War, is called *The Long Week-End* and subtitled 'Part of a Life', which suggests a sequel.

This three-hundred-page book comprises three unequal parts, each further subdivided into a number of short chapters. The first part, 'India', has nine chapters and covers his childhood up to the definitive separation from his family and the land of his birth when he went to school at the age of eight. The second part, 'England', devotes nineteen chapters to his difficult acclimatization to Britain, and his school years. The final section, 'War', describes, in forty-three chapters, the appalling ordeal which brought him ephemeral glory and indelible scars. In these pages the predominant feeling is one of cold anger – not hatred, depression or ironic contempt, but a rage against his parents, teachers, instructors and superiors; against the whole world, and ultimately against himself. Luckily, the reader is swept away by Bion's extraordinary vitality, which reassures us that human beings have the capacity, somehow, to survive. Happily, there is also much evidence of Bion's curiosity, and his astute amusement at all aspects of the world.[59]

Bion began writing the autobiography in the hope of extending his thinking during the epistemological period. The first sentence of the Preface informs us that his 'intention has been to be truthful'. But absolute pride had been mellowed by years of experience, and he recognizes that it is possible only 'to be "relatively" truthful'. Alongside the aim for 'scientific truth', the aim of epistemology, he gives space to 'aesthetic' and 'psycho-analytic' truth – in other words, he aims to 'achieve, in part and as a whole, the formulation of phenomena as close as possible to noumena'. By any account, it is a strange autobiography indeed.

Bion also informs us that he did not choose the autobiographical genre but had found himself led to it by the very nature of his psychoanalytic work. Only by recognizing and analysing the countertransference was he was able to escape the confusion created by the projective identification he encountered in groups. The work that followed from the group period confirmed this as analysing psychotic and borderline pathologies brought him face to face with the unutterable and 'proto-mental' aspects of experience. What a psychoanalyst writes about others is always more distorted than what he can write about himself: 'I write about "me". I do so deliberately because I am aware that it is what I should do anyhow. I am also more likely to approximate to my ambition if I write about the person I know better than anyone else – myself' (Bion, 1982, p. 8). So the book is basically about one man's relationships, not about the many people, groups and institutions who are nevertheless mentioned by name. Had he been able to, Bion would perhaps have preferred to use abstractions to create himself as a unique subject of observation and writing.

Since the noumenon, the absolute and ultimate Truth, is unknowable, knowledge can be gained only from renouncing the desire to seize truth in its totality. Every attempt to fulfil this desire necessarily dissects reality according to a 'vertex' – not only is it limited to the point of view of our field of vision, but because we refuse to acknowledge the reality of such limitation, we cannot 'know' from other points of view. Bion's life has meaning only in its entirety, but it had to be represented in terms of artificial sections which do not correspond to his reality. In the autobiography Bion divides the first twenty-four years of his life into three periods. For each of these he establishes a basic point of view. The analyst oversteps his limits when he tries to grasp a situation in its entirety, just as the small child can know only part of the reality which he shares with adults.

Fortunately, the analyst is able to carry out a 'non-pathological splitting' in order to apprehend or see things as they are usually seen only by babies, children or adolescents. When he writes about the results of his observation, the analyst brings together the adult and polymorphous parts of himself. Psychoanalytic truth and aesthetic truth are brought together and become almost identical.

Bion follows a chronological sequence, beginning with the oedipal years of childhood. He considerably narrows his point of view by means of the 'non-pathological' splitting which enables him to take the perspective of himself as a child. The first chapters are particularly concerned with the time when he was with his mother, father and sister, and he leaves aside the knowledge of the wider family circle about which he wrote, much later, to his fiancée.

The first chapters are set in India, and it is this location which, at the outset, is of central importance. Although it is very short, the section called 'India' is surprising in its sensual and emotional intensity. Everyone who met Bion remembers his 'perfectly English' education and manners, but these concealed an irrevocably Anglo-Indian background which eventually re-emerged in his later years. Bion left India, never to return, at the age of eight. By that time he had built up a store of memories and experiences which added to the richness of his personality. The second word of the autobiography is 'ayah', his Indian nurse; this word becomes part of the special vocabulary of experience of this background. Decades later, as he read Indian mythology, Bion realized that this wizened old woman had already taught him about Indo-Aryan mythology through the marvellous stories she used to tell him. She had given him cultural models to contain his overflowing imagination, and he had assimilated them. He was to turn to them again in maturity in the process of constructing an original intellectual system of thought.

From a very early age Bion responded with all his senses to the land of his childhood, and in the autobiography he describes the intensity of the monsoon, the cries of the wild animals, the semi-desert landscapes, the dazzling light, the noonday silence, the shade of the large trees; 'None the less I loved India. The blazing, intolerable sun – how wonderful it was!' (Bion, 1982, p. 29). It was partly in search of his roots that Bion settled in Southern California. He was never to return to the land of his birth. Towards the end of his life he had accepted an invitation to return to Bombay. Bombay had been the final stop on the long train journey he made with his mother, and was the port at which they embarked for England. He died two months before he was due to go. How close was he to returning to India in order to die there?

The second section of the autobiography, 'England', covers the years between his arrival at school and his departure for France. The sudden break in the narrative here reprises the deep rupture – almost as deep as the caesura of birth – constituted by being sent away to school. Virtually overnight the child Wilfred found himself 'paralysed, stupefied and completely alone' in an English school for boys.

The autobiography is written by an old man. During his eight years of analysis Bion had had plenty of time to reflect on, and to integrate, his adolescent emotions. He had made extensive use of his childhood memories in writing the literary trilogy. He was now aiming to document his life as much as to disclose it; he also hoped to commemorate the tragic ordeal that befell his generation.

Bion had the strength of mind to refuse to become compliant and to maintain, until his last days, the 'bloom of rebellion' (Lejeune, 1980). Despite the variety and familiarity of the events he describes, his perspective remains fresh. At the beginning of the book the author, like the average reader, knows nothing about army life. With the reader he shares the shock and trauma of war. He describes a heroic form of survival, and explains the price that was to be paid for withstanding the strain. The narrative is one of both life and art, for life merges and unifies, while art discriminates and selects.

Bion compares his autobiographical project to writing a biography – he employs the same method for understanding his life as he applied to understanding his patients. Biography had been his project for his patients, whereas the autobiography was to initiate a new project for himself. He aimed to write about himself as if he was writing about someone else, but would it be possible to write the narrative of a life whose end was yet to be thought? Bion came up against the problem of the uncertainty of the narrative's closure. In the end he wrote only half of what he planned as a complete work. Unable to complete the life, he condenses chronology in order to finish the first volume with himself in his forties.

Bion decided to be his own judge. He surrenders his ego to our curiosity, as he presents it to his own lucid and concerned conscience. In its style, the autobiography is more of a salvation than an exploration. Salvation is to be found through an acknowledgement of blame; the recognition of original guilt finally leads him to the liberation of absolution.

Far from bringing him the glory and success he had hoped for, the Second World War brought with it a series of blows to his self-esteem and a tragic personal loss. If the passage of time had healed the scars of an ungenerous fate, it had not healed the wound of his sense of guilt for a terrible loss, despite years of analysis and a second marriage. In 1983 Francesca Bion published 'Another Part of a Life' with the title *All My Sins Remembered*. Bion had been unable to progress beyond Betty's death, Parthenope's birth and his difficulties in being psychoanalysed.

The autobiography traces the destiny of a man whose life evokes the contradictions of a Shakespearian protagonist. The author, still shocked to find terrible cruelty within him, quotes Hamlet's lines as his parting words: 'The fair Ophelia – Nymph, in thy orisons be all my sins remembered' (Act III Scene 1).[60] Hamlet utters these words at the end of the famous soliloquy, several weeks after the memorable night when he has vowed to avenge his father and decided to simulate madness in order to carry out his plan of revenge. The ghost has informed him of the sexual relationship between his mother, Gertrude, and his uncle, Claudius, but Hamlet becomes disturbed, and turns against Ophelia instead of turning against his mother's incestuous adultery. The violence with which he attacks Ophelia is the violence which he cannot express to his mother.

The action is suspended, and Shakespeare advances the narrative by bringing a theatre on to the scene and thereby doubling his dramatic and narrative space. Hamlet greets the actors and asks them to perform Aeneas's narrative to Dido, 'and especially when he speaks of the murder of Priam'. Listening to them, Hamlet conceives the idea of having them perform *The Murder of Gonzago*, with some lines of his own added to the original story. Once the actors have left, he begins another soliloquy. He is amazed at the way an actor can bring so much of his soul to the text that he can bring about a complete transformation. He is fascinated and disgusted by the weakness of the flesh, a femininity which is the queen of dissimulation. The whole tragedy continues to focus on the relation between femininity and acting. If the sensuous woman is an actress and a whore, the actor is artificially but genuinely moved. Bion had also known an actress: Betty Jardine.

The book is named with full awareness of the meaning of the text. Bion knew how to construct the language of this final page, where he joins his imagination to Shakespeare's. We, the readers, can deduce his despair at times of desolation and remorse by following Hamlet's thoughts. Shakespeare doubles the action by providing, within the scene, a place from which it can be observed from behind a curtain, thereby creating a metaphor for theatrical space. The space of the action contains within it a space from which action can be observed, and both these are contained within the encompassing space which unites spectators with actors on stage. The autobiography shows us the backstage space of a man who played a central part on the psychoanalytic scene.

Thanks to the actors, Hamlet is able to take action – to act. The famous soliloquy which ends with 'all my sins remembered' is suspended between the point at which he has made a decision and the point at which he meets Ophelia again. The action is suspended while the protagonist gives us an insight into his inner drama. He thinks of a basic unresolved conflict between acting (that is, to kill and to be) and submitting (that is, not to kill and not to be). Suicide is a compromise solution to the dilemma. If Hamlet were to kill himself he would destroy Gertrude within him, while punishing himself at the same time. Another alternative – to die and/or to sleep – emerges as one solution. Death might bring the misfortunes of life to an end, just as sleep brings release from the problems of the day. But dreams will trouble the release of sleep, as there is a process which transmutes the problems of the outside world into the inner world of the psyche. Hamlet berates himself for his cowardice over suicide when he sees Ophelia. He can renounce the temptation to suicide only when he has brought about the death of his beloved. The great cruelty of which Bion accuses himself was directed against his beloved daughter Parthenope.

Francesca Bion thought that this 'sad testimony of a search for self' would probably give a false impression of the man she had lived with. She decided to add to the autobiography more than twice its length in family correspondence in order to show 'the other side of genius'. She successfully manages to fill the autobiography's thirty-year blank space with evidence of flourishing creativity and fulfilment.

The text is undoubtedly an autobiography, since author, narrator and protagonist are one and the same man. Wilfred R. Bion, whose name appears on the books' covers, tells the story of his personal history with particular emphasis on the history of his personality. The autobiographical text shifts our overall perspective on the work as a whole. We can now see two different spaces: one dedicated to 'science' in so far as science can make advances in psychoanalytic knowledge; the second a literary space in which the reader needs to respond in terms of aesthetic conventions. Even more important is the fact that the autobiography alters the meaning of Bion's earlier work by a process of deferred action, because the rest of his work is then also to be read in terms of autobiography.

Epilogue

At first Bion thought that he would spend only three or four years in California; in fact he stayed and worked there until 1979. Around the end of the August of that year, the couple returned to England – it seems that they wanted to be closer to the children. Bion chose to live near to his old university and Queen's College. He still had a few old friends at Oxford. He was setting up a new private practice when he was diagnosed as having a serious illness. He died of leukaemia on 8 November 1979, only two months after returning to the town which, for the British, embodies a tradition of intellectual integrity and work stretching back to the Middle Ages. Bion was cremated and his ashes were buried at the cemetery in Happisburgh, near the high cliffs overlooking the North Sea. From adolescence onwards he had grown attached to Norfolk and, his wife tells us, he was always happy there. His sudden death was a shock to his family, friends, past analysands and admirers.

Death facilitates the task of the biographer and commentator. Freed from the crushing presence of the author, he can read in his own way. The author loses his right to control the use of his texts. A new space of relative freedom emerges from which we can reinterpret – or, even better, re-create – the work.

We began reading Bion before he was a famous psychoanalyst, when he was still considered a strange Kleinian. At that time his name was a sign around which the initiated could rally, and only a few enthusiasts studied his work, almost in secret. To a very high degree Bion possessed the ability to make connections; he was also able to go straight to the heart of the matter. In his work we find a profound and demanding intellect and an acute but icy sensitivity, encountering a fascinating and intriguing inner experience.

We have read Bion without leaving aside any aspect of his work, and found a consistent connection running throughout his writings. Thought and emotion are mutually supportive. Bion found the language of creative imagination after working with the language of abstract reasoning. Although he approached the world through several conceptual systems and forms of expression, the variety of his writings is the manifestation of a more fundamental concern which determines their differences and is the cause of their correlation. We have related Bion's work to the work of other well-known thinkers to show how he was inspired by them, how he responded to them, how his thinking created turbulence as it surpassed the limits of his predecessors.

But these complementary views have overturned tradition and transformed the way in which we see the world. Through his leaps of the imagination and his obsessive repetitions Bion tirelessly explored many wide-ranging themes. He remained equally committed to two opposing tendencies: simplicity and complexity. This frequently led him to inimitable conclusions: familiarity made strange, and the unknown made familiar. Bion wrote with an exhilarating terror of not being understood. He preferred to be a man of paradoxes than to be a man of prejudice. He would open up one train of thought, then break off, only to take it up again later. He never explicitly spelled out the continuity which, he maintained, was implicit in his work. But how is truth to be told if it resides in delusion?

Bion's work does not yield up its continuity at first glance; it emerges little by little as one reads it. Bion did not identify completely with his output; by remaining to some extent an onlooker, he was able to plan and organize the effect of his work. Each passage is constructed in relation to its reception. The reader's point of view was taken into account from the beginning of the text. His work is never very different from a work of fiction, in which the quest of an enigma maintains the suspense. The journey becomes an upwardly spiralling movement in which previous points are continuously recapitulated and taken further.

Bion has extended our pleasure in learning. He is one of those writers whose work can be recognized straight away. In a few hours, they connect us to their respective worlds. They address us directly, and captivate us. The success of their work can be gauged by the way they re-create our relation to everyday life. We leave

Bion with a feeling that our moments of work might be like scientific research, that our emotions and memories might become the basis of a work of art. As a psychoanalyst he began at the beginning of things, and he found a new path for psychoanalysis. He remains a real pioneer of modern psychoanalytic practice.

NOTES

1   Anzieu (Anzieu, 1986) suggests that Wilfred Bion may have been descended from Jean-François Bion, first a country priest and then chaplain on a convict ship. Moved by the courage of the Huguenots thus condemned to deportation, he eventually reached Geneva early in the eighteenth century, embraced the Reformation and became a vicar in England. Bion was delighted, in the course of his journey to Brazil, to discover others with the same name (Bion, 1983, p. 219). He does not seem to have followed up the Greek derivation of his surname; there is no mention of Wilfred Bion in the *Encyclopaedia Britannica*, only references to two Bions from Ancient Greece, a poet and a philosopher. Our research has uncovered one Bion family in the *Dictionnaire des familles françaises*. The family belonged to the *haute bourgeoisie* of the Rouerge, and at the end of the nineteenth century they were allowed to join their name to the Marlavagne. There are references to Bion families in the *Dictionnaire historique et biographique de la Suisse*.

2   Bion, the training analyst, does not appear to have come across Freud's essay 'A child is being beaten', which explains how acting out can take the place of awareness of the fantasies which underlie sexual perversion.

3   Bion mentions nothing about the fantasies that accompanied this childhood masturbation. Melanie Klein confirms, from 1932 onwards, that childhood masturbation fantasies contain the earliest fantasies of sadism aimed at the parents. Later in the autobiography he often gives the impression that he had never had a father, a mother or, even less, a sister. Their obliteration might be a kind of 'final solution' to the oedipal predicament. As a solution it resembles the psychotic's destruction of the thinking apparatus as a means of 'undoing' the oedipal predicament.

4   An appreciation of Bion published in the *Old Stortfordian Newsletter* gives an account of his prep school years: 'As a shy and namby-pamby eight year old, straight from India, he had held strong views that the only civilised way to spend a cold wet winter's afternoon was to sit reading a book by the fireside, and not to play muddy games outside . . . Among his peers he was revered as the toughest of the tough: they were blind to his latent sensitivity . . . Classroom subjects apart from history and literature did not inspire him and he lodged comfortably about half way down the end of term form order . . . Already he possessed that intellectual curiosity which was to render him an outstanding polymath. But it was with rugger and water polo

that his name at that time was associated. He was a formidable Captain and leader of the scrum.' (in Pines [ed.] 1985, pp. 386–7.)

5   We are grateful to Dr Eric Trist for introducing us to Hadfield's work, and we have also drawn on H.V. Dicks's well-documented study *Fifty Years of the Tavistock Clinic.*

6   The historical context of Bion's psychiatric work in the Second World War is described in R.H. Ahrenfeldt, *Psychiatry in the British Army in the Second World War.* The author had never met Bion and describes the history from the perspective of the army authorities, particularly that of Rees. The book therefore offers a salutary alternative to the generous enthusiasm of other writers, such as Eric Trist, who were directly influenced by Bion, and gives a point of view that contrasts with that of his autobiography.

7   In the 1930s a number of Oxford and Cambridge intellectuals were receptive to Marxism. In that era of severe economic recession, Marxism seemed to offer the only radical solution, and it was also at this time that the Soviet Union recruited a number of spies from among the upper-middle-class youth at Cambridge.

8   Trist offers another explanation. When Bion was responsible for the officers' mess he discovered that the accounts had been mismanaged and a person of rather high rank seemed to be involved. General Rees knew that Bion would not let the matter be settled 'with discretion', so he opted to get rid of him. Bion had a reputation for being strict about regimental conduct.

9   Jacques Lacan was the first person to alert the French to the advances taking place in military psychiatry in England. He spent September 1945 in London to find out more. His intuition enabled him to admire greatly the article written by Bion and Rickman in November 1943, 'which is only six newspaper columns, but which will be noted in the history of psychiatry'. He had a long interview with the two pioneers. Here are his impressions: 'these two men, of whom it could be said that the flame of creation burns within – in one as if frozen in an immobile and moonlike mask, accentuated by the fine commas of a black moustache, which, no less than the large physique and the swimmer's chest that hold it up, contradict Kretschmer's formulae, when everything tells us that we are in the presence of one of those beings who are solitary in even their highest achievements, and as we find confirmed in this man's adventure in Flanders, where he followed his tank, switch in hand, into the breach, and paradoxically thus forced the iron gates of fate . . .' Jacques Lacan, 'La psychiatrie anglaise et la guerre', *Évolution Psychiatrique,* 1947.

10   Parthenope was the name of one of the mythological sirens, half-woman, half-bird, renowned for the musical gifts which tempted and tormented sailors. According to the legend, when they were

unable to seduce Ulysses they threw themselves into the sea, and Parthenope's body was washed ashore in the Bay of Naples. The Ancient Greeks gave her name to the city that was to become Paleopolis. Bion came across the name in Virgil, one of his favourite poets.

11 Toynbee was born in London in 1989, and educated at Winchester and Oxford. Between 1919 and 1955 he taught at London University – first Greek history, then international history. His main work is the twelve-volume *Study of History*, written between 1934 and 1961. The main thesis of the study is that civilizations arise like creations; a civilization declines when its creative power diminishes. Toynbee does not share Spengler's pessimistic vision: he does not consider that the decline of civilizations is inevitable.

12 We hesitate to establish tenuous links of influence when Bion himself does not cite them as such. However, we are thinking of Kurt Lewin, who applied the principles of Gestalt theory to individuals and then to groups. From 1938 onwards, working in Berlin, Lewin carried out extensive research, having extended the notion of a dynamic field to the context of small groups. When Bion met Trist, the latter had come across some of Lewin's works (Trist, in Pines [ed.] 1985, p 5). We know that Bion consulted Trist extensively during his formulation of the theory of groups. The term 'group dynamic', which Bion uses as the title of his last article in his writings on groups, was first used in 1944 by Lewin. Lewin had considerable influence in the USA. His clinical method, known as the T-Group, was actually quite similar to Bion's, even though their theoretical formulations were quite different.

13 Trotter's famous work *Instincts of the Herd in Peace and War* was written during the First World War, from the point of view of the many psychosociological insights gained from that context. Freud cites Trotter's book with immense respect in his well-known essay on *Group Psychology and the Analysis of the Ego*. Bion was in a difficult situation, as it was his work, more than any experimental tests on group behaviour, that served to minimize the theoretical significance of the man who had taught him surgery, and whom he had so greatly admired.

14 According to Laplanche and Pontalis in *The Language of Psycho-analysis*, the primal scene is a scene of sexual intercourse between the parents which the child observes or infers on the basis of certain indications and phantasies. It is generally interpreted by the child as an act of violence on the part of the father. If the phantasy of the primal scene is accepted as generic to group behaviour, it seems that we could compare the basic assumption dependence with the phantasy of intrauterine life, the basic assumption pairing with the phantasy of

seduction, and basic assumption fight–flight with the phantasy of castration. It seems strange that Bion never applied the concept of envy retrospectively to group dynamics, whereas he considered that envy played a most fundamental role in psychosis.

15 When the Kleinians tried to analyse schizophrenics, the notion of psychotic countertransference was developed. They wanted to apply the concept of projective identification to these unusual transference phenomena. As a corollary to this, they conceived of the countertransference as a research tool, since the analyst's emotional response could be a means of access to the patient's consciousness. Bion was the first to demonstrate, in 1952, that projective identification was as valuable a concept for the group analyst's countertransference. Much later the idea was taken up by both Racker and Grinberg in Argentina.

16 See G. Bléandonu, *L'École de Melanie Klein* (1985). It should be noted that the only source of information on Klein in relation to Bion is to be found in Phyllis Grosskurth's biography, *Melanie Klein* (1985). The source of Grosskurth's information for this biography is Francesca Bion. In other words we have, in effect, only one version of the relationship between Bion and Klein.

17 Derived from their papers given in the Controversial Discussions in 1943–4.

18 This intuitive leap was never explained, just as we still do not know why Klein targeted anxiety first, and followed her intuition to the end. Meanwhile it was Klein who had given Bion his lead. She had conceived of the 'normal disturbances of the processes of thinking' that arise in the paranoid-schizoid position. She had noted, particularly, the deleterious effect that persecutory anxiety and excessive schizoid mechanisms can have on the beginnings of intellectual development, believing that certain kinds of intellectual deficiencies should be considered as part of the schizophrenias.

19 Wittgenstein was born in Vienna and later became a British citizen, like Melanie Klein. He fought in the First World War and worked in the medical corps in the Second, much like Bion.

20 When aggressive drives are, provisionally, dominant, the drives of love and hate may become confused; good objects are experienced as being mixed or confused with bad objects. This creates extreme anxiety, as the mixing creates the feeling of a threat of complete destruction of the self.

21 We note the approximate nature of this psychopathology: Bion treated and talked to only adult schizophrenics. Although Klein maintained that schizophrenia is more common in children than was thought in 1930, this illness is usually found in adolescents and young adults. In describing the psychopathology of early childhood, Bion outlined more of a theory of childhood psychosis than of schizophrenia.

Frances Tustin realized this, and went on to apply her teacher's theories to childhood autism.

22 In her 'Notes on symbol formation' Segal employs the concept of symbol formation proposed by Klein in relation to her theory of the two positions. In the paranoid-schizoid position, symbolic equations are formed as one part of the self is totally and projectively identified with the object. This process, in which the symbol is treated as an object, underlies the concrete thinking of the schizophrenic.

23 By employing the term 'hysterical hallucinations' Bion makes explicit reference to the *Studies in Hysteria* (1895). At that time Freud considered the possibility of such things as hysterical psychoses, and many of his clinical cases have a similar nosography to Bion's patient during his long analysis. We leave aside discussion of the question of the successful psychoanalytic treatment of schizophrenia: successes might simply indicate that the 'trees' of hysteria have been mistaken for the 'wood' of psychosis.

24 The title of the article 'On arrogance' (1957b) places arrogance foremost. According to Bion's theory, pride becomes self-esteem when the life instincts predominate, and becomes arrogance under the influence of the death instinct. Bion conceived of arrogance in a similar way to the Hellenic concept of *hubris*. In her article 'Some reflections on *The Oresteia*' (1963), Klein considers *hubris* an insolent pride which grasps for more, bursts bounds and breaks the established order.

25 It is interesting to compare this reconstruction with that of Winnicott, who developed a concept of the good-enough mother, whereas Bion's concept is of an understanding mother who contains within herself and has clarity of thought. In 1945 Edward Glover criticized Klein for idealizing the mother's behaviour, having wanted to prove that the mother is good in reality and cannot be blamed for the infant's essential unhappiness. Ten years later Bion and Winnicott, who both had the advantage of a Kleinian training, conceptualized the infant with a mother's care as a dyad – a logical extension of object-relations theory, which implies an interaction between them.

26 Regarding these adjectives, let us note that Bion's intellectual universe, like Klein's, practically ignores perversion. It would seem to us, however, that the non-psychotic personality is as perverse as it is neurotic. Perhaps the late interest in borderline cases was a way of compensating for this oversight. We find this confirmed in *Second Thoughts*, where Bion refers to a well-known article by Meltzer which links anal masturbation to projective identification. Bion confirms that, like some borderline personalities, the man with the imaginary twin had been able to develop this perverse aspect on the intellectual level, and to become a 'pseudo-mature personality'.

27 Bion seems to refer to materialists such as Karl Vogt. This nineteenth-century German philosopher formulated the famous dictum: 'The brain produces thoughts as the liver produces bile, or the kidneys produce urine'.

28 It is not always clear what Bion is referring to, as he uses the term function in relation to his new theory as often as he uses it in relation to its usage in psychology and physiology: for example, as in the case of intellectual or alimentary functions.

29 Love and Hate refer back to a long-standing philosophical tradition, but crucially here to an essay written in 1937 by Melanie Klein and Joan Riviere, 'Love, hate and reparation'. In their attempt to discover the fundamental sources of emotions, the authors chose hate, 'the force of disintegration and destruction which tends towards privation and death', and love, 'a form of harmonization, unification, which tends towards pleasure and life'. In this way Bion links up love and hate with the mother's reverie. The 'K link' is his personal and innovatory contribution to the theory.

30 We cannot give a full account of *Cogitations* here: it is a large work which covers twenty years' writings. There is an excellent review of the book by André Green (*International Journal of Psycho-Analysis*, vol. 72 [1992]: 285). The only reservation I have about this subtle and knowledgeable review is its attempts to separate Bion from the other (unidentified) Kleinians who, by implication, were wrong. Green mentions that the fact of having known Bion personally, unlike myself or most readers, may have coloured his emotional response to the book.

31 We dwell on this concept, which was an idiosyncratic preoccupation of Bion's. However, he did not follow up its origin and development as a concept. In *Learning from Experience* he simply suggests that the reversible perspective is essentially linked to the 'selected fact', yet it is the latter which gives coherence to the scattered elements of the paranoid-schizoid position and, by so doing, ushers in the depressive position; whereas from *Elements of Psychoanalysis* onwards, reversible perspective is limited to the realm of pathology.

32 'For the model for the growth of $\overset{Q}{\underset{+}{}}$ I shall borrow from Elliott Jaques's concept of the reticulum' (Bion, 1962b, p. 92). Bion was inspired by a little-known article by Jaques, 'Disturbances in the capacity to work' (*International Journal of Psycho-Analysis*, vol. 41 [1960]: 357–67). Jaques's aim was very close to that of Bion, as he sets out here a theory of intellectual work, notably that of the psychoanalyst. He defined work as mental energy employed in reaching a goal set by the pleasure principle by means of the reality principle. Jaques differentiates between six stages, which he describes in terms of the concept of an

'integrating reticulum' which combines a multitude of conscious and unconscious elements.

33 The index of *Learning from Experience* contains only numerous references to 'emotion', whereas the index to *Elements of Psychoanalysis* contains only references to 'feeling'.

34 Mach is best known for his critique of Newtonian mechanics, which greatly influenced Einstein.

35 An interesting comparison could be made between René Thom's 'catastrophe theory' and Bion's 'catastrophic change'. In fact Bion's concept is probably closer to Kurt Goldstein's Gestalt theory of 'catastrophic reaction'.

36 This symbol is undoubtedly the capital letter. But the significance of zero is also connoted, as its typographical representation resembles that of the fifteenth letter of the alphabet. In mathematical usage zero represents the point of origin, which bears certain resemblances to Bion's concept. In another context entirely, the title of a well-known erotic novel, *The Story of O*, reminds us that this vowel, in its roundness, can also symbolize the female sexual organs.

37 Meltzer has noted that the statement 'if it could be said that' leads us to confuse the problem of the limits of thinking with the limits of language. On a psychoanalytic level this is manifested by a confusion between the objects of the imagination (of the subject about which we are thinking) and the objects of internal reality (those which exist inside us). Meltzer thought that Bion's project fails here because of his confusion between the absent object or no-thing, and the internal object or no-thing. But again we have to ask ourselves if the confusion is Bion's or if it is the confusion of the psychotic as described by Bion?

38 When Bion uses the concept of the 'real self', the work of D.W. Winnicott inevitably come to mind. Winnicott, another analyst who was also influenced by Melanie Klein at the beginning of his work, formulated the concept of a 'true self' with a somewhat mysterious meaning, defined essentially in opposition to the 'false self'. Bion and Winnicott also ascribe different roles to 'illusion'. Whereas Bion gives it a rather negative meaning, defining illusion as an aspect of hallucination, Winnicott thinks of illusion as of great value, as part of the process of transitional and cultural phenomena. It is interesting that neither Bion nor Winnicott refers to one another's work in their writing, although they both created original theories starting from a more or less Kleinian perspective.

39 Our word 'intuition' derives from the Latin *intuor*, meaning 'to observe attentively' – once again Bion uses a visual, and thus a sensory, metaphor to describe consciousness of mental phenomena.

40 In one of his Brazilian Lectures Bion affirms that his use of O was not identical to the zero of mathematics. O resembles zero while remaining quite different from it. In analysis there must be a space analogous to the pause (or silence) in music.

41 André Green links Bion's description of the union with O (at-one-ment), with 'absolute primary narcissism' as described by Freud. Bion's 'union with O' distances him from Kleinian theory, according to which there may be narcissistic states but there is no primary narcissism. This concept is more closely linked to Freud's second topography, in which he describes a primary state of life, of which intrauterine life is the prototype. But we shall see that Bion's concept of the 'caesura' is radically different from Freud's.

42 Bion describes psychological states which are not unlike those encountered in yoga. He was certainly very interested in the Orientalism which flourished in Western culture in the 1950s and 1960s, especially in the growing popularity of Indian culture and religions. He was, of course, originally from the Punjab himself. The Indian philosophies that became popularized in the 1960s were another discourse on and technique of mysticism and ecstatic experience.

Later Bion spells out his sense of recognition as he finds aspects of his work confirmed in the *Baghavad-Gita*, specifically the grid and the great myths of knowledge from Eden to Babel; and this recognition is discussed in the Brazilian Lectures, where one participant asks him 'whether there is any connection between the concepts of desire and memory in your work and similar concepts in Indian writing' (Bion, 1973-4, pp. 31-3).

43 Bion sets out to demonstrate that psychotic-like defence mechanisms have erected permanent and institutionalized lying as a specific social ailment. He seems to accord the lie a status between neurosis and psychosis, just as Freud does for perversion. The statement that 'neurosis is the negative of a lie (perversion of truth)' expresses his fundamental thesis on this point.

44 Bion uses the term Establishment to refer to the group of people who exercise power and responsibility by virtue of their social status, and because of their intellectual and emotional qualities. Ideally, their social status depends on their qualities. Otherwise the dictionary definition of the Establishment would be more accurate: 'A powerful group of individuals who defend their privileges and social position'.

45 The nineteen volumes of this Indian epic history tell of the Indo-European invasion of the Ganges basin. The *Bhagavad-Gita* is the well-known sixth volume; Bion makes great use of it in the literary trilogy and in the Brazilian conference papers.

46 The legend as told in the twelve books of Virgil's quasi-historical epic poem on the origins of Rome, *The Aeneid*, identifies Palinarus as helmsman of Aeneas's ship. In he fifth book the fleet sets sail from Sicily to Italy, and Venus promises her son Aeneas a safe journey. Only one of his crew will be drowned, a sacrifice which will guarantee the lives of the others. Palinarus, alone on deck, falls prey to the god of sleep, and while he is trying to keep a steady gaze on the stars in order to navigate, he begins to fall asleep. He clings fast to the helm, but a sudden movement of the ship pushes him overboard. Nobody hears his cries as he falls, and he is drowned.

47 In his Brazilian Lectures Bion returns to this metaphor several times. Inspired by neurophysiology, he conceives of a human being whose (encephalitic) brain develops no further than the thalamus. In that case, the brain would be a subcortical structure connected to physiological processes. A being of this kind would experience what we call feelings, but would the feelings be a kind of fear, love or hatred that our cortex has protected us from experiencing? A patient whose behaviour was governed by his thalamus alone would dream, but be unaware of the sounds and contents of his dreams. On the other hand, a patient like this might be able to know what happens when there is no gap between thinking and doing (Bion, 1973–4, p. 26).

48 It is at this point that the opposition between Freud and Bion becomes most explicit and obvious: 'In his book on the *Trauma of Birth* Rank has energetically tried to demonstrate the connection between the infant's earliest phobias (fears) and the effect of the events of birth. But I cannot say that he has succeeded. He can be criticized on two counts; firstly that he bases his analysis on the hypothesis that the infant, at birth, receives determining sensory impressions, especially of a visual nature . . . Moreover, this hypothesis has not been proven and it seems very unlikely' (*Inhibitions, Symptoms and Anxiety*, p. 59).

49 Bion could not have forgotten that Freud proposed the concept of the splitting of the ego towards the end of his life, in the context of thinking about psychosis and fetishism. It can be no coincidence that Bion returns, in the grid, to the notion of the construction on which Freud had written an essay immediately before his 'Splitting of the ego in the process of defence' (1938).

50 At this point in the fiction Roland represents Bion at various stages of his life: one at which he had abandoned Betty as she was about to give birth, and one at which he had tried to separate a calf from its mother by leading it to Munden (Bion, 1982, p. 58). At one stage he kept a screen memory of a girl who had supposedly been raped by German soldiers in the First World War (ibid., p. 210).

51 Bion implies that England has been conquered by Communists, probably Soviets. Rosemary declares that this is not capitalist England (Bion, 1975, p. 20), and that the workers have been liberated (ibid., p. 6).

52 DU derives from the German term for the second-person-singular familiar form of 'you'. Bion uses it because of its German connotations, and because there is no familiar form of address in the English language which carries the meaning of the archaic 'thou'. or the French *tu*. This bizarre being interrupts in a sinister way, like the return of the repressed, like an encounter with an 'enemy German' in World War One conducted only in schoolboy German, a very rudimentary form of dialogue (Bion, 1982, p. 251).

53 In their 'Key' to the *Memoir of the Future* the Bions tell us that Auser was a young officer who died on 11 August 1918 at Amiens (Bion, 1981, p. 12). But if we are to believe the autobiography, this officer's name was Asser. In the trilogy a slip of the pen condenses the names of two very different officers: Asser and Hauser. Bion never tried to conceal the fact that he never liked Asser, who was an officer under his orders in World War One, but that he was impressed by his fervent patriotism and his heroic death (he preferred to be killed leaving his tank than to surrender). Asser was a year younger than Bion and had just joined the regiment, whereas Hauser had been a member of the regiment from the beginning.

54 We are particularly indebted to Henri Fourtina's doctoral thesis on psychoanalysis and language in Great Britain, presented in 1987 at Grenoble. Chapters 5, 6 and 7 are specifically about the *Memoir of the Future*.

55 Bion opens up discussion on the concept of a psychic envelope. It is not surprising to find a number of references to this concept in his autobiography, *The Long Week-End*. Possibly the most fruitful approach to this would be through Didier Anzieu's concept of the *Skin Ego*, but here we will simply note some of the references that Bion makes in his autobiography:

- 'to make my last year at the prep school one in which I began to break through what I see in retrospect to have been an intolerable exo-skeleton of misery' (p. 54);
- 'But I was imprisoned, unable to break out of the shell which adhered to me' (p. 104);
- 'the fellow in the shell-hole had his mouth wide open, the skin stretched – *by* the mouth?' (p. 138);
- 'Gradually in the following days I grew a protective skin' (p. 172);
- 'I had my childhood and schoolboy culture. It gave me something, but neither the discipline of repetitive command, nor the "heaven" of middle class England, nor an exo-skeleton taking the place of a

> skeleton for an endo-skeletonous animal can serve; still less in the domain of the mind' (p. 194);
> - 'I was only a part of the skin on a boxer's knuckles' (p. 213);
> - 'I felt some residual belief adhering rather as egg-shell adheres to the newly hatched chick' (p. 244).
>
> Finally Bion often makes a pun in French, using 'couvre-toi de flanelle' as a substitute for 'couvre-toi de gloire!' (from the French novel *Tartarin de Tarascon* by Alphonse Daudet), a pun which depends on the 'covering' of glory being substituted by the humble material flannel, which provided only a mundane and physical covering, not a metaphorical protection.

56 This point is discussed in Meg Harris's essay 'The Tiger and O' in *Free Associations* 1, 1985.

57 The seventeenth-century religious writer John Bunyan is remembered chiefly for *The Pilgrim's Progress*, which traces the Christian's progress towards the Celestial City, overcoming innumerable obstacles. Bion makes specific reference to his concept of the Slough of Despond.

58 Bion makes several references to Pound, the American poet and critic who was his contemporary. He particularly admired his ability to unite erudite poetry with an almost conversational style, and his emphasis on 'melopocia', the rhythm and sonority of language. His work is also surrounded by a particular aura due to the fact that he was diagnosed as a schizophrenic and hospitalized several years after the war.

59 Since we have drawn widely on the autobiography to present biographical information, we will not discuss the book's contents but turn to the form and the project of writing. We have found two books by Philippe Lejeune useful: *Le pacte autobiographique* (Paris: Éditions du Seuil, 1975) and *Je est un autre* (Paris: Éditions du Seuil, 1980).

60 For further exploration of this, see André Green's wonderful book *Hamlet et Hamlet; une interprétation psychanalytique de la représentation* (Paris: Balland, 1982).

BIBLIOGRAPHY

Place of publication is London unless otherwise indicated.

GENERAL

Abraham, K. (1908) 'The psycho-sexual differences between hysteria and dementia praecox', in *Selected Papers of Karl Abraham*, International Psycho-Analytic Library No.13, 1949. Hogarth.

Ahrenfeldt, R.H. (1958) *Psychiatry in the British Army in the Second World War*. Routledge & Kegan Paul.

Anzieu, D. (1986) 'Beckett et Bion', *Revue de Psychothérapie Psychanalytique de Groupe* 5–6: 286.

—— (1989) *The Skin Ego*. Yale University Press.

Assoun, P.L. (1981) *Introduction à l'Épistémologie freudienne*. Paris: Payot.

Bair, D. (1979) *Samuel Beckett*. Paris: Fayard.

Bléandonu, G. (1970) *Les Communeautées thérapeutiques*. Paris: Éditions du Scarabée.

—— (1985) *L'École de Melanie Klein*. Paris: Le Centurion.

Davis, P.J. and Hersh, R. (1985) *L'Univers mathématique*. Paris: Gauthier-Villars.

Dicks, H.V. (1970) *Fifty Years of the Tavistock Clinic*. Routledge & Kegan Paul.

Fourtina, H. (1987) *Psychanalyse et langage en Grande-Bretagne. Théories/Écriture*, University of Grenoble III, unpublished thesis.

Freud, S. (1895) 'Project for a scientific psychology', in James Strachey, ed. *The Standard Edition of the Complete Works of Sigmund Freud*, 24 vols, Hogarth, 1953–73, vol. 1, pp. 295–397.

—— (1911) 'Formulations regarding the two principles of mental functioning', *S.E.* 12, pp. 215–26.

—— (1919) '"A child is being beaten": a contribution to the study of the origin of sexual perversions', *S.E.* 17, pp. 177–204.

—— (1921) *Group Psychology and the Analysis of the Ego. S.E.* 18, pp. 65–143.

—— (1923) 'Neurosis and psychosis', *S.E.* 19, pp. 149–53.

—— (1925) *Inhibitions, Symptoms and Anxiety*, *S.E.* 20, pp. 77–178.

—— (1938) 'The splitting of the ego in the process of defence', *S.E.* 23, pp. 273–8.

Freud, S. and Breuer, J. (1893) *Studies in Hysteria, S.E.* 2.

Gathorne-Hardy, J. (1977) *The Public School Phenomenon*. Hodder & Stoughton.

Green, A. (1982) *Hamlet et Hamlet: une interprétation psychanalytique de la représentation.* Paris: Balland.

—— (1992) 'Review of *Cogitations* by W.R. Bion', *Int. J. Psycho-Anal.* 72: 285.

Grinberg, L. *et al.* (1975) *Introduction to the Work of Bion.* Perthshire: Clunie, Roland Harris Educational Trust.

Grosskurth, P. (1986) *Melanie Klein.* Maresfield Library.

Grotstein, J. (ed.) (1981) *Do I Dare Disturb the Universe?* Beverly Hills, CA: Caesura.

—— (1993) 'Towards the concept of the transcendent position: reflections on some of "The Unborns" in Bion's *Cogitations*', *Melanie Klein and Object Relations* 11: 57–75.

Hadfield, J. (1923) *Psychology and Morals.*

—— (1935) *Psychology and Modern Problems.*

—— (1954) *Dreams and Nightmares.* Harmondsworth: Penguin.

—— (1962) *Childhood and Adolescence.* Harmondsworth: Penguin.

Hume, D. (1739) *A Treatise on Human Nature.*

Jaques, E. (1960) 'Disturbances in the capacity to work', *Int. J. Psycho-Anal.* 41: 357–67.

Kant, I. (1781) *Critique of Pure Reason.*

Klein, M. (1932) *The Psycho-Analysis of Children. (The Writings of Melanie Klein,* vol. 2). Hogarth/Institute of Psycho-Analysis, 1975.

—— (1936) 'Weaning', in *Love, Guilt and Reparation. (The Writings of Melanie Klein,* vol. 1, *1921–1945).* Hogarth/Institute of Psycho-Analysis, 1975.

—— (1946) 'Notes on some schizoid mechanisms' in *Envy and Gratitude. (The Writings of Melanie Klein,* vol. 3). Hogarth/Institute of Psycho-Analysis, 1975, pp. 1–24.

—— (1957) 'Envy and Gratitude' in *Envy and Gratitude and Other Works. (The Writings of Melanie Klein,* vol 3). Hogarth/Institute of Psycho-Analysis, 1975, pp. 176–235.

—— (1963) 'On the sense of loneliness', in *Envy and Gratitude. (The Writings of Melanie Klein,* vol. 3). Hogarth/Institute of Psycho-Analysis, 1975, pp. 300–313.

—— (1963) 'Some reflections on "The Oresteia"', in *Envy and Gratitude. (The Writings of Melanie Klein,* vol. 3). Hogarth/Institute of Psycho-Analysis, 1975, pp. 275–99.

Klein, M. and Riviere, J. (1937) *Love, Hate and Reparation.* Hogarth Press.

Klein, M. Isaacs, S. and Riviere, J. (1952) *Developments in Psycho-Analysis.* Hogarth.

Lacan, J. (1947) 'La Psychiatrie Anglaise et la guerre', *L'Evolution Psychiatrique.*

Laplanche, J. and Pontalis, J.B. (1973) *The Language of Psycho-Analysis.* Hogarth/Institute of Psycho-Analysis.

Lejeune, P. (1975) *Le Pacte autobiographique*. Paris: Seuil.
—— (1980) *Je est un autre*. Paris: Seuil.
Lewin, K. (1938) *Gestalt Theory*.
Lyth, O. (1980) Obituary of Bion, *Int. J. Psycho-Anal.* 61: 269.
Meltzer, D. (1978) *The Kleinian Development III*. Perthshire: Clunie.
—— (1966) 'The relation of anal masturbation to projective identification',
    in E. Bott Spillius, ed. *Melanie Klein Today*, vol. 1: *Mainly Theory*.
    Routledge, 1988, pp, 102–116.
Miller, E. and Crichton-Miller, H. (eds) (1940) *The Neuroses in War*.
    Macmillan.
Money-Kyrle, R. (1961) *Man's Picture of His World*. Duckworth.
Morin, E. (1970) *Journal de Californie*. Paris: Seuil.
Paton, H.J. (1936) *Kant's Metaphysics of Experience*. Allen & Unwin.
—— (1947) *The Categorical Imperative*. Hutchinson's University Library.
Pines, M. (ed.) (1985) *Bion and Group Psychotherapy*. Routledge & Kegan
    Paul: The International Library of Group Psychotherapy and Group
    Process.
Poincaré, H. (1908) *Science and Method*. Walter Scott Publishing Co.
Rank, O. (1929) *The Trauma of Birth*. Kegan Paul, Trench & Truber.
Rawlinson, H. (1948) *The British Achievement in India*. William Hodge.
Rosenfeld, H. (1965) *Psychotic States*. Hogarth.
Schmid, A.F. (1978) Une philosophie de savant: Henri Poincaré et la
    logique mathématique. Paris: Maspero.
Segal, H. (1950) 'Some aspects of the analysis of a schizophrenic', in *The
    Work of Hanna Segal – A Kleinian Approach to Clinical Practice*.
    Free Association Books, 1986, pp. 101–120.
—— (1957) 'Notes on symbol formation', in *The Work of Hanna Segal –
    A Kleinian Approach to Clinical Practice*. Free Assocation Books,
    1986, pp. 49–65.
Toynbee, E. (1934–1961) *A Study of History*. 12 vols. Royal Institute of
    International Affairs.
Trotter, W. (1920) *The Instincts of the Herd in Peace and War*. T. Fisher
    Unwin.
Tustin, F. (1981) *Autistic States in Childhood*. Routledge & Kegan Paul.
Williams, M.H. (1985) 'The tiger and O: a reading of Bion's memoir and
    autobiography', *Free Associations* 1: 33–56.
Wittgenstein, L. (1922) *Tractatus Logico-Philosophicus*. Routledge.
—— (1953) *Philosophical Investigations*. Blackwell.
Yourcenar, M. (1980) *Mishima ou la vision du vide*. Paris: Gallimard.

Works by Bion

1940 '"The war of nerves": civilian reaction, morale and prophylaxis', in E. Miller and H. Crichton-Miller, eds *The Neuroses in War*. Macmillan.

1943 'Intra-group tensions in therapy: their study as a task of the group', *The Lancet* (27 November); reprinted in *Experiences in Groups* (1961).

1946 'The Leaderless Group Project', *Bulletin of the Menninger Clinic* 10, 3 May: 77.

1948 'Psychiatry in a time of crisis', *Brit. J. Med. Psychol.* XXI(2): 81.

1948-51 'Experiences in groups', *Human Relations* I-IV, reprinted in *Experiences in Groups* (1961).

1950 'The imaginary twin', presented to the British Psycho-Analytical Society in November 1950 as Bion's membership paper; reprinted in *Int. J. Psycho-Anal.* (1955); reprinted in *Second Thoughts* (1967a).

1952 'Group dynamics: a review', *Int. J. Psycho-Anal.* 32(2); reprinted in *Experiences in Groups* (1961).

1953 'Notes on the theory of schizophrenia', presented at the Eighteenth International Psycho-Analytic Congress; reprinted in *Int. J. Psycho-Anal.* 35 (1954); reprinted in *Second Thoughts* (1967a).

1955 'Language and the schizophrenic', in *New Directions in Psycho-Analysis*. Tavistock.

1956 'The development of schizophrenic thought', *Int. J. Psycho-Anal.* 37; reprinted in *Second Thoughts* (1967a).

1957a 'Differentiation of the psychotic from the non-psychotic personalities', *Int. J. Psycho-Anal.* 38; reprinted in *Second Thoughts* (1967a).

1957b 'On arrogance', presented at the Twentieth International Psycho-Analytic Congress, Paris; reprinted in *Int. J. Psycho-Anal.* 39 (1958); reprinted in *Second Thoughts* (1967a).

1958a 'On hallucination', *Int. J. Psycho-Anal.* 39; reprinted in *Second Thoughts* (1967a).

1958b 'Attacks on linking', *Int. J. Psycho-Anal.* 40(5-6); reprinted in *Second Thoughts* (1967a).

1961 *Experiences in Groups and Other Papers*. Tavistock.

1962a 'A theory of thinking', *Int. J. Psycho-Anal.* 43(4-5); reprinted in *Second Thoughts* (1967a).

1962b *Learning from Experience*. Heinemann Medical Books; reprinted Karnac, 1984, also reprinted in *Seven Servants* (1977).

1963 *The Elements of Psycho-Analysis*. Heinemann Medical Books; reprinted Karnac, 1984, also reprinted in *Seven Servants* (1977).

1965 *Transformations*. Heinemann Medical Books; reprinted Karnac, 1984, also reprinted in *Seven Servants* (1977).

1966 'Catastrophic change', *Bulletin of the British Psycho-Analytical Society* 5(v); also in *Attention and Interpretation* (Chapter 12) (1970).

1967a *Second Thoughts*. Heinemann.

1967b 'Notes on memory and desire', *Psycho-Analytic Forum* 2(3) (Los Angeles, CA); reprinted in E. Spillius, ed. *Melanie Klein Today*. Routledge.

1970 *Attention and Interpretation*. Tavistock; reprinted Karnac, 1984, also in *Seven Servants* (1977).

1973-4 *Bion's Brazilian Lectures* Nos 1 & 2. Rio de Janeiro: Imago Editora.

1975 *A Memoir of the Future, Book One: The Dream*. Rio de Janeiro: Imago Editora; reprinted Karnac, 1990.

1976 'Evidence', *Bulletin of the British Psycho-Analytical Society* 8; reprinted in *Clinical Seminars and Four Papers* (1987).

1977a *A Memoir of the Future, Book Two: The Past Presented*. Rio de Janeiro: Imago Editora; reprinted Karnac, 1990.

1977b *Seven Servants: Four Works by Wilfred Bion*. New York: Jason Aronson.

1977c *Two Papers: The Grid and the Caesura*, originally presented as talks to the Los Angeles Psychoanalytic Society in 1971 and 1975 respectively. Rio de Janeiro: Imago Editora; reprinted Karnac, 1989.

1977d 'Emotional turbulence', paper given at the International Conference on Borderline Disorders, Topeka, Kansas (March 1976), published in the book of the conference, P. Hartocollis, ed. *Borderline Personality Disorders*. New York: International Universities Press; reprinted in *Clinical Seminars and Four Papers* (1987).

1977e 'On a quotation from Freud', in P. Hartocollis, ed. *Borderline Personality Disorders*. New York: International Universities Press.

1978 *Four Discussions with W.R. Bion*. Perthshire: Clunie.

1979a *A Memoir of the Future, Book Three: The Dawn of Oblivion*. Perthshire: Clunie; reprinted Karnac, 1990.

1979b 'Making the best of a bad job', *Bulletin of the British Psycho-Analytical Society* 20; reprinted in *Clinical Seminars and Four Papers* (1987).

1980 *Bion in New York and São Paulo*. Perthshire: Clunie.

1981 *A Key to a Memoir of the Future*, with Francesca Bion. Perthshire: Clunie; reprinted Karnac, 1990.

1982 *The Long Week-End 1897-1918*. Abingdon: Fleetwood.

1985 *All My Sins Remembered* and *The Other Side of Genius*. Abingdon: Fleetwood.

1987 *Clinical Seminars and Four Papers*. Abingdon: Fleetwood.

1990 *A Memoir of the Future* (see 1975, 1977a, 1979a, 1981 above). Karnac.

1992 *Cogitations*. Karnac.

INDEX

A Memoir of the Future, trilogy, 235, 249-64 passim
Abraham, Karl: analysis of Klein, 93; 'The psycho-sexual differences between hysteria and dementia praecox' (1908), 129; part-object, 138
abstraction, evaluation of, 161-2
action, relation to function, 150
adaptation syndrome (Selye), 246
adolescence, emotional turbulence in, 242
aesthetics, 202-3
alpha elements: in misunderstanding, 179-80; in processes of mental growth, 184
alpha function, 142; in verbal thought, 122; as representing an unknown, 150; of knowledge, 151-2; emotions underlying, 160; theory of, 173; and dreams, 175, 176
analyst: and group method, 61, 87; emotional response of, 107, 198; relationship with schizophrenic patient, 118-19; effect of projective identification on, 124-5; and attacks on linking, 136-8; and use of the grid, 169-72; role of, 197, 245-6; and difficulty of note-taking, 217; should suspend memory and desire, 221-4, 244; own training analysis, 222
Anzieu, Didier, 155
Argentina, conference (1968), 233-4
aristocracy, and basic assumption pairing group, 76

army: 21st Army Corps, Normandy (1943), 64; Bion joins 5th Tank Battalion (1916), 25; Bion's work with (Second World War), 49; use of psychology and psychiatry, 51-3, 58; Bion's project for officer selection, 55-9; treatment of war neuroses at Northfield, 59-60
Army Medical Corps, Second World War, 52-3
arrogance, 135, 281 note 24
art: Bion's use of, 196-7; analogy with analysis, 200-1
asceticism, in psychoanalysis, 220-4
'Attacks on linking' (paper), central to theoretical development, 105
Attention and Interpretation (1970), 188, 193, 215, 218, 239, 241-2
autobiography, 265-9, 270-1; limitations of, 6; *see also Long Week-End, The*

Babel, Tower of, 185
Baghavad-Gita (Mahabharata), 234, 284 notes 42 and 45
basic assumption: in group therapy, 70-3; limitations of, 75-6
basic assumption groups, 85-6; types of, 72-3; emotions in, 73-5; dependency (Chinese model), 80-1; fight-flight (Greek state model], 80; pairing (Jewish model), 81
Beckett, Samuel, Bion's work with (1934-6), 44-6